GOOD NEWS IN HISTORY
Essays in Honor of Bo Reicke

Professor Bo Reicke
Photo, Daniel Reicke, 1980

GOOD NEWS IN HISTORY
Essays in Honor of Bo Reicke†

With a Contribution by Professor Reicke

Edited by
Ed. L. Miller

Scholars Press
Atlanta, Georgia

GOOD NEWS IN HISTORY

Essays in Honor of Bo Reicke

Edited by
Ed. L. Miller

©1993
Scholars Press

Library of Congress Cataloging in Publication Data
Good news in history: essays in honor of Bo Reicke/ edited by Ed. L.
   Miller; with a contribution by Professor Reicke.
      p. cm. — (Scholars Press Homage series)
   ISBN 1–55540–882–6 (alk paper)
   1. Bible. N.T.—Criticism, interpretation, etc. 2. Bible. N.T.—
Theology.   I. Miller, Ed. L. (Ed. LeRoy), 1914–   .   II. Reicke,
Bo Ivar, 1914–   .   III. Series.
BS2361.2.G66   1993
225.6—dc20   93–17977
                                                                      CIP

Printed in the United States of America
on acid-free paper

Es muß . . . betont werden, daß im Bericht des Matthäus über das leere Grab nicht mythologische Phantasie, sondern ergreifende Wirklichkeit zu finden ist, wenn alles nur in die richtige Perspektive eingesetzt wird.

Ausgangspunkt muß die vielseitige historische Bezeugung der Auferstehung Jesu vom Tode bilden. Nicht nur die Frauen am Grabe, nicht nur die Apostel und nächsten Jünger, sondern auch eine große Menge von Zeugen werden im Neuen Testament zur Bestätigung der Wirklichkeit und Tätigkeit des Auferstandenen angeführt. Vor allem ist hier Paulus zu erwähnen, der seit der Bekehrung bei Damaskus die Macht und Kraft des Auferstandenen immer wieder spürte und in seinem Briefwechsel mit den Korinthern allerlei Erscheinungen Christi vor älteren und jüngeren Zeugen aufgezählt hat. In diesem Lichte erweist sich die Auferstehung Jesu Christi als historische Tatsache und nicht bloß als fromme Phantasie.

Das leere Grab war ein materielles Ergebnis dieser nachher empirisch festgestellten Auferweckung Jesu vom Tode.

Bo Reicke

From a sermon preached on Easter Sunday, April 19, 1987, in the Evangelisch-Lutherischen Kirche in Basel, shortly before Professor Reicke's death on May 15.

Contents

viii

Preface

All of the essays in the present volume are by former students of Professor Bo Reicke, late Professor of New Testament at the University of Basel, Switzerland. By this volume, presented *in memoriam*, the authors desire to express on behalf of all his students their gratitude for his direction and instruction, as well as for his example of personal faith and humanity. Professor Reicke's doctoral students eventually numbered over forty, and the ten included in this volume are representative of their many nationalities and varying theological perspectives.

Aside from Professor Reicke's mastery of the New Testament and its time, his students enjoyed the happy opportunity of working under one who was, in his dealing with them, always patient, kind, and accessible. Some could tell of innumerable meetings with Professor Reicke in the coffee shop on the top floor of the University Library, or informal gatherings at local *Weinstuben* following an evening seminar in which Greek and Latin was translated from *Enchiridion Patristicum*, and all could attest to the hospitality extended by Professor Reicke and his wife Ingalisa when they opened their home on a regular basis to students. Indeed, the Reickes were always sensitive to the needs of their students, and over the years many a personal problem was resolved by their concern and intervention.

Though the essays in this volume cover a wide range of issues and otherwise differ in length and technicality, they relate in one way or another to the New Testament. The title of the volume, *Good News in History*, suggests the common conviction of the authors that history is the stage upon which God is accomplishing the salvation of his people, a conviction reflected also, and pervasively, in the writing and teaching of Professor Reicke. It is especially a pleasure to be able to include, in translation, a piece by Professor Reicke himself. His article, "Unity and Diversity in New Testament Theology," expresses perhaps better than any other of his writings the central concerns of his approach to the New Testament. And his students have on innumerable occasions seen on the chalkboard the diagram that appears in that article (p. 185 of the present volume)!

I wish to thank John S. Meyer, Damian Baumgardner, Michael McCloskey, and Erik M. Hanson (successive assistants in the Theology Forum at the University of Colorado), as well as Dr. Paul T. Keyser, and Rev. Garry DeWeese for their indispensable help in the preparation of the present volume. Also appreciated has been the continuing and always helpful counsel of Prof. Bruce N. Kaye and Prof. David Moessner, both contributors.

Ed. L. Miller

Abbreviations

ANF	*Ante-Nicene Fathers*
ANQ	*Andover Newton Quarterly*
ATR	*Anglican Theological Review*
CBQ	*Catholic Biblical Quarterly*
DNTT	*The New International Dictionary of New Testament Theology*
ET	*Expository Times*
GOTR	*Greek Orthodox Theological Review*
HTR	*Harvard Theological Review*
JBL	*Journal of Biblical Literature*
JBR	*Journal of Bible and Religion*
JES	*Journal of Ecumenical Studies*
JJS	*Journal of Jewish Studies*
JR	*Journal of Religion*
LCC	*Library of Christian Classics*
NT	*Novum Testamentum*
NTS	*New Testament Studies*
NTT	*Norsk Teologisk Tidsscrift*
NPNF	*Nicene and Post-Nicene Fathers*
RB	*Revue Biblique*
RE	*Real-Encyklopädie der klassischen Altertumswissenschaft*
SE	*Studia Evangelica*
SJT	*Scottish Journal of Theology*
TDNT	*Theological Dictionary of the New Testament*
TTZ	*Trierer theologische Zeitschrift*
TZ	*Theologische Zeitschrift*
VC	*Vigiliae Christianae*
ZNW	*Zeitschrift für die neutestamentliche Wissenschaft*

Good News for the "Wilderness Generation": The Death of the Prophet Like Moses According to Luke[1]

David Moessner

Professor of New Testament, Columbia Theological Seminary
Decatur, Georgia

It has become a maxim in the halls of New Testament scholarship that Luke ascribes no particular atoning significance to the crucifixion in his account of the salvation-history fulfilled in Jesus of Nazareth.[2] The most one can maintain is that

---

[1] First appearing as a seminar working paper, "Jesus and the 'Wilderness Generation': The Death of the Prophet Like Moses according to Luke," Society of Biblical Literature 1982 Seminar Papers, ed. K. H. Richards (Chico, Calif.: Scholars Press, 1982), pp. 319-340, reprinted here with minor revisions.

[2] In the interim of a decade since this study was first written this "maxim" has remained proverbial. However, due to the growing influence of literary-critical approaches, the "firm" conclusion is now being challenged, especially in Roman Catholic circles, as by R. J. Karris, "Luke 23:47 and the Lucan View of Jesus' Death," JBL, 105 (1986), pp. 65-74; idem, Luke the Theologian: Aspects of His Teaching (New York: Paulist Press, 1985), pp. 210-213; J. Neyrey, The Passion According to Luke: A Redaction Study of Luke's Soteriology (New York: Paulist, 1985), esp. pp. 184-192. Cf. my Lord of the Banquet (Minneapolis: Fortress Press, 1989), esp. pp. 322-324; idem, "'The Christ Must Suffer,' the Church Must Suffer: Rethinking the Theology of the Cross in Luke-Acts," Society of Biblical Literature 1990 Seminar Papers, ed. D. J. Lull (Atlanta: Scholars Press, 1990), pp. 165-195; idem, "The Christ must Suffer": The Center of Luke's Theology (forthcoming). No attempt has been made to update the vast number of studies bearing on the significance of Jesus' death that have appeared since the end of the 1970's. The thesis of the following study is intended to address only one angle of the larger dimension of Luke's portrayal of the crucifixion. See the surveys by, e.g., F. Bovon, Luc le théologien: Vingt-

2   *Good News in History*

the author of Luke-Acts has included a few traditional formulae which speak of vicarious sacrifice or redemptive blood (e.g., Luke 22:19b-20; Acts 20:28).[3] While it is conceded that *suffering*—both for Jesus (e.g., 9:22; 12:50; 13:33; 17:25; 18:31; 22:15, 19-20, 22, 37; 24:7, 25-27, 46; Acts 3:18, 24; 7:52; 8:32-35; 13:27; 17:3; 26:22, 27) and his disciples (e.g., Luke 9:23-25; 12:11-12; 14:26-27; Acts 9:16; 14:22; 20:23; 21:11-14)—plays an important role in the overall plan of God,[4] the

---

cinq ans de recherches (1950-1975) (Neuchâtel: Delachaux & Niestlé, 1978), pp. 175-181; C. H. Talbert, "Shifting Sands: The Recent Study of the Gospel of Luke," *Interpretation*, 30 (1976), pp. 389, 391; W. G. Kümmel, "Current Theological Accusations Against Luke," *ANQ*, 16 (1975), pp. 134, 138; *Introduction to the New Testament*, revised ed., tr. H. C. Kee [Nashville: Abingdon Press, 1975), p. 149. Cf. I. H. Marshall, *Luke: Historian and Theologian* (Exeter: Paternoster, 1970), pp. 169-175; H. Flender, *St. Luke: Theologian of Redemptive History* (London: SPCK, 1967), pp. 157-162; *contra*, L. Morris, *The Cross in the New Testament* (Exeter: Paternoster, 1965), pp. 63-143.
   [3] See n. 2 above. On traditional formulae, e.g., Kümmel, "Current Theological Accusations Against Luke," p. 138: "While Luke by no means entirely removes the redemptive significance of the death of Jesus he does not stress it." For earlier estimates, see, e.g., P. Vielhauer, "On the 'Paulinism' of Acts," in *Studies in Luke-Acts*, ed. L. E. Keck and J. L. Martyn (Nashville: Abingdon Press, 1966), p. 45 (first appearing in 1950/51); H. Conzelmann, *The Theology of Saint Luke* (London: Faber, 1960), pp. 201-202; U. Wilckens, *Die Missionsreden der Apostelgeschichte* (Neukirchen: Neukirchener Verlag, 1961), p. 216: "Der Tod Jesu hat keine Heilsbedeutung, und damit fehlt der lukanischen Christologie überhaupt jede inhaltliche Soteriologie." Other more recent views include, e.g., R. Tannehill, "A Study in the Theology of Luke-Acts," *ATR*, 43 (1961), pp. 195-203 (Jesus' self-humiliation on the cross is atoning "for us" as a basis for the church's communion and for bequeathing the Kingdom to the apostles); R. Zehnle, "The Salvific Character of Jesus' Death in Lucan Soteriology," *TS*, 30 (1969), pp. 420-444 (the whole life and death as exemplary causality or medium of God's graciousness, but the crucifixion is not an efficient cause of atonement); A. George, "Le sens de la mort de Jésus pour Luc," *RB*, 80 (1973), pp. 186-217 (the saving efficacy of the cross through martyrdom leading to the New Covenant in the plan of God); A. Büchele, *Der Tod Jesu im Lukas-Evangelium* (Frankfurt/Main: Knecht, 1978) (the saving efficacy of cross through repentance elicited by the power of the forgiving love of God revealed in the whole life and death of Jesus); F. G. Untergassmair, *Kreuzweg und Kreuzigung Jesu* (Paderborn: Schöningh, 1980) (the exemplary death along with the whole life offering "vertical" communion with God in the divine visitation of Jesus); D. L. Tiede, *Prophecy and History in Luke-Acts* (Philadelphia: Fortress Press, 1980), pp. 97-125 (the necessity to suffer/die as a Scriptural warrant in the plan of God); J. A. Fitzmyer, *The Gospel According to Luke: I-IX* (Garden City, N.Y.: Doubleday, 1981), pp. 219-221 and *passim* (the cross is an eschatological event in the whole drama of the salvific plan in the life of Jesus which highlights the necessity of the suffering Messiah); J. M. Ford, "Reconciliation and Forgiveness in Luke's Gospel," in *Political Issues in Luke-Acts*, ed. R. J. Cassidy and P. J. Scharper (Maryknoll, N.Y.: Orbis, 1983), pp. 80-98 (the whole ministry as atonement for outcasts and interceding as the new high priest for all sinners on the new Day of Atonement on the cross and as an efficacious martyr's intercession). Of those surveyed, only Ford singles out the cross in a direct connection with atonement for the *judgment* of God upon *sin*.
   [4] Kümmel, "Current Theological Accusations Against Luke," p. 138: Luke's "chief interest lies in the fact that the death of Jesus corresponds to the will of God"; Flender, *St. Luke*, p. 158: Jesus' "suffering is not only a human crime permitted by God, but was planned by his living,

real emphasis within the divinely ordained journey of salvation from Galilee to Jesus' "taking up" in Jerusalem is nevertheless upon that final stage of the resurrection or exaltation. "The exaltation of Jesus is the supreme saving event in Luke's eyes, since it is the act whereby God confirms the status of Jesus."[5]

Yet we may wonder whether attributing such a prominent idea as suffering and death simply to the "will of God" does justice to the critical function Luke accords this reality in the structuring of his salvation narrative. The whole path of Jesus is portrayed as one of rejection and cross-bearing in which those who cannot share in this suffering are excluded from the "gaining of life" (Luke 9:23-24; 14:26-27; cf. 9:58; 13:31-33; etc.). Jesus is reported to be "totally controlled" by the death awaiting him (12:50),[6] and if, as seems probable, 22:43-44 are to be regarded as ancient, if not authentic,[7] this death is indeed depicted as an agonizing ordeal of the greatest magnitude. Moreover, what protrudes at every crucial turn of events in the Acts is the fate of the disciples-apostles to follow their Master in the way of *suffering*: First the apostles (4:3, 18, 21; 5:17-26, 33, 40-41), then Stephen (6:9-14; 7:54-8:3), then the whole congregation of disciples (8:1; 11:19) are persecuted for the "sake of the name" (e.g., 9:16); and it has been pointed out that Paul's conversion is actually a calling to suffer (9:16), with his final trip to Jerusalem patterned after the way to the cross (e.g., 20:22-23; 21:11-14, 30-36).[8] When we are told repeatedly by Luke that both Jesus' and his followers' suffering fulfills a divine "must" (δεῖ) (9:22; 13:33; 17:25; 22:37; 24:7, 26, 44-46; Acts 1:16; 9:16; 14:22; 17:3; 23:11), then we may legitimately question whether this necessity is to be construed simply as the path of the "righteous" or of the martyr(s) which leads to glory.[9] Does not Luke himself perhaps supply a more specific and pivotal

---

active will"; Marshall, *Luke*, p. 172, commenting on the "Servant" Christology of Deutero-Isaiah in Luke: "In the Servant in fact we see the supreme case of a person who goes to suffering by the will of God."

[5] Marshall, Luke, p. 169; cf. Flender, *St. Luke*, pp. 159-162; Conzelmann, *Theology of St. Luke*, pp. 199-206; Talbert, "Shifting Sands," p. 389; H. Franklin, *Christ the Lord* (London: SPCK, 1975), pp. 58-67.

[6] See, e.g., on συνέχω, H. Köster, TDNT, VII, pp. 884-885.

[7] B. M. Metzger, A Textual Commentary on the Greek New Testament (London: United Bible Societies, 1971), p. 177 (ancient, but not original); I. H. Marshall, *Gospel of Luke* (Exeter: Paternoster, 1978), p. 832.

[8] H. J. Cadbury, The Making of Luke-Acts (New York: Macmillan, 1927), pp. 231-233; G. Bouwman, *Das dritte Evangelium* (Düsseldorf: Patmos, 1968), p. 74; for survey and literature, see esp. A. J. Mattill, "The Jesus-Paul Parallels and the Purpose of Luke-Acts: H. H. Evans Reconsidered," *NT,* 17 (1975), pp. 15-46, esp. pp. 30-37.

[9] Cf., e.g., Talbert, "Shifting Sands," p. 389: "In Luke-Acts Jesus' death is viewed primarily

content to his "will of God?"

Professor Bo Reicke has never been one simply or glibly to accept "assured results" without his own penetrating and remarkably unprejudiced investigation of the pertinent data. It is in gratitude to his even-handed approach to New Testament exegesis—a reputation which distinguished Professor Reicke among his peers—that the following study of the meaning of Jesus' death is undertaken. If this modest re-evaluation attains even a modicum of the admirable standard he has set, it must be gratefully credited to the inspiration of his own considerable and careful analyses of the Lukan *corpus*.

The suggestion offered here is that in the final two-thirds of his Gospel, Luke presents the journey of Jesus as a fulfilled or "new" Exodus to Jerusalem. His death, like Moses' in Deuteronomy, *must* occur in order to effect deliverance for a stiff-necked, disobedient nation. As such, this death, like that of Moses, expresses God's judgment upon this rebellion and, therefore, atones for the sin of the people. But because Jesus is the eschatological prophet like Moses (Deut. 18:15-19) whom God raises and exalts from the dead, his death enables and ushers in the final consummated salvation of the Exodus deliverance, granting Israel a second opportunity to receive this life even as this life is extended to the nations (the Acts). The focus will be limited to Luke 9-24 and to Peter's speech in Acts 3:12-26 where the motifs of the prophet like Moses are explicitly developed.[10]

Part I will provide a quick overview of Moses' calling in Deuteronomy with special attention to the role that his death plays.[11] Part II will argue that Luke 9:1-50 presents a fourfold Deuteronomic Exodus typology[12] which governs the

---

as part of the divine plan and as a martyrdom of a righteous man, which serves as the dominical basis for Christian suffering"; cf. F. Schütz, *Der leidende Christus* (Stuttgart: Kohlhammer, 1969), pp. 97-112.

[10] The only other citation of Deut. 18:15-19 in Luke-Acts is Acts 7:37; but the context for and thrust of Stephen's speech is not an evangelistic communication of the effect of Christ's life and death but rather a defense of the Christian community's relation to Israel's history of salvation. Thus the positive significance of the crucifixion is not treated there directly. For the Exodus typology in Acts 7, see L. T. Johnson, *The Literary Function of Possessions in Luke-Acts* (Missoula, Mont.: Scholars Press, 1977), pp. 70-76.

[11] Our methodology in both Parts I and II will follow a literary analysis of the text as *story*, as defined by the Russian "Formalists" (see, e.g., *Readings in Russian Poetics,* ed. L. Matejka and K. Pomorska [Cambridge, Mass.: MIT Press, 1971], pp. 3-37; *Russian Formalism,* ed. S. Bann and J. E. Bowlt [Edinburgh: Scottish Academic Press, 1973], pp. 6-19, 26-40, 48-72). For an application to the New Testament, see N. R. Petersen, *Literary Criticism for New Testament Critics* (Philadelphia: Fortress Press, 1978), pp. 24-92, esp. pp. 33-48.

[12] For our understanding of typology, see L. Goppelt, *Typos: Die typologische Deutung des Alten Testaments in Neuen* (Darmstadt: Wissenschaftliche Buchgesellschaft, 1966). Analysis of

portrayal of Jesus in the remainder of the Gospel. Part III will marshal evidence to contend that an *atoning* import is the only logical one for the death of Jesus within the argument of Acts 3:12-26. Although limitations of space prevent a more comprehensive investigation of the significance of Jesus' crucifixion, it is hoped that the imprint of the career and atoning death of the Prophet like Moses will emerge clearly as a pregnant picture of the Lukan "will of God."

I

Moses has led the pilgrim tribes of *all Israel*[13] to the borders of the Promised Land in the valley opposite Beth-peor (Deut. 3:29; cf. 34:6). There, under the baneful shadows of the Nebo massif (32:49-50; cf. 1:37; 3:27; 4:21-22), he takes the people through a renewal of the covenant at Mt. Horeb by leading them back in memory to their momentous revelation at that mountain and their ensuing wilderness wanderings from Kadesh-barnea (1:6-11:32).[14] Before the recitation and expounding of the Law (12:1-26:19), it already becomes manifest that in these two seminal experiences Moses' lot to *suffer* and *die* was irrevocably cast.

When at the mountain God began to speak to the gathered assembly of Israel out of the midst of the fiery cloud (4:12-13, 33, 36; 5:4, 22, 24; 9:10; 10:4), the people were so terrified that they implored Moses to mediate the voice (φωνή, LXX) of Yahweh for them (5:4-5, 22-31). This then becomes Moses' great calling, to utter the voice of the Lord to the people (e.g., 4:5, 14, 40; 5:27-28, 30-31; 10:5; 32:46-47; cf. 30:2, 8; etc.)[15] by teaching them all his commandments that they

---

the "form-content" of the journey "section" in Luke (9:51-19:44) in current exegetical discussion has ossified into a static "journey" form into which Luke has "poured" the content of various sayings of Jesus. By using the "Formalist" notion of "plot motivation" and "plot device" (cf. n. 11), we will be attempting to show that Luke has dynamically structured the "story-stuff" of the journey around a fourfold movement within a Deuteronomic Exodus typology.

[13] 1:1; 5:1; 11:6; 13:11; 18:6; 27:9, (14); 29:2, (10); 31:1, 7, 11 (twice); 32:45; 34:12.

[14] This portrait of his calling is indebted heavily to G. von Rad, *Old Testament Theology*, tr. G. M. D. Stalker (New York: Harper & Row, 1962-65), I, pp. 289-296; *Deuteronomy* (London: SCM Press, 1966), *passim*. For questions of tradition and redaction, cf., e.g., H. W. Nicholson, *Deuteronomy and Tradition* (Oxford, England: Blackwell, 1967), esp. pp. 18-36; M. Weinfeld, *Deuteronomy and the Deuteronomic School* (Oxford, England: Clarendon Press, 1972), esp. pp. 179-189, 320-370; N. Lohfink, "Darstellungskunst und Theologie in Dtn. 1:6-3,29," *Biblica*, 41 (1960), pp. 105-134, esp. pp. 107-110.

[15] Cf. von Rad, *Old Testament Theology*, I, p. 294: "The most impressive corroboration of this all-embracing mediating office of proclamation is of course the fact that the corpus of Deuteronomy is put into the form of words of Moses (and so not of Jahweh) spoken to Israel"; cf. Lohfink, "Darstellungskunst und Theologie," p. 106, n. 4.

might live in the land which they were to possess as an inheritance of the covenant to Abraham, Isaac, and Jacob (1:8; 6:10; 9:5, 27, 29; 29:13-15; 30:20; 34:4). But though they had promised fidelity to Moses' God-given word (5:27), even while Moses is still on the mountain speaking "face to face" with God (cf. 34:10), the people at the base rebel by worshiping an image, the golden calf (9:8-21; cf. 4:15-19). At once the Lord's anger is so overwhelming that only Moses' suffering submission in the intercession of 40 days and nights can appease his wrath sufficiently to save the people from total annihilation (9:18-20, 25-29; 10:10-11).

So the Lord continues his promise to them by sending Moses onward from Horeb at the head of the people to the land of promise (10:11; 1:7). But, it would seem, to no avail. Despite the searing discipline (4:36) of seeing the very glory of God on the mountain (5:24) and hearing his great voice from the cloud of fire (4:11) the people are intractable in defying Moses' authority. At Kadesh-barnea, some eleven days journey (cf. 1:2), all Israel and especially her "men of war" (2:14-16) spurn the voice of the Lord through Moses and spite Moses' leadership altogether as they "murmur" against the call to battle and then go up against the Lord's command (1:19-46). With that, two epoch-making judgments fall upon Moses and his egregious entourage: (i) Only the *children* (παιδίον) (1:39; cf. vss. 34-38; 11:2; 31:13) of the assembled people at Horeb will become the future possessors of the land; the entire older generation will be wiped out (1:35; 2:14-16); (ii) "On account of"[16] (1:37; 3:26) the people's intransigence Moses *must suffer* the anger of the Lord, the anguish of being choked off from the land of promise, and thus ultimately *die* without the promised deliverance—all *because of* the sin of his people (1:37; 3:26; 4:21-22; cf. 9:18-20, 25-29; 10:10-11; 31:2, 14; 32:50-52; 34:4).

These two themes sound the double-beat leitmotif of a dirge which undertones the whole of Deuteronomy. The first reverberates as the relentless, interminable stubbornness of all Israel to heed God's voice through Moses, even from the moment they left Egypt (e.g., 9:6, 7, 13, 27; 10:16; 12:8; 29:19; 31:27). They have been "rebellious"[17] (1:26, 43; 9:7, 23, 24; cf. 21:18, 20; 31:27) as long

---

[16] 1:37, *bighlal*—δι' ὑμᾶς; 3:26, *lema 'an*—ἕνεκεν ὑμῶν; see, e.g., T. W. Mann, "Theological Reflections on the Denial of Moses," *JBL*, 98 (1979), esp. p. 486.

[17] *marah* (Hi.); *sarar*—ἀπειθεῖν, -ῆς; cf. Mann ("Denial of Moses," p. 484) on *marah*: "It seems to have been introduced into the vocabulary of the wilderness theme by the Deuteronomist."

as Moses has known them (9:24). They are "evil" or "presumptuous"[18] (9:4-5, 27;
17:13; 18:20, 22; 19:16; 25:2), "sinful"[19] (5:9; 9:18, 21; 15:9; 19:15; 21:22; 23:21-
22; 24:15-16; 30:3), "proud"[20] (8:14; 17:20), slow to believe and "hearken"[21]
(9:23; cf. εἰσακούω, 1:43; 9:23; 21:18), refusing discipline and training[22] (4:10-14,
36; 5:5, 23-30; 8:2-5, 16-17; 9:6-29; 11:2-12) without "understanding"[23] (32:28;
cf. 4:6; 11:2). They need new "eyes to see and ears to hear" (29:4); or, as Moses
himself sums up, they are *en masse* a "stiff-necked," "faithless," and "crooked
generation" (32:5, 20; 1:35). Only against this refrain can the echo of Moses'
suffering and death, be heard as a clarion call to effect deliverance precisely
through this means. For it is not the case that the younger generation, the
"children" on the mountain who take possession of the land, are blameless while
their "fathers," the "men of war," receive the punishment. Rather, it is striking how
this generation at the "border" is lumped with their predecessors as one solidary
mass of a disobedient, perfidious people, such that their sin is at once linked to that
of their "fathers" on the one side, but also to the necessity of Moses' tragic fate on
the other.

At three strategic junctures in the story time[24] the necessity of Moses' death
is woven into the progression and ultimate completion of the *present* generation's
deliverance. (i) Moses' suffering mediation and intercession for the people at Horeb
is forged to Yahweh's sentence at Kadesh-barnea: Moses' cry for relief from the
"burden and strife" of a contrary people "at that time" (i.e., Horeb, 1:9) is
granted—ironically, if not heartlessly—in the subsequent and explicit announcement
of his death (1:9, 12 → 34-40; cf. 9:7-21 → 22-24). Though the present generation
was only "children who this day have no knowledge of good and evil" (1:39),
nonetheless they are made culpable for that grave disobedience: "The Lord was
angry with me also on account of *you*" (1:37). "When the Lord sent you from
Kadesh-barnea then *you* rebelled against the Lord" (9:23). (ii) As if to dispel any
notion that Yahweh's anger was assuaged by the death of the older evil generation
or that the Exodus continued to the borders of Canaan through the "uprightness"
or innocence of Caleb or Joshua or the "children" of the mountain, the narrator has

---

[18] *rasha'; zadhon; resha'* (Hi.) —ἀσεβ-, -εια, -ημα; ἀσεβεῖν.
[19] *'avon; chata'*—ἁμαρτία.
[20] *rum*—ὑψωθῆς.
[21] *shama '*—εἰσακούειν.
[22] E.g., 8:5: *yasar* (Pi.)—παιδεύειν.
[23] *tebunah*—ἐπιστήμη.
[24] In contrast to "plotted time"; see nn. 11 and 12.

Moses repeat Yahweh's sentence to him *"at that time"* (3:23),[25] i.e., *when the possession of the Trans-Jordan area was completed.* Moses' plea to enter into the land is met with "anger on *your* account" (3:26a). *Because of* the sin of the audience Moses is addressing, he must die (3:27). (iii) The third announcement removes any vestige of the possibility that Moses' death is, after all, merely parallel to the main event of deliverance, or that his denial outside the land is simply an example "of the tragic dimension of human experience."[26] After reviewing the affairs at Beth-peor following the time of the second declaration of his demise (4:1-9), Moses harks back to the revelation of Yahweh at Horeb to warn against apostasy, and uses that watershed event with its sequel at Kadesh-barnea (4:10-19) to summarize and typify his audience's present state of affairs *"this day"* (4:20b). They stand freed from their bondage in Egypt, ready to pass over into the land, to be sure (4:20), but—again—Moses must die, precisely because "on account of you,"[27] Yahweh "swore that I should not cross the Jordan nor enter into the good land which the Lord your God is giving you as an inheritance. For *I* must die in this land, *I* must not cross the Jordan, but rather *you* shall cross over that *you* may take possession of that good land" (4:21-22).[28]

In short, without Moses' death they would not receive the gracious act of deliverance that Yahweh is now bringing to pass[29] (cf. 31:2,14; 32:48-50;[30] 34:4) even as they are forewarned not to continue their rebellious ways once they have entered the land, lest they meet the same fate as their fathers (4:23-28). Thus at each of the three critical turns in the developing story *Moses' death* moves the action of Yahweh's deliverance forward to its climax at the boundaries of the land and enables the people to cross over to their promised inheritance.[31]

---

[25] See 3:29-4:1.

[26] So Mann ("Denial of Moses," p. 486), referring to H. Barzel, "Moses: Tragedy and Sublimity," *Literary Interpretations of Biblical Narratives,* ed. K. R. R. Gros Louis *et al.* (Nashville: Abingdon Press, 1974), p. 129.

[27] For the three parallel synonymous expressions (1:37; 3:26; 4:21), see S. R. Driver, *Deuteronomy,* revised ed. (Edinburgh: Clark, 1902), p. 27.

[28] The emphatic "I" is twice sharply contrasted to the emphatic "you."

[29] Driver, *Deuteronomy,* p. 71.

[30] Usually ascribed to the P account; cf., e.g., von Rad, *Deuteronomy,* p. 201; Mann, "Denial of Moses," p. 483.

[31] The suggestion is not that a developed, theoretical explanation of Moses' death as atoning or redemptive is offered in Deuteronomy. Yet within the plotted dynamics of the story, Moses' death is indispensable to the enactment of the Exodus deliverance and occupation of the land, an event which *must* be accomplished as an execution of Yahweh's wrath/judgment and, consequently, an explanation of the *raison d'être* of Moses' denial. For interpretations of

The pen-portrait is now distinct. Moses has emerged as a *suffering mediator*, sent from Horeb to lead the "faithless" and "crooked generation" of "children" to the promised salvation by *dying* outside the land. More precisely, we can distinguish a fourfold dynamic to his prophetic vocation:

(i) On the mountain, Moses' calling to be the mediator of God's life-giving words (the Law) on the Exodus journey is revealed most formidably by the voice (φωνή) out of the fiery cloud to the gathered assembly of *all* Israel.

(ii) From the mountain the persistent *stubbornness* of the people to hearken to this voice is divulged through its distortion into the *image* of the golden calf; this defiance in turn illustrates the unwillingness of the people to "hear" this voice from the beginning.

(iii) Accordingly, while Moses is still on the mountain, and as he descends and is *sent* on the Exodus, his calling is disclosed to be a *suffering journey to death*.

(iv) As a result, his calling does not effect deliverance for all those who follow him to the Promised Land but only for the new people of the land, the "children of the mountain."

At the core of this dynamic is the double-stroke of Israel's stiff-necked opposition to the voice of the Lord through Moses and the consequent tragic fate of this prophet. As later generations of Deuteronomist historians colored his career,[32] Moses' death outside the land was a *necessary* punishment for the sin of all Israel—even of the "children" who, like their fathers, proved themselves to be the "stubborn" and "crooked" "wilderness generation."

"vicarious" in a "substitutionary" and/or "representative" sense, see, e.g., von Rad, *Old Testament Theology*, I, pp. 294-295; G. E. Wright, "Exegesis of Deuteronomy," in *Interpreter's Bible*, ed. G. E. Wright *et al.* (Nashville: Abingdon Press, 1953), II, pp. 339-340.
[32] See nn. 14 and 25.

II

It has long been recognized that Luke's account of Jesus' mountain transfiguration (9:28-36) introduces his subsequent "journey" to Jerusalem (9:51-19:44).[33] But from a literary standpoint the whole of 9:1-50 performs such a function through Luke's[34] carefully carved continuity in audience and scenery. In this way, before Jesus' journey to his "taking up" is signally announced (9:51), Luke sets forth a four-fold Exodus typology of the prophetic calling of Jesus which conforms closely to that of Moses in Deuteronomy, as we have outlined it above. This typology in fact becomes the *organizing principle* for the rest of the story in the Gospel. As the scheme is set out, it is important to bear in mind that the correspondence in "type" is not a function of a mechanical, rote-like parallelism in the sequence of events or description of details. It is *not* suggested that a one-to-one analogy in the chronology of episodes in Deuteronomy exists in Luke 9:1-50 or in the following journey and events in Jerusalem, or that every event or subject in the one has a mirror image in the other. Rather, what we discover is a profound correspondence in the calling, execution, and fate of the calling of the one who is the Prophet like Moses (Deut. 18:15-19), effecting a New Exodus for a renewed people of God.

(i) Only Luke of the three Synoptists speaks of Jesus' transfiguration taking place "while he was praying" (9:28b, 29a); like Moses Jesus is one who speaks directly with God.[35] As his robes begin to "flash like lightning" (ἐξαστράπτω) and

---

[33] So, e.g., Conzelmann, *Theology of Saint Luke*, pp. 57-59; J. H. Davies, "The Purpose of the Central Section of Luke's Gospel," *Studia Evangelica II* (Berlin: Akademie, 1964), pp. 164-165; D. Gill, "Observations on the Lukan Travel Narrative and Some Related Passages," *HTR*, 63 (1970), pp. 218-221; C. C. McCown, "The Geography of Luke's Central Section," *JBL*, 57 (1938), pp. 64-66; P. Schubert, "The Structure and Significance of Luke 24," *Neutestamentliche Studien für Rudolf Bultmann*, ed. W. Eltester (Berlin: Töpelmann, 1954), pp. 181-182.

[34] Or perhaps his sources'. For more recent bibliography on Luke 9, see, e.g., R. C. Tannehill, *The Narrative Unity of Luke-Acts: A Literary Interpretation* (Philadelphia: Fortress Press, 1986), I, esp. pp. 303-316; see also the first paragraph of n. 2 above. For Luke 9:7-50 and especially Herod's perplexity (9:9) as raising the question of Jesus' identity and in 9:10-50 depicting Jesus' authoritative status in preparation for the "Teacher *par excellence*" of the journey section, see J. A. Fitzmyer, "The Composition of Luke, Chapter 9," *Perspectives on Luke-Acts*, ed. C. H. Talbert (Danville, Va.: Association of Baptist Professors of Religion, 1978), pp. 149-152.

[35] It may be objected that since Luke alone presents Jesus at *prayer* in other instances (e.g., 3:21; 5:16; 6:12; 9:18), and that Exodus also portrays Moses speaking directly with God (e.g., 19:9-13), this detail does not say very much, if anything at all. But this feature takes on added weight within the *interlocking* picture of Jesus with the Moses of Deuteronomy (see below) in which the Mosaic portrait is clearly distinguished from the J and E accounts in Exodus (cf., e.g.,

the "appearance" (εἶδος)[36] of his face is altered, suddenly (ἰδού) Moses and Elijah "appear" "in glory" (ἐν δόξῃ) with him (9:29b-31a). Luke alone would have his readers behold *three* glowing personages who must have created quite a spectacle for the unwitting observers. As with the Horeb theophany, the mountain was "burning with fire" (cf. Deut. 4:11-12, 15, 33, 36b; 5:23). Again it is only Luke who states that the three disciples saw Jesus' glory (τὴν δόξαν αὐτοῦ) (cf. Deut. 5:24). Peter, dumbfounded and stumbling over every word, suggests that they make three tents (9:33b) when, just "as he was speaking," a *cloud* [37] comes and "over-shadows" them (9:34).[38] The disciples are "frightened" as the cloud engulfs them and a "voice from the cloud" (φωνή . . . ἐκ τῆς νεφέλης) declares, "This is my Son, my Chosen One, *hearken* to him" (αὐτοῦ ἀκούετε) (vs. 35). Now it is the heavenly voice (φωνή) of Horeb which, Moses reminds the people time and time again, is their life (Deut. 4:11-13, 33, 36; 5:22-26; 8:20; 18:16; cf. for the future, 4:30; 13:4, 18; 15:5; 26:14, 17; 27:10; 28:1, 2, 9, 13, 15, 45, 62; 30:2, 8, 10, 20). To hearken is to live, to disobey is to die. And not only to this voice in Moses but also in the "prophet like" him who shall "arise" (ἀνίστημι) "among his brethren" after him are they to "*hearken* to him" (αὐτοῦ ἀκούσεσθε) (18:15b).[39] Here it is curious that of the three versions of this heavenly voice, only Luke in both diction and word-order matches the Septuagint of 18:15b.[40] Thus, like all Israel, who on the mountain hundreds of years earlier witnessed the authoritative revelation of the *divine voice* through Moses, so now on the mountain the three disciples, representing the "Twelve" and hence the twelve tribes of all Israel, witness the definitive revelation of the divine voice through Jesus, God's chosen Son. *Like Moses Jesus is called to mediate the voice of God.*

As Jesus determines to head for Jerusalem (9:51), Luke sketches a portrait of one whose authority can only be described adequately as the "voice of God." "On the way" (9:57-10:20) Jesus issues orders and sends out ambassadors on a

---

von Rad, *Old Testament Theology*, I, pp. 291-295). That Jesus is often at prayer merely shows the consistency of Luke 9:28-36 with the rest of the Lukan presentation.

[36] Cf. Ex. 24:10, 17 LXX—only Luke has this verbal link with the Exodus account.

[37] Cf. Ex. 40:35 LXX; Psalms 90(91):4 LXX; 139(140):7 LXX; Prov. 18:11 LXX.

[38] Whether the disciples, or Jesus and Moses and Elijah, are implied, is not decisive for our thesis; cf. Marshall, *Gospel of Luke*, p. 387.

[39] It must not be overlooked that the *authority* of the prophet like Moses is tied *directly* to Moses' authority *revealed at Horeb* (18:16-17).

[40] *If* any direct textual dependence is involved, this parallel would seem to indicate familiarity with the Septuagint account rather than any deliberate "change" of Matthew or Mark, especially given the latters' divergent emphases (see n. 57).

mission that brooks no rival. His command to follow him transcends any observance of the Law as it is currently perceived and enforced (9:59-60);[41] the *words* of his emissaries bear such a force that to heed (ἀκούω)[42] them is to make effective the eschatological life of the rule of God (10:5-6, 9), while to reject them already unleashes the verdict of the final judgment (10:10-12, 13-15, 16, 17-20). When confronted by one of the leading authorities of the covenant Law, there is no doubt that as Jesus finishes his parable of the uncompassionate priest and Levite with "Go and do likewise" (10:37b) he claims for himself the *authority* to declare where the life of the Law is present and where it is not (10:25-37). The conclusion is unavoidable that the "dead who are to bury their own" (9:60) are those who are missing the eschatological life of the life-giving Law in the Kingdom entourage of the "teacher" who utters directly the will of God (10:25, 28, 37; cf. vs. 38).

Between the two Deuteronomic pillars[43] of the *Shema* (10:27a—Deut. 6:5) and the Decalogue (18:20[44]—Deut. 5:16-20) Luke fills in his portraiture of a prophet-teacher whose own word defines "what one must do to inherit eternal life" (10:25; 18:18). Mary, who "was hearkening to his *word*," "has chosen the better part" (10:39b, 42); Jesus' words to the crowds are wiser than Solomon's and greater than Jonah's as they (and not his miraculous deeds) evoke the eschatological blessing of God's rule for those "who hear the word of God" in him "and keep it" (11:28, 29-36; cf. vss. 14-27); to the Pharisee leaders of the people comes the prophetic indictment that "you pass by justice and the love of God; these you ought to have done without neglecting the other things. . . . It shall be required of this generation" (11:42, 51b, 37-41, 43-50, 52); and to his disciples (cf. 12:1b) Jesus claims in his own presence to be an eschatological messenger who, according to their reception of him, will determine their fate in the court of God himself (12:8-9; cf. vss. 1-7, 10-12, 22-34). That is to say, he speaks for God: "Fool, this night your soul is required of you" (12:20); or, "It is your Father's good pleasure to give you the Kingdom" (12:32b); or, "Blessed is that servant whom his lord finds so doing when he comes" (12:43). It is no wonder that this "Lord" (13:23) who journeys on through the towns and villages toward Jerusalem, teaching in their

---

[41] See, e.g., W. Grundmann, *Das Evangelium nach Lukas* (Berlin: Evangelische Verlags-anstalt, 1961), p. 205.

[42] ποιέω (e.g., 10:25, 28, 37; 11:42) and φυλάσσω (11:28; 18:21) are the other key verbs.

[43] M. D. Goulder's expression in "The Chiastic Structure of the Lucan Journey," *Studia Evangelica II*, p. 196.

[44] Luke's order matches the Septuagint.

streets (13:22), controls the door into the banquet hall of salvation: "You will weep
. . . when you see Abraham . . . and all the prophets in the Kingdom of God but
you yourselves thrust out" (13:28, 23-27, 29-30). Only those who follow by
actually *hearkening* to his *word* will avail themselves of the covenant life fulfilled
in their midst (14:35; cf. 14:1-34; 15:1-2, 3-32). To the proud, prestigious, and
presumptuous[45] of Israel comes the categorical warning: "They have *Moses* and
the prophets, let them hearken to them. He [Abraham] said to them, 'If they do not
hearken to Moses and the prophets neither will they be convinced if someone
should rise from the dead'" (16:29, 31, 1-13, 14-18, 19-30; 17:1-10, 11-19, 20-37;
18:1-8, 9-14, 15-17). What Luke presents, then, is *eschatological halakhoth* from
the mouth of one who not only stands in the line of Moses and the prophets, but
will also consummate them through the raising up of this voice from the dead.
Jesus speaks with nothing less than the authority of the author of the Law
himself!—"Do this and you will live" . . . "and receive . . . in the coming age
eternal life" (10:28b; 18:30).

As the journey episodes intensify as Jesus nears Jerusalem, the life he bears
and speaks is manifest among those who submit to his authority: "Your faith has
saved you" (18:42); "Today salvation has come to this house" (19:9); "If these
were silent the very stones would cry out" (19:40). It is thus when he enters the
Temple that he is ensconced there by the people (λαός)[46] as *the teacher* of Israel
(19:47-48). He is the one who has the authoritative *word* to which the chief priests,
scribes, and elders (cf. 9:22) can only protest, "By what authority [ἐξουσία] do you
do these things? Who gave you this authority?" (20:2); ". . . they were not able in
the presence of the people to catch him by what he said" (20:26a); ". . . they no
longer dared to ask him any question" (20:40; cf. 20:1-8, 9-19, 20-26, 27-39, 41-
44, 45-47). This prophet-teacher, then, who "stirs up the people, teaching
throughout all Judea, from Galilee even to this place" (23:5) must die. Yet not even
death can prevent this voice from declaring the decisive life-giving word from God
as foretold by "Moses and all the prophets" (24:25-26, 44-47). For by virtue of the
resurrection and glorification of this prophet the apostles will stand up in
Solomon's Portico to announce that what Moses had prophesied in Deut. 18:15-19
has at last been culminated (Acts 3:22-23). Now even Peter, of the trembling trio

---

[45] Including the "disciples"; see below on (iii), in Part II.
[46] For Luke's use of λαός, see P. S. Minear, "Jesus' Audiences according to Luke," *NT*, 16
(1974), pp. 81-109.

on the mountain, will boldly resound to "all the people" of Israel the thunderous voice from that mountain: *"Hearken to him"* (Deut. 18:15b → Luke 9:35b → Acts 3:22b).

(ii) It is only Luke of the Evangelists who dares mention that while Jesus is transfigured "in glory" with Moses and Elijah the disciples sleep (βεβαρημένοι ὕπνῳ) (9:32a)![47] Only *after* they have "awakened" (vs. 32b) do they "see" Jesus' glory and the two prophets. Moreover, Luke does not spare Peter and his companions further embarrassment when Peter, astir with "greatness in the air," thinks that the group needs a "booth" for each of the "glorious" figures—"not knowing what he was saying" (9:33b). It is then, *"as he was speaking"* (9:34a), that a *cloud* comes and the "voice out of the cloud" commands the terrified disciples to obey the voice of God in Jesus, his elect Son. Like the people of Israel on Horeb who in their stubborn resistance to obey the voice of God through Moses had to be disciplined by the shock of the thundering voice from the fiery cloud (Deut. 4:36), so the disciples in their stuporous response to the voice of God through Jesus also have to be overwhelmed by the traumatic voice from out of the cloud. Luke continues (vs. 36) that "after the voice had *spoken* Jesus was found alone" and the disciples "were mute," telling no one in those days (ἐν ἐκείνας ταῖς ἡμέραις) anything of what they had seen (ἑώρακαν). For they could say, with the speakers in Deut. 5:24b, "We have this day [ἐν τῇ ἡμέρᾳ ταύτῃ] seen [εἴδομεν] God speak with human beings and humans still live!"

It may be objected that this second analogy hardly holds together when it is recalled that in fear of their own lives the Israelites eagerly accepted Moses' mediation of the divine voice on the mountain, in contrast to the halting ambivalence of the disciples who do not even comprehend the "life and death" matters in their midst at all. But what we are presenting is a typological correspondence far more fundamental than a specific sequence or episode within a momentous revelation. To penetrate these deeper dimensions it will be necessary to see how Luke's casting of the disciples on the mountain is, like Deuteronomy, carefully engrafted into the behavior of the crowd below on the plain (9:1-27, 37-50).

In 9:1-6 Jesus "sends" out the Twelve with "power" (δύναμις) and "authority" (ἐξουσία) to continue the same activity in which he himself has been engaged, sc. healing and preaching the Kingdom of God (vs. 2; cf. 9:11). Herod's stance to both Jesus' and his emissaries' amazing feats is then dovetailed into this sending out

---

[47] For linguistic issues, cf. Marshall, *Gospel of Luke*, p. 385.

(9:7-9): Herod has "heard of all the things that were being done"; folks are buzzing with speculation that "John the Baptist had been raised [ἠγέρθη]" or that "Elijah had appeared [ἐφάνη]" or that "one of the prophets of bygone days had arisen [ἀνέστη]"⁴⁸ (cf. ἀναστήσω, Deut. 18:15, 18); as for Herod, he is at a loss for what to think—he must "see" (ἰδεῖν) this Jesus for himself (9:9; cf. 23:6-12)! The disciples' activity here is without doubt identified with Jesus' fame; to hear about their work is to force a decision about Jesus.⁴⁹ They appear to be one with their master in the power and authority granted them.

The Twelve return (9:10) and report, but no response is given by Jesus except that he takes them "apart" to Bethsaida. The "crowds" (ὄχλοι) (vs. 11), however, who have thronged Jesus for some time now,⁵⁰ learn where he is going and follow him. While it is not explicitly stated that these crowds represent the same group which is voicing its opinions about Jesus (9:7-8), it is nevertheless interesting that at this point, after he has spoken about the Kingdom of God, healed,⁵¹ and with his disciples fed these crowds in a desert place (ἐν ἐρήμῳ τόπῳ) (vs. 12b; cf. ἐν τῇ ἐρήμῳ, Deut. 8:2), Jesus asks his disciples just what these *crowds* are thinking about him (9:18). They report almost verbatim the same sentiments that are troubling Herod's ears (vs. 19). The popular feeling is that Jesus is a great prophet, comparable to the greatest of the Old Testament figures. The reader is led to believe, then, that these opinions are emerging essentially from the same crowds. Peter, on the other hand, not content to be marked by such commonality, goes beyond this stance, acknowledging Jesus to be God's own "anointed" (τὸν χριστὸν τοῦ θεοῦ) (9:20). But unlike the other Synoptists no praise or blessing by Jesus is accorded this insight; no period of private correction and teaching is awarded the confession.⁵² Instead, Jesus, "charging" and "commanding" them to silence and in the same breath (εἰπών)⁵³ telling them that "the Son of Man must suffer many things . . . ," *continues on* by telling (cf. ἔλεγεν, vs. 23)⁵⁴ *all* that they too must

---

⁴⁸ This phrase is unique to Luke.

⁴⁹ This is a vivid illustration of the *shaliach* concept; cf. Luke 9:10: οἱ ἀπόστολοι. See C. K. Barrett, "*Shaliach* and Apostle," in *Donum Gentilicium,* ed. H. Bammel and W. D. Davies (Oxford, England: Clarendon Press, 1978), pp. 88-102.

⁵⁰ E.g., 6:17, 19; 7:9, 11, 12, 24; 8:4, 19, 40, 42, 45.

⁵¹ These first two activities match those of the Twelve (9:2).

⁵² Contrast Mark 8:31-32 and Matt. 16:17-19, 21, 24-28.

⁵³ Cf., e.g., W. Grundmann, "Fragen der Komposition des lukanischen Reiseberichts," *ZNW,* 50 (1959), pp. 255-256.

⁵⁴ Cf. Marshall, *Gospel of Luke,* p. 373: "He went on to say"; for this use of the imperfect cf. F. Blass and A. Debrunner, *A Greek Grammar of the New Testament and Other Early*

suffer if they want to save their lives by following him (9:23-26). The sequence here is quite different than in Mark and Matthew. For Luke presents one continuous scene in which the *same crowds* remain close by as a theatrical backdrop for the disciples' performance. This lack of interaction of Jesus with his disciples might appear to "level" them with the masses, to join them with the popular currents of the crowds. *All* must follow Jesus and *all* alike must suffer. Yet however different this picture, without Mark and Matthew as foils, and stylistic variances notwithstanding, Luke's account is straightforward and intrinsically logical. The disciples *are* distinguished from the crowds confessionally and spatially by a relative privacy where Jesus is praying "alone," in addition of course to their commissioning (9:1-6) and special assistance in feeding these multitudes (9:12-17).

But as we pursue the advancing lines of the plot, this suspicion is borne out as the disciples' solidarity in power and authority with Jesus takes marked turns in the opposite direction. The divergences in audience and sequence with Mark and Matthew do indeed become signposts of a fundamentally different terrain which lies ahead. The great tableau of Jesus' following which extends from 9:10-27 climaxes with Jesus prophesying to all that some among them will not "taste death" before they "see [ἴδωσιν] the Kingdom of God" (vs. 27). "Now about eight days after *these sayings*," Peter, James, and John—in spite of themselves—"see" (εἶδον) Jesus' *glory* on the mountain (vs. 32). "The next day" when they have descended, Jesus is met by a "great crowd" (ὄχλος πολύς) (9:37b) only to learn from one of them (ἀπὸ τοῦ ὄχλου) (vs. 38a) that his *disciples* "were unable" (οὐκ ἠδυνήθησαν) (vs. 40) to heal this man's "only son" (cf. vs. 38b). Jesus' response: "You faithless and crooked generation!" (ὦ γενεὰ ἄπιστος καὶ διεστραμμένη) (vs. 41a). Here Jesus lumps his disciples together with one solid mass of a disbelieving, perverse people. Indeed, just as earlier the people's faithless twisting of God's commandment in the case of the golden calf revealed their disobedience when Moses descended the mountain, so now, as Jesus descends the mountain, the disciples' faithless twisting of their divinely bestowed power and authority with the man's only son reveals the disobedience of the whole generation. Moreover, Moses' charge to the people that they are a "stubborn and crooked generation" (γενεὰ σκολιὰ καὶ διεστραμμένη) (32:5), and "a perverse [ἐξεστραμμένη] generation, children in whom there is no faith [οὐκ ἔστιν πίστις]" (32:20), is matched here by Jesus: In both, the zealous anger of the Lord who confronts an obdurate generation "in the wilderness" comes to expres-

---

Christian Literature, tr. and rev. Robert W. Funk (Chicago: University Chicago, 1961), sec. 329.

sion. And Moses' cry of desperation at Horeb, "How can I bear alone the weight and the burden of you and your strife?" (1:12), is echoed remarkably again by Jesus here at the base of the mountain: "How long am I to be with you and bear you?!" (Luke 9:41).[55] Jesus laments that he must endure this faithless mass any longer; even the disciples, who hardly more than a week earlier had confessed his Messiahship, are pulled into and identified with this crooked lot. They in fact are the very provocateurs of this outburst. Their "impotence" at the base of the mountain becomes a striking demonstration of their ambivalence at the top. The *whole generation*, disciples and all, are like their Horeb counterparts—one disobedient, rebellious mass.

That this portrayal is not happy coincidence is startlingly confirmed as the scene unfolds. Luke moves at a quick pace. While the crowds "marvel" at the "majesty [μεγαλειότης] of God and all that he was doing" (9:43), Jesus tells his disciples again in sobering if not stern words, "Let these words sink into your ears [ὦτα]. . . ." (9:44). The disciples fare no better this time than with Jesus' first prediction of his passion as Luke stresses, in four different phrases, their incapacity to grasp these words: They (a) do not "understand" (b) that which has been "concealed" from them, (c) "in order that they should not perceive"; and (d) "they were *afraid* [cf. vs. 34b] to ask him about this saying" (9:45). They are like their frightened wilderness predecessors who remain slow to believe and *hearken* (Deut. 9:23; 32:20), a people "without understanding" (32:28), even though they had witnessed the "majestic" (μεγαλεῖος) (11:2-7) deliverance of God. Despite the mighty signs in their midst and the glory on the mountain, they re-embody the people of whom Moses so well observed: "You have seen all the things the Lord did . . . the signs and those great wonders. Yet the Lord has not given you a heart [καρδία] to know or eyes to see or ears [ὦτα] to hear, even to this very day" (29:2b-4).

But as with the Israelites, the disciples' and the whole generation's "crooked" disobedience is not simply summed up by uncomprehending unbelief. For immediately Luke continues on at the same time and in the same "crowded" arena with the disciples arguing which of them is the "greatest" (9:46-48). That they could squabble about their own importance in the midst of these crowds just when they had failed miserably at casting out a "demon" (δαιμόνιον) (vs. 42) from one

---

[55] The disciples are "at strife" in 9:46-48 (see below); see n. 57 for the different import of this lament in Matt. 17:17 and Mark 9:19.

of their *children* seems almost as if Luke here has resorted to "burlesque." With the powerful perception of a prophet Jesus penetrates all the way to their "hearts" (εἰδὼς . . . τῆς καρδίας αὐτῶν) and places a "child" (παιδίον) by his own side (9:47). The point: Unless one can humble his or her puffed-up heart, and *"in my name"* associate with, i.e., "receive" (δέχομαι), a person as small (μικρότερος) and insignificant as a child, that one will be unable to "receive" Jesus and thus also the One who has "sent" Jesus (9:48). There is no point in being at Jesus' side unless one is humble enough to be at a child's side. The rebuke to the disciples could hardly be more scathing. They are failing to obey Jesus' voice through "proud and patronizing hearts."

That this is the pith of the problem in its Lukan context is illustrated by the next pericope which again continues on, uninterrupted in setting. John "answers" that they (i.e., the disciples) "saw [εἴδομεν] someone casting out *demons* [δαιμόνια] *in your name*"; they "forbade him, because he does not follow *with us* [ἀκολουθεῖ μεθ᾿ ἡμῶν]" (cf. 9:11, 23). Not only are the disciples blind and deaf to the true authority of Jesus' voice, but their presumptuousness also makes them numb to Jesus' discipline. What they "see" in this Jesus who performs mighty works is foremostly that which makes themselves "mighty" as well. That is to say, they cannot recognize and fall in line with Jesus' authority structure but insist that "true following" (cf. 9:23-27) requires a falling in line with them. The resonance of ἐν τῷ ὀνόματί σου (9:49) with ἐπὶ τῷ ὀνόματί μου (9:48) is loud and clear. Jesus' retort is also equally unequivocal. He forbids them to "forbid" the person who is working "in Jesus' name"[56] since such a person is obviously not "against" the disciples but is "for them" (9:50). Jesus' pointing to the child in vs. 48 as an object lesson in submission to his authority has been of no account whatever. The disciples are too caught up in their own "prominence" to *stoop* to the side of the child. They are like their obstinate antetypes—refusing discipline and training (Deut. 9:6-29; cf. 4:36; 5:23-30; 8:2-5, 14-20; 11:2-7). Their glimpse of Jesus' divine glory on the mountain has revealed their own self-"glory" on the plain (Deut. 5:24; Luke 9:32).[57] We are now in a position to see how the incidents at the base of the

[56] There is no indication by Jesus that his authority is being abused by the "unknown" exorcist.

[57] A comparison of the *disciples* in the corresponding Matthean and Markan passages discloses that only Luke reflects a developed complex of Exodus motifs which determines the whole *tenor* and *structure* of the story of Jesus: Mark 9:14-50—the disciples are *bound* to Jesus through their confessing, albeit naive and insufficient, faith and as such are set apart from the unbelieving and, in part, even hostile crowds; Matt. 17:14-18:35—even more than in Mark the

mountain interpret the behavior on the summit and in fact all that precedes the
ascent (9:1-27). The contrast of the disciples with the "unknown exorcist" could not
be starker. He has the power and authority to exorcise *demons* because he works
in Jesus' name, *he has submitted to the divine voice in Jesus.* This incident (9:49-
50), which at first seems to be attached arbitrarily by Luke, indeed renders Jesus'
lament and charge in 9:42 fully comprehensible. The disciples are unable to
exorcise the demon from the child because they have not submitted to this divine
voice, and they *cannot* because their "hearts" are bloated beyond response to the
"child" in their midst. They are at *base* no different from the rest of the "twisted,
unbelieving generation" of the crowds. Thus what we have is the same fundamental
distortion of the divine voice as at Horeb. In both, the command to hearken to the
authority of the Lord through his mediator is completely contorted to the authority
of their own imagination: As the *image* of the molten calf divulges the rebellious
refusal to obey the voice of God in Moses, so the *image* of self-importance of the
disciples reveals their stubborn refusal to obey the voice of God in Jesus. The idol
of the one is as real as the idol of the other. Thus *in both Deuteronomy and Luke
9 the reluctance and fear of listening to the voice of God on the mountain is truly
a foreboding revelation of the "wilderness generation" on the plain.* And the
incomprehension, strife, conceited hearts, imperviousness to discipline, etc., all
become salient signs of "this generation's" crooked unbelief. We can schematize
this basic dynamic of response in both Deuteronomy and Luke 9:1-50 as follows:
Reluctance and Fear of Hearing the Voice on the Mountain → Stubborn Perversion
of this Voice on the Plain → Incomprehension, Strife, Conceit, Rejection of
Discipline, etc. by the Whole Generation. What was true of the miraculous signs
for the wilderness people of God becomes true again for the "wilderness
generation" in Luke: "You have been rebellious against the Lord from the day that
I knew you" (Deut. 9:24; cf. 8:3, 15-20).

At several pivotal points in the developing contour of the "voice of God" to
Jerusalem, Luke again presents a Jesus who confronts the "wilderness generation"
which, like their "fathers," forms an obstinate monolith of resistance. In 11:14-54,
although encountering five types of response, Jesus levels them all to one *mass* of
an "evil generation" (vss. 29, 50-51).[58] "Marvelling" amazement (vs. 14b), a

---

disciples are distinguished from the *unbelieving* and *perverted* crowds (17:17a) by their faith and
responsibilities as *guardians* of that faith.

[58] Although only "others" (11:16a) are "seeking a sign," Jesus accuses the *whole generation*
of this (vs. 29).

charge of alignment with "Beelzebul" (vs. 15), "testy" skepticism (vs. 16), naive, uncommitted admiration (vss. 27-28), and censorious "amazement" (vs. 38) all stand condemned at the final judgment for failing to *repent* at the "sign" of the preaching of the one greater here in their midst (vss. 29-32). Smaller groups (vss. 15-16), a nameless individual (vss. 27-28), and Pharisees (vss. 37-54; cf. vs. 37a—"while he was speaking") all emerge from the burgeoning crowds of "this generation" (ἡ γενεὰ αὕτη) (vs. 29) to be spattered by the "blood of all the prophets shed from the foundation of the world . . . from the blood of Abel to the blood of Zechariah" (vs. 51a). It is precisely "this generation" which "consents to the deeds of *your fathers*" (vs. 48). Whereas in 9:1-50 it was the *disciples'* inability and lack of *authority* which spark Jesus' indictment of the crowds (9:41), it is now the resistance to Jesus' *ability* and *authority* from the individuals, groups and leaders of the crowds themselves which provokes this same rebuff. "Yes, I tell you, it shall be required of *this generation*" (vs. 51a).

As the crowds swell to the "thousands" (12:1) Jesus turns alternately to the disciples (12:1b, 22) and the masses (12:15, 54) to warn them to discern and heed the "sign" (cf. 11:16) in their midst that is already "on the way" to "accuse" them before the "judge" (12:58). The crowds of this generation have already become like their leaders, "hypocrites" (12:56 → 12:1 → 11:37-54). By refusing to repent they will bring upon the whole nation (cf. the fig tree)[59] destruction "normally" associated with their "worst sinners" (13:1-5); a calamity experienced by *some* is a ready illustration of the calamity awaiting *all* (vss. 3, 5)!

Farther along the way (cf. 17:11) Jesus is confronted again by a stubborn generation that seeks a "sign" (17:20-21 → 11:29). He does not mince his words when he tells "the Pharisees" that the Kingdom of Salvation (cf. 17:19) they are searching for is already in their midst. The leaders of "this generation" remain like their "unknowing" followers (cf. 11:29-36, 43-46; 12:55-57),[60] calloused to the "effective presence" of the Kingdom already "here" in their presence (cf. ἰδοὺ ὧδε, 17:21 → 11:30b, 32b). So Jesus once again turns to his disciples to admonish them not to fall prey to a *generation* that, once they have inflicted his suffering and rejection (17:25), will continue as the generations of Noah and of Lot to "eat and drink, buy and sell," etc., totally hardened to the redemptive warning of the past

---

[59] E.g., Hos. 9:10; Joel 1:7; Jer. 8:13; 24:1-8; Mic. 7:1.

[60] 12:57 intimates an unwitting acceptance of *someone else's judgment*, most likely from their leaders, 12:1.

and oblivious to the future day of the Son of Man (17:24, 30). Such a day will not come when "folk say to *you*, 'Look, here [ὧδε] it is!'" (17:23 → 21 → 12:54-57 → 11:30b, 32b, 16).

With the sights of Jerusalem in full view Jesus weeps for a people who have remained blind to the "things that would lead to peace" (19:41-42). Jerusalem, symbol of God's covenant salvation and yet also of a nation's stiff-necked rejection of God's messengers (13:33-35), proves itself again to be the "wilderness generation" that spurns the Exodus *visitation* (ἐπισκπή) of God (19:44b → 9:31 → Ex. 3:16 LXX; Gen. 50:24-25 LXX). Therefore, as in 587 B.C.E., and already predicted by Moses (Deut. 4:25-28; 28:45-68[61]), God will *visit* them for destruction (cf. Jer. 6:15; 10:15; Isa. 29:6). In the Temple Jesus proceeds to etch this nation's behavior into the "people's" minds; their leaders are like the impudent tenants of a vineyard who, repeatedly mistreating the owner's messengers, force him to give the vineyard to others (20:9-18, esp. vs. 16).[62] It is no coincidence that Luke begins his Acts with Jesus' charge to the "wilderness generation" at the mountain—now echoed ironically by Peter—"save yourselves from this 'crooked generation'" (Acts 2:40b → Luke 9:41 → Deut. 32:5), and closes his story with the prophet's foreboding pronouncement of a "blind," "deaf," and "hard-hearted" people: "This people's heart has grown dull. . . . Therefore . . . this salvation of God has been sent to the Gentiles; they will hearken [ἀκούσονται]" (Acts 28:27a, 28; Paul citing Isa. 6:9-10).

(iii) It is only Luke of the Gospel writers who discloses that while the disciples slumber Moses and Elijah converse with Jesus about his "exodus" (ἔξοδος) "which he was to fulfill in *Jerusalem*" (9:31). We have already seen that Luke explicitly links Jesus' words about bearing a cross and losing one's life directly to the mountain glorification (9:23-27 → 28). These words are in turn an amplification of the Son of Man's *suffering rejection* and *death* at the hands of "elders, chief priests, and scribes" (9:22), that is, by the Sanhedrin in Jerusalem. Moreover, in the context of 9:51 where "the days" (plural) of his "taking up" in Jerusalem are (literally) "becoming completely full," that is, "had already arrived,"[63] it is certain that the exodus Jesus fulfills in Jerusalem is also one that

---

[61] For these Deuteronomistic traditions, see O. H. Steck, *Israel und das gewaltsame Geschick der Propheten* (Neukirchen-Vluyn: Neukirchener Verlag, 1967), pp. 139-143.

[62] See F. W. Danker, *Jesus and the New Age* (St. Louis: Clayton, 1972), p. 201.

[63] Cf. Acts 2:1 for the best analogy; cf. also Davies, "Purpose of the Central Section of Luke's Gospel," and Schubert, "Structure and Significance of Luke 24," pp. 184-185, for the

he fulfills on his way *to* Jerusalem, i.e., through a *journey* to that city. Hence his exodus is both a "going out" *to* as well as a "departure" *from* Jerusalem. *Like Moses, then, Jesus' calling to a journey of suffering and death is revealed to those on the mountain who would follow him to reach the "promised land" of salvation* (Deut. 1:6-9; 10:11; Luke 9:22-25 → 32 → 51).

As Jesus descends and is met by the "wilderness generation" his cry of desperation, like Moses' lament, reveals the palpable *necessity* of his suffering. "How long must I be with you and put up with you?" voices the sentiment not of a normal mortal but of one who is clearly reckoning with a departure from "this generation"[64] in the imminent future. This necessity is suddenly voiced again, and in the most ironic of settings. As the chorus of the *crowds of people* marvel approval, Jesus tries to shake his disciples from the snare of sin by warning them of these same people into whose hands he is about to be "delivered" (παραδίδωμι) (9:44b;[65] cf. 9:23, 25, 18). It is not only the Sanhedrin that is going to force Jesus' death, but so is this same *twisted generation*! The base of the mountain again confirms what has already been divulged at the top. And it now becomes transparent that Herod's beheading of John the Baptist along with his desire to "see" Jesus (9:9 → 23:8) is an omen of ill on par with the "crowds'" (9:11-19) or the "disciples'" (9:20, 27, 28-36, 37-50) ability to "see" Jesus. Consequently, together with Herod symbolizing the hardened nation, the disciples' desire to dismiss rather than feed the λαός in the wilderness is, like the Exodus antetype (Deut. 8:2-5, 14-17), a poignant demonstration of the whole generation's stubborn refusal to accept discipline and hence to heed the voice of the mountain revelation. The grounding for the death of Jesus is thus already the same as for Moses in Deuteronomy. *Because of* the intransigent sin of the people, a resistance so powerful that even gestures of redemption are twisted around to strife, jealousy, and conceit, Moses/Jesus *must suffer and die.*

As Jesus and his retinue continue onward from the mountain on the New Exodus, the various *dramatis personae* of the "wilderness generation" emerge along Jesus' path to merge eventually into one solid front of disobedience and even hostile opposition. As they cross over into Samaria, the disciples can only think of

---

linguistic relation of 9:51 to 9:31.

[64] See M. Dibelius, *Die Formgeschichte der Evangelien* (Tübingen: Mohr, 1919), p. 278.

[65] 9:23-25, along with probable paronomasia on ὁ υἱὸς τοῦ ἀνθρώπου with χεῖρας ἀνθρώπου (cf. J. Jeremias, "παῖς θεοῦ," in *TDNT*, V, p. 715), indicates a *generic* sense of "man," or the *generation* of Jesus' day; cf. 17:25.

calling down more of that "glorious fire" of the mountain (9:29-34) to vindicate their own status as the mighty men of war for their Messiah-Deliverer (9:54—Deut. 1:41; 2:16). But for Jesus' stiff rebuke the disciples would "gird on his weapons of war and go up and fight!" (Deut. 1:41). Jesus must warn all who would wish to follow that his journey will be one long trek of rejection, not unlike that through the Samaritan village—"without any place to lay his head" (9:57-58). His own ambassadors will be like "lambs in the midst of wolves" (10:3; cf. vss. 6b, 10-12, 16b).

At table fellowship with the leaders of "this generation" the one greater than Solomon and Jonah who is "here" links them to the *persecution* and *murder* of all the prophets throughout Israel's history. Luke records that as he departed, "the scribes (οἱ γραμματεῖς) and the Pharisees began to oppose him fiercely . . . waiting to catch him in something he might say" (11:53-54). The plot thickens instantly when Jesus goes directly to warn his disciples of the "leaven of the Pharisees which is hypocrisy" (12:1). This infectious influence, which engages Jesus as a "teacher" while simultaneously undermining the "something greater," will be fully exposed (12:2). Those who endure will undergo persecution and trial (12: 4-7, 11-12); but their allegiance will be rewarded by acclaim before the throne of God (vss. 8-9). They should therefore not be in fear of those who, at most, can *kill* the body (vs. 4). Rather, they are to fear God and submit to his chosen ambassador (vss. 5, 8-10). As the large audience scene unfolds, however, it becomes alarmingly apparent that the large band of disciples are succumbing more and more to this leaven. They are told not only that slovenliness in preparing for the coming judgment will result in disaster (12:35-48), but that this judgment is also *already* in their midst, straining relentlessly to its fulfillment (vss. 49-53). For Jesus himself *has come* (vss. 49, 51) to cast eschatological fire right through the center of the households of Israel (vss. 52-53). As the "accuser" is "on the way" these households "from now on" will be torn asunder (vss. 58, 52a)! Stiff-necked opposition to his sending is now welling up so ominously that Jesus is becoming engulfed by the "baptism" of death (vs. 50). That "immersion" in the obdurate "wilderness generation" at the mountain is developing inexorably towards eruption. The destiny of this judgment is inescapable; it is becoming all-consuming and explosively real. "How I wish it were already ignited!" (vs. 49a).[66]

---

[66] Cf. Marshall in noting the relation between the coming fire of judgment upon the world and Jesus' baptism of death: "His baptism is the pre-condition for what is to follow" (*Gospel of Luke*, p. 547).

Opposition to Jesus intensifies even as he intensifies his warning to disciples and crowds and puts his "hypocritical adversaries to shame" (13:15, 17). In 13:31-35 Jesus learns that Herod already has a "death warrant" out on his life. Undeterred, he tells these Pharisees, in effect, that indeed Herod will have his day (cf. 23:6-12), but not until he has journeyed on his divinely ordered sending as a prophet to the heart of a stubborn nation (vss. 32-33). With this prophet's lament and cry of judgment in vss. 34-35, it has become certain that the judgment required of "this generation" for all the murders of Israel's prophets and messengers is due to its killing of the prophet Jesus who forms the "omega point" of this entire history. Luke follows immediately with another instance of "this generation's" determination to impede Jesus in his Exodus sending (14:1-6; 13:31-35 → 11:53-54). The leaders and their "many" (14:16) are already on the brink of exclusion from the Kingdom banquet which Jesus' journey is inaugurating (esp. vss. 15, 17, 21-24). When, at some point later on the journey (cf. 14:25), the Pharisees scoff at Jesus' talk of crisis and ultimate obedience and the dangers of prestige and wealth, he retorts with a parable mirroring the "many" with its influential leaders who have become so immune to the signs and warnings of the present time that not even the raising up of a prophet from the dead can jolt them into repentance (16:14-31). Thus it happens that the solid front of lepers of the Jewish nation (17:11-19) becomes emblematic of what already has become abundantly evident: Jesus "must [δεῖ] *suffer* many things and be rejected by *this* generation" (17:25). Jesus must die.

At 18:31-34, Jesus informs the "Twelve" that the imminent journey "up to Jerusalem" will bring to fruition everything written about him by the prophets. But "this generation" remains obtuse (18:34; cf. 9:44b). With the monolithic house of scorn in place (19:7, πάντες; cf. vss. 14, 20-27, 39-40, 44b), it is not long, once Jesus has entered the Temple, that the forces of opposition are set in motion. Representatives of each of the three functionary groups of the Sanhedrin are actively *plotting* to kill Jesus (19:47). And with Luke's mention of the "scribes" (γραμματεῖς) (vs. 47) we encounter once again the Pharisees and the Pharisee-scribes whom Jesus had arraigned *at table* on the journey for their hypocrisy as leaders of the λαός—and whom he will again so indict (11:43-46 → 14:7-11 → 20:45-47; cf. 20:19-20, 39-40).[67] But just when these plotters again appear in the picture (22:2),

---

[67] As in 20:47 it is the Pharisee-scribes of 11:47-52 who will receive the "greater condemnation" for their detrimental influence upon the people; *pace* J. A. Ziesler, "Luke and the Pharisees," *NTS,* 25 (1978-79), pp. 146-157.

the story takes what must surely be a most ironic twist. Judas, one of the *"Twelve"* (22:3), makes the decisive move to "deliver" Jesus over to the scribes and chief priests (cf. 22:48). What Jesus had forecast to the "wilderness generation" at the base of the mountain (9:44) and disclosed privately to the Twelve (18:32) is now consummated by one from this innermost band of followers (παραδίδωμι)[68] (22:48 → 22:3 → 18:32 → 9:44). Instead of Jesus the accuser handing the crowds over to the judge (12:57-59), one of his own disciples will hand him over to the judges of the Sanhedrin!

And yet Luke has prepared his readers for this development. Already at the mountain the disciples had demonstrated their solidarity with the generation of "men" into whose *hands* Jesus is to be delivered to death (9:44). And on the journey they had certainly fared no better! Now as Jesus prepares to eat the passover meal as an anticipation of his *suffering* (22:15; cf. 17:25; 9:22), the *hands* of *this generation* are once again with him *at table* (22:22 → 14:1 → 11:53-54; cf. 9:44). *"Woe* to that man by whom he is delivered over!" (22:22b → 11:42-52). Jesus again declares that his death must take place according to the will of God (22:22a → 9:44-45), and the disciples again begin to argue which of them is the greatest (22:24-27 → 9:46-48)! That they could quarrel over their own importance in the pall of Jesus' death can only serve here to seal their incorporation with the "wilderness generation" whose leaders are epitomized by their *striving for rank at table* (11:43; 14:7-11; 20:46). Not only this, but when Peter of the mountain triad is told that he is going to deny that he even "knows" his master, he protests that he is ready to go with Jesus to prison and death—again "not knowing what he was saying" (22:33-34; cf. vss. 54-62; 9:33b).

Luke continues to move at a quick pace. While praying on the mountain (Olivet) Jesus comes over to his disciples to discover that instead of "alert" and "ready" (21:34-36 [cf. 22:33] → 12:37, 40), they are *sleeping* (22:45-46 → 9:32)! Suddenly the band of chief priests, Temple police, and elders of the people—led by one of the *Twelve*—descends upon Jesus to spirit him away to the house of the high priest. Only Peter follows at a distance, soon to deny his "Lord" *three times* (22:54-62). The assembly of the leaders of the people then condemn Jesus for claiming to be the "Son of God," thereby acknowledging negatively what the voice on the mountain had already declared (22:70-71 → 9:35), and lead him before

---

[68] On the disciples' involvement, see especially P. S. Minear, "A Note on Luke xxii: 36," *NT*, 7 (1964-65), pp. 128-134.

Pilate where they accuse him of perverting the people and of threatening Caesar through his own royal aspirations (23:1-5). With that, Pilate sends Jesus to the nation's "king" who, now "seeing" Jesus (23:8 → 9:9), joins his soldiers in mocking this "Christ" (23:11; cf. 9:20). Jesus is then shuttled back to Pilate to stand one final time before the crowd, now called interestingly enough, "the people" (ὁ λαός) who in turn stand with their leaders and the chief priests (23:13). The whole nation is assembled: The people, their leaders, their priests, their king, their Gentile governor of the kings of the nations (22:25) all condemn Jesus to death. *Three times* Pilate tries to persuade release of Jesus, but each time it falls on the deaf ears of a nation that is unrelenting to the end: "For they all cried out together, 'Away with this man. . . . Crucify him, crucify him. . . .' And they were urgent . . . and their voices prevailed" (23:18, 21, 23). At last Pilate delivers him over (παραδίδωμι)(23:25 → 18:32 → 9:44) to their will. "This generation" has spoken: Jesus must die.

Luke then recites the drama of the "wilderness generation" at the mountain. One by one, in a mounting suspense of stubborn resistance and twisted treachery, the "hands of people" link to form the Exodus people who force the death of the prophet Jesus in Jerusalem. It is indeed a "faithless and crooked generation" (9:41). And while it has become obvious that the external circumstances and immediate causes of Jesus' death are anything but parallel to Moses' death in Deuteronomy, nevertheless the *theological* explanation of the basis or cause of their deaths is the same:[69] *Because of* the intransigent disobedience of the people to the voice of God in his messenger-prophet, God has determined that Moses/Jesus *must die*. It is only in the light of this perspective that the curious juxtaposition in Acts of the *accusations* against the entire nation with the pronouncements of the *necessity* of God's foreordained plan in the Scriptures can be clarified (2:23-23a, 31; 3:13b-15-18, 20 24; 4:10-11; 25b-27-25a, 28; 7:51-52a-52b; 10:39b-42-43; 13:28-27, 29; cf. 5:35-39). As Peter crisply states in 2:22-23, "Men of Israel . . . this one, delivered

---

[69] Curiously, even the *plotted* portrait of this calling is similar. As later generations of Deuteronomists impressed the passion of Moses as the signet for the whole (1:9, 12; 1:37; 3:25-28; 4:21-22), so Luke posits premonitions of the deadly resistance to come (2:34-35; 4:16-30; 5:35; 6:16). And in both, notices of Moses'/Jesus' suffering and death are concentrated before and after the giving of the Law/eschatological *halakhah* (Deut. 1:37; 3:25-28; 4:21-22; 9:18-21, 25-29; 10:10; 31:2, 14, 23; 32:48-52; 34:4 — Luke 9:22, 23-25, 31, 41, 43b-45, 51; 18:31-34; 19:47; 20:9-18, 19, 20, 26; but cf. 12:49-50; 13:31-33; 17:25). Consequently in Luke as in Deuteronomy, the *necessity* of Moses'/Jesus' suffering and death is first adumbrated and then announced in advance of the fuller mountain manifestation of the monolithic disobedience.

up according to the determined plan and foreknowledge of God, *you* crucified and killed through the hands of lawless folk"; or, for example, ". . . *you* killed the author of life whom God raised from the dead. . . . Moses said, 'The Lord your God will raise up for you a prophet like me from among your brothers and sisters'" (3:15a-22a, quoting Deut. 18:15a).

(iv) Of the Synoptists, only Luke links the figure of a child directly to the mountain revelation (9:47-48). Only the childlike can heed the "voice" of the mountain and "receive" this Jesus who has been sent by God from the mountain (vs. 48). Already in 9:23-25 Jesus had set forth the indispensable conditions of this receiving or of this following him on his exodus to Jerusalem. People must deny themselves, take up their crosses daily and follow him (vs. 23); for those who wish to "save" their lives will in fact lose them (vs. 24a). In 9:46-47 the disciples try desperately to "save" their lives, promoting rather than denying themselves. With the *child* at his side, Jesus conveys in essence that such behavior can only lead to destruction of life, as it stifles the life-giving liberation of the prophet's exodus to death and exaltation. That is precisely why the "anonymous exorcist" (vss. 49-50) is "for" (ὑπέρ) the disciples since his *childlike* submission is a powerful promotion "for" the following Jesus demands.

It is the case with this fourth line of the typology as well that it functions as a constitutive principle for the rest of Luke's story in his Gospel. For, side by side with the ever-growing resistance, Luke counterposes a steadily increasing stream of "Wisdom's" (see 7:35) or "Abraham's" (cf. 13:16, 28; 16:22; 19:10) *children* who for a time, in submitting to Jesus' authority, do crack the "monolith" into the divided house of Israel (cf. 12:51-53). Already in contrast to the mission of the Twelve and especially to the behavior of the disciples on the mountain and with the Samaritan village, the narrator describes the return of the Seventy (-two) messengers in tones strikingly reminiscent of the "anonymous exorcist" (9:49-50). Like him, they evince the authority to cast out "demons" (δαιμόνια) (9:49-50; 10:1-20) "in your [Jesus'] name" (ἐν τῷ ὀνόματί σου) (9:49; 10:17) and thus are likened by Jesus to the submission of the "child" (παιδίον, νήπιοι) (9:47-48; 10:21). Immediately the story of the "wise and learned" lawyer follows as a foil to the childlike Samaritan who illustrates what submission to Jesus the teacher entails with respect to "the Lord your God" and "your neighbor" (10:25-37; esp. vss. 25, 27).

As he presses onward (cf. 10:38; 13:22), women (10:39; 13:10-17), the crippled and infirm (13:10-17, 32; 14:1-6, 21), tax collectors and "sinners" (15:1-2;

28 *Good News in History*

cf. vss. 3-21; 16:19-31), and "foreigners" (17:11-19; cf. 13:29; 14:23) all display the childlike reception of Jesus which is tantamount to the flow of Abraham, Isaac, and Jacob and all the prophets into the Kingdom of God (13:22-30, esp. vs. 28). Therefore, in the midst of this current, Jesus' "woe" to the disciples in 17:1-3a against the "falling away" of "these little ones" (τῶν μικρῶν τούτων) (vs. 2b) is to be felt. With Luke's use of οὗτοι, these "little ones" are most probably pictured right in the midst of the disciples.[70] Either literal children, or more probably the "poor" and "outcast," i.e., the "least" in society, are signified here, especially since Luke has thrust a constant parade of these "weak" and "powerless" before his readers' eyes from 14:1 (*viz.*, 14:1-6, 21-24; 15:1-32; 16:19-31). Once again the symbol of the *child* in their midst (9:46-48) is a graphic warning of the response required to receive the life in their midst. As we have already seen, the disciples now are facing the grave danger of succumbing to the hindering leaven of hypocrisy. They must "take heed" lest their inflated image destroy the servant status to which Jesus has called them (17:7-10 → 9:46, 49-50; cf. 17:3b-4, 5-6; 12:41-48). "For the one who is *the least* [ὁ μικρότερος] *among you all*, that is the one who is great" (9:48b).

With the two countermovements continuing to crescendo (cf. 17:11-19, 20-21, 22-18:8), Jesus points a parable to "some who were confident in themselves that they were righteous, while snubbing others" (18:9-14). Whereupon the disciples "look down" upon children coming to Jesus (18:15) in a manner frightfully familiar in the Pharisee's disdain for the "sinner" tax collector in vss. 9-14, esp. vs. 11. As in 9:46-48 Jesus places the children (παιδία) by his side and chides the disciples for hindering them: ". . . of such is the Kingdom of God. Truly I say to you, whoever does not receive the Kingdom of God like a child [ὡς παιδίον] cannot enter into it" (18:16-17).

Jesus' approach to Israel's center is marked by a childlike following—of the blind man who "sees" (18:35)[71] and of a "sinner" tax collector, "small of stature," who repents (19:3, 8)—against the backdrop of the "citizens" who "do not want this man to reign over us" (19:14).[72] Jesus exclaims that salvation has come to these children of Abraham "today" (19:10; 18:42b); but as for that mass of rebellion, when the journeying king returns, "bring them here and slay them before me" (19:27b). Jesus is then heralded as king by the great company of disciples who

---

[70] Marshall, *Gospel of Luke*, p. 641.

[71] The "blind" man *follows* in contrast to the "rich" man (18:18-30) who cannot.

[72] The *journeying* "nobleman" in 19:12-14 mirrors Jesus' journey "to receive a kingdom" (vs. 12): 9:51 → 22:69.

were looking for the Kingdom of God to appear straightaway as Jesus rides "triumphantly" into Jerusalem (cf. 19:11, 34-40). The people are electric with expectation as he teaches in the Temple with an uncanny authority (19:48b; 20:19, 26, 40; 21:38; cf. 18:43b). Yet in spite of all this, Jesus strikes an entirely contrary pitch by warning of doom and destruction; the people are to "watch" and "pray" unceasingly, lest through "carousing and drunkenness" they fall into the eschatological crisis that will come upon them suddenly like a snare (21:8-36). "Truly I say to you, *this generation* will not pass away until all has taken place!" (vs. 32). At the Passover table Jesus again interjects a somber note into an atmosphere charged with anticipation of great and glorious things (22:15, 21-23, 24). Once again he must resort to the image of the child to fight the disciples' misguided vanity. And yet again his words fall on deaf ears. Not even his warning of "Satan's sifting" of Peter (and the others, ὑμᾶς, vs. 31) pierces the veil of a proud generation that is slow to believe and hearken, a people that will take its "teacher" to the cross.

The events which follow are now well known. The λαός of the "wilderness generation" (9:13b) consolidate behind their leaders to execute a false prophet who was to have "redeemed" Israel (cf. 24:19-21). Thus even as the innocent children of Mt. Horeb were later to blend into the crooked generation of their forebears to necessitate the death of Moses at the end of the Exodus journey, so now even the "children" of Jesus' Exodus journey are incorporated into "this generation" of the people of Israel to compel Jesus' death at the end. Once the period of Acts begins, Luke will no longer distinguish various groups like tax collectors and sinners, the righteous and the little folk, etc. but speak rather of the "men of Israel" (e.g., vs. 2:29) or "peoples of Israel" (4:27) or "this crooked generation" (2:40). And though he underscores the leaders' role in both volumes[73] and describes a childlike submission by a "lawless one" even as Jesus hangs alongside him as one "reckoned with the lawless" (22:37; 23:42), yet the spectacle before Pilate and the accusations against the people in Acts make it clear that in Luke's presentation the *whole generation* has coalesced into an obdurate folk that demands Jesus' death. Like Moses, Jesus must die.

But the story of this Prophet like Moses is not at an end. Just as through Moses' death the "children" of the first Exodus do enter the land of the promised

---

[73] Luke 6:7, 11; 7:30; 9:22; 11:47-12:1; 16:14; 19:47; 20:19, 26, 40; 22:2, 4, 52; 23:6-12, 51; 24:20; Acts 4:10; cf. 4:27.

deliverance, so now through Jesus' death the "children" of the New Exodus enter the life of the fulfilled deliverance of the covenant of Abraham (Acts 3:18, 24-25). Though the people, like their forerunners hundreds of years earlier, acted in "ignorance" (Acts 3:17—Deut. 29:4; 32:28-29; cf. 4:6; 11:2), they now have the unprecedented opportunity to have their sins "blotted out" and to receive "times of respite" from the judgment of God which come from the "presence of the Lord" (3:17, 19b-20a). For now Peter dares to announce the fulfillment of Moses' words in Deut. 18:15-19 and to assert unabashedly, "And it shall be that every one who does not *hearken* to that prophet will be destroyed from the people" (3:23). Once again only those who submit to this voice will receive the life which now flows through the powerful presence of the "name" (3:16, 6).[74] And, like Moses, it is now through the command of this prophet "to repent and turn around" (3:19a), that the people may at last be delivered from the "evil" (πονηρία) (3:26—Deut. 4:25; 9:18; 28:20; 31:29) of a froward generation. *Those days*[75] proclaimed by "Moses" (3:22-23) and "all the prophets" (vs. 24) have—finally—come to their fulfillment.

In keeping with the Deuteronomic Exodus typology, it is significant that Luke places Peter's speech in Acts 3 in the midst of the blessings of the covenant to the ancestors now perceived to fulfill the description of life in the "land" *à la* Deut. 30:1-10. Moses had predicted that this stubborn people would be punished by exile but would later be restored to the land with even greater blessing (e.g., 28:36-38, 63-68; 29:28).[76] Now in Acts 2-5: (a) The *gathering* of the dispersed people of Israel from all the corners of the earth in Deut. 30:1b, 3b-5 begins to be fulfilled at the Feast of First Fruits in Jerusalem (2:5-12). It is primarily from this group that the first "believers" are drawn (2:14-41; cf. 3:11); (b) the "crooked" hearts (2:40) of the Horeb covenant people are "cleansed" through the baptism of the Holy Spirit as they turn and repent and thus fulfill Deut. 30:6a LXX (1:5; 2:1-4, 37-41; cf. 3:19, 26); (c) those whose hearts are purged hearken to the preaching of the apostles to bring about the obedience to the voice of the Lord as Moses envisions in Deut. 30:2, 8, 10 (2:37, 41-42; 4:4; 5:25-26, 32; cf. 3:21-24); (d) the sins of this young community are "released" or "removed" (ἄφεσις in the sense that their ill effects are "cured" or "counteracted" [ἰάομαι] according to the prediction

---

[74] Cf. the presence of the Lord in his "name" in Deuteronomy, e.g., 12:5, 11, 21; 14:23-24; 16:2, 6, 11; 18:5, 7, 19-20!; 21:5; 26:2.

[75] Cf. Luke 9:51, "the days of his taking up."

[76] Though not termed a "New Exodus," the return is both a restoration and a consummation of the first Exodus; and in 28:68 the people will *again* be enslaved in Egypt.

of Deut. 30:3a LXX (2:38; 5:31; cf. 3:19, 26); and (e) the "singleness" or "oneness" of "heart and soul" that characterizes the restored-covenant community fulfills Moses' prophecy of the *oneness* or *wholeness* of heart devoted to the Lord in Deut. 30:2, 6, 10 (4:32; cf. 2:42, 44). Now all of these points are fittingly summed up in the *eating* and *rejoicing* "before the Lord" by the young "First Fruits" community: "Day by day, attending the Temple together and breaking bread in their households, they partook of food, full of joy and with a singleness of heart, praising God and finding favor with the whole people" (2:46-47a). Here at last the crowning of the first Exodus in Deuteronomy in the eating and rejoicing at the central place "before the Lord" (Deut. 26:1-11) finds its full fruition in the eschatological jubilation of the New Exodus Life.

III

Several additional points in Peter's speech in Acts 3 cohere with the Deuteronomic Exodus-New Exodus typology and thus enhance the portrait of Jesus' death that we have presented above.

(i) It is curious what little reference is made in 3:12-26 to the *resurrection*. Only in vs. 15b does Peter state that "God raised him [i.e., "the author of life"] from the dead," while vs. 13a speaks of Jesus' "glorification." In both verses the divine action *reverses* the *result* of the action of the people, *viz.*,"delivering up," "denying," and "killing" God's "servant," "the Holy and Just one" (vs. 14), and "the author/pioneer of life." Because of this reversal the one who was dead is now alive again and therefore, as one vindicated by God, is present to infuse life into the body of a lame man (vss. 1-12). There is no indication whatsoever that this raising from the dead itself releases the people from the guilt and consequent punishment for the death of this *innocent* man Jesus (cf. "holy and just," vs. 14; Pilate wanted to release him, vs. 13b; a "murderer" instead was released, vs. 14b).

(ii) The *people's* guilt, in fact, is stressed in vss. 13, 14, 15, 17, and 19. In vs. 19 this guilt is explicitly acknowledged as still *in effect* by virtue of the call to "repent" and "turn around" "with the *result* that" (εἰς . . . ὅπως ἄν) (vss. 19, 20a). As is well known, the dominant idea in the Judaism of Jesus' day was that only when acknowledgment/confession of sin accompanied a sacrifice, or when a confession of guilt preceded the death of a criminal/Law breaker, did the sacrifice/death effect atonement.[77] By the conjunction of vs. 18—Jesus' *suffering* (i.e., death)—with vs.

---

[77] See, e.g., E. Löhse, *Märtyrer und Gottesknecht* (Göttingen: Vandenhoeck & Ruprecht,

19 (οὖν), it is now certain that the call to repentance is coupled to the guilt of the *death* of Jesus.[78] That is to say, without this repentance the "blotting out of sin" and "times of respite/reprieve" (vss. 19-20) would not become effective in the lives of the hearers, as vs. 23 reiterates. The idea is all but explicitly uttered that "by virtue of"/"by means of" Jesus' death this removal/forgiveness of sin (vs. 19) coupled with the eschatological fulfillment of salvation (vs. 20) is *now* a reality and available to the hearers.

(iii) This understanding of Jesus' death is supported further by vs. 26 where the purpose of the first sending of Jesus, God's "servant," is to "bless you by turning each of you from your evil." The following progression in thought is summed up in this verse. (1) A potent power of *blessing* is now (cf. the present, εὐλογοῦντα) in force (vs. 26b); εὐλογέω here resonates with the blessing (εὐλογηθήσονται) that was to be fulfilled as the *raison d'être* of the "covenant" to "Abraham" and "your fathers" (vs. 25).[79] (2) This promise of blessing has already been *fulfilled* in Jesus, God's servant (vs. 26), since: (a) "The God of Abraham and Isaac and Jacob . . . and of our fathers" has *already* "glorified"/"exalted" his servant (vs. 13a); (b) *"You* are the sons and daughters of the prophets and of the covenant" (vs. 25a), and this God has already sent his servant to *"you first"* with this blessing (vs. 26); (c) This sending was long ago foretold by "all of the prophets, from Samuel onward, who spoke and proclaimed *these* days" (vs. 24). "These days" are linked both forward to the "sons and daughters of the prophets" of vs. 25a (sc. descendants of those prophets of vs. 24) and backward by the copula (καὶ) at the beginning of vs. 24 to the *first* prophet, *viz.*, Moses, who predicted the "prophet like me" (vss. 22-23). It is clear, therefore, that God's servant who has already been sent in vs. 26 is also the fulfillment of the *prophet like Moses*. (3) Hence it follows that the *primary referent* of the "raising" (ἀναστήσας) in vs. 26 is to the ἀναστήσει of vs. 22, to the prophet's calling and life and not to the "raising up from the dead."[80] This interpretation harmonizes perfectly with the frequent

1955), pp. 25-29.

[78] See, e.g., G. Stählin, *Die Apostelgeschichte* (Göttingen: Vandenhoeck & Ruprecht, 1963), p. 66.

[79] Recall the importance of this expectation in Deuteronomy; see the beginning of Part I above.

[80] As E. Haenchen (*The Acts of the Apostles,* tr. B. Noble and G. Shinn [Oxford, England: Blackwell, 1971], p. 210), F. F. Bruce (*The Book of the Acts* [Grand Rapids, Mich.: Eerdmans, 1954], p. 94), and Stählin (*Apostelgeschichte*, p. 69) also maintain; cf. also 13:33. It is unlikely that the *aorist* "sent" (ἀπέστειλεν) of vs. 26 refers to the present sending of the risen Christ

sense of the aorist participle in tandem with the aorist verb as signifying what *precedes preceding* in time/sequence. Consequently, Jesus' mission to Israel was to "turn away" the people from their (collective) *evil*, and this mission is still in effect in the blessing available to the hearers in the present. (4) Since vs. 26 sums up the fulfillment of the covenant and the prophets, it is significant that the *only* event within the mission of Jesus foretold by these prophets which is *explicitly* said to be *fulfilled* (ἐπλήρωσεν) is the *suffering* (death) of God's "Christ" in vs. 18. As it has already been noted that the reference to "ignorance" in vs. 17 does not remove their guilt and its consequences (vs. 19), this means that the only aspect of this mission which is singled out and tied, on the one side, to the cause for repentance (vss. 18-19), and, on the other side, to the active power available to remove the cause of this guilt (i.e., "your evil"), is Jesus' *death*.

(iv) In light of i-iii above, the heavy concentration of accusation against the people in vss. 13b-15, 17, followed immediately by the *offer* of forgiveness and eschatological rest from judgment in vss. 19-20, takes on added importance. Between these two realities of guilt and release stands the *pivot* verse 18—the *death* of "the Christ." And this fulfillment is depicted in vs. 26 as an energetic power of blessing, not simply an attitude or subjective mindset of God. In other words, God's graciousness has *not* simply overlooked the "tragic" and "ignorant" mistake of the Jewish people;[81] the event of dying was integral to the breakup of the corporate evil (vs. 26). "You killed . . . that your sins may be blotted out . . . to bless you!"

(v) In contrast to Jesus' warnings and pronouncements of judgment upon the *whole* nation which we traced in the journey and the Temple teaching, there is no such blanket condemnation here. The "times of respite" are already available; the *power* to turn from the monolithic evil has already been unleashed. The *evil* and *crooked* generation of Luke 11:29 and Acts 2:40 has been broken apart by the repentance/faith of 3000 people of Israel from all over the world (2:5-12, 41; cf. 4:4; 5:14). Now the proclamation is that the unrepentant *individual* will be cut off *from* the *people* (3:23). And through most of the remainder of Acts the final judgment denotes the universal assize of the living and the dead (e.g., 10:42; 17:31; 24:15, 25; cf. 2:20). Only at the end in 28:25b-28 do the ominous tones of blanket

---

through the apostles since vs. 20 speaks of a *future* sending (ἀποστείλῃ) at the "consummation of all things" which *follows* (ἄχρι) the *present* "receiving" of "Christ Jesus" by or in "heaven" (vs. 21); *pace* G. Schneider, *Die Apostelgeschichte*, (Freiburg/Breisgau: Herder, 1980-82), I, p. 330.
    [81] E.g., Vielhauer, "Paulinism," p. 45.

denunciation revive the threat of a general destruction of Israel which Jesus had pronounced (but cf. Acts 7:51-53; 13:41; 18:6; 20:26). When this observation is joined to the intrinsic relation between Jesus' baptism of *death* and the *judgment* of the nation in Luke 12:49-53 that we delineated above,[82] then here is one more indication that the "divine must" of Jesus' *death* is central to the removal of the divine judgment hanging over the "stiff-necked" nation.[83]

To conclude, in the last two-thirds of his Gospel and at the beginning of Acts, Luke portrays a Jesus who, like Moses, must *die* to effect the good news of deliverance for his people. But now this *divine "must"* is fulfilled in the eschatological prophet like Moses whose death, consummating Moses and all the prophets, delivers the people at last from the stiff-necked resistance of the "wilderness generation." "For this means life to you" (Deut. 30:20b).

---

[82] See (iii) in Part II.

[83] Note how Jesus' identity/solidarity with *sinners* reinforces this connection: e.g., Luke 3:15-17, 21-22; 5:27-39; 7:36-50; 13:10-17; 15:1-32; 19:1-10; 22:39-46; 23:39-43.

The Silence of Jesus in the Passion

Evelin Albrecht

Oberkirchenrätin, Evangelisch-Lutherische Kirche
Oldenburg, Germany

In two places of his passion narrative Mark (and following him Matthew also)[1] calls attention to the silence of Jesus in response to the accusations of his adversaries, first at the trial before the Sanhedrin (Mark 14:55-64) and second before Pilate (Mark 15:1-5). It is striking, however, that although in both places Jesus responds with silence to his accusers (Mark 14:60b-61a follows vss. 57-59; Mark 15:4-5. follows vs. 3), in direct relation to this silence comes a word of revelation (14:62, 15:2). It seems therefore that Jesus himself diminishes the effect of his silence,[2] but Mark stresses the silence in spite of this. The intent of this paper is to explain this silence.

Other literature has produced two explanations for the silence. The first is derived from the content of the Gospel. The viewpoint has gradually developed that the presentation of the suffering of Jesus is prefigured in the Old Testament picture of the Suffering Just One.[3] This conception of the silence of Jesus has found far

---

[1] On the dependence of Matt. 26:62ff. and 27:11-14 on the Markan material, and also on the mention of the silence of Jesus in the passion story by Luke and John (Luke 23:6-12; John 19:9b), see the closing section of this paper.

[2] So E. Linnemann, *Studien zur Passionsgeschichte* (Göttingen: Vandenhoeck & Ruprecht, 1970), p. 110.

[3] Cf. J. Ernst, *Das Evangelium nach Markus* (Regensburg: Pustet, 1981), p. 455; R. Pesch, *Das Markus-Evangelium* (Freiburg/Breisgau: Herder, 1976), p. 436; D. Lührmann, "Markus 14:55-64: Christologie und Zerstörung des Tempels im Markus-Evangelium," *NTS*, 27 (1981/82),

wider acceptance than the previously accepted idea of the Suffering Servant in Isa. 53:7.[4] The verses concerned with the silence of Jesus in Mark 14:60-61 and 15:4-5 are therefore more often interpreted from Ps. 37:14-16 LXX and Ps. 38:13 LXX. On the other hand, it is obvious that this understanding of the silence of the Just One (or the Suffering Servant) is influenced by knowledge of the corresponding verses from Isaiah, though not by a direct quotation of these verses or through similar phrases.[5] Consequently, the Christian community, in view of its understanding of the Old Testament picture, would stress the silence of Jesus. This, however, does not explain the tension between the silence and the words of revelation in 14:62 and 15:2.

Therefore a second explanation is often given which is derived through a traditional historical analysis of the entire passion history. This analysis—mostly from word-statistical or style-critical methods—results in a manifold division of the text into single verses and sections. Therefore the statements about the silence of Jesus are often assigned to other pre-Markan traditions rather than to the verses of the accusations themselves (Mark 14:57-59). Moreover, they are not always assigned to the same level as the words of revelation in Mark 14:62 and 15:2. The Evangelist Mark is seen then as a redactor who merely coupled the traditions and perhaps revised them, more or less.[6]

The discussion of these questions will not be expanded further in this paper, though through all these attempts at explanation the question still remains as to why the silence of Jesus was either added or retained despite the tension with his words of revelation. The presumption that Jesus was actually silent in the face of the accusations is no final answer.[7] This paper's point of departure is therefore the present form of the Markan text, without presuming that the text is fabricated by Mark. It is presumed, however, that Mark had in fact used existing traditions, which account for the occasional remaining unevenness,[8] but on the other hand did

---

p. 460; *et al.*

[4] Cf. E. Klostermann, *Das Markus-Evangelium* (Tübingen: Mohr, 1950), p. 155; W. Grundmann, *Das Evangelium nach Markus* (Berlin: Evangelische Verlagsanstalt, 1980), p. 413; W. Maurer, "Das Messiasgeheimnis des Markus-Evangeliums," *NTS*, 14 (1967/68), p. 522.

[5] Cf. W. Schenk, *Der Passionsbericht nach Markus* (Gütersloh: Mohn, 1974), p. 239.

[6] Cf. Pesch's synopsis of the different opinions, *Markus-Evangelium*, pp. 7-10.

[7] This can remain only a presumption and, even if true, the question cannot be answered as to why the tradition has maintained this silence in the trial at the same time as the self-revelation of Jesus.

[8] Cf. H. Räisänen, *Das "Messiasgeheimnis" im Markus-Evangelium: Ein radaktionskritischer Versuch* (Helsinki: Finnish Exegetical Society, 1976), pp. 167-168.

not simply place the various traditions next to one another. With this understanding our examination will be based on the objective order of the verses in their context and on the entire order of the Markan Gospel.

I

According to Mark 14:60b Jesus remained silent and made no answer to the not entirely unanimous accusations which were raised before him (in 14:58) concerning his sayings about the Temple. Following this is the accusation that he claimed not only that he would rebuild the Temple (an expectation of the Messianic Age which was already present in the Qumran texts and Jewish-apocalyptic literature, 4QFlor. 1:1-13 and Targum Isaiah 53:7),[9] but also that he would destroy the old Temple. The Messianic claim of Jesus is here brought into question, which as such need not be a ground for accusation or condemnation, but which by the reference to the "destruction of the Temple" places Judaism itself into question.[10] Following the silence of Jesus, which Mark particularly emphasizes through his double use of "he was silent and did not answer,"[11] comes the direct question of the High Priest, "Are you the Christ, the Son of the Blessed?" This inquiry is not a change of subject, since (as in 14:58) it likewise refers to the Messianic claims of Jesus.[12] Jesus acknowledges this in vs. 62 with a quotation from Ps. 110:1 and Dan. 7:13. This claim of power as the coming Judge of the World is seen as blasphemy and leads to his condemnation (compare the parallel claim of power to forgive sins in Mark 2:1-12). The central theme in this passage is therefore the Messianic claim of Jesus which he first responded to with silence and then with the acknowledgement that he is the Coming Son of Man.

This double answer, silence and then in fact acknowledgement, in this particular case is attributed to Jesus but can also be found in Mark's Gospel with reference to others, particularly in the disagreement with the demons and in the

---

[9] Cf. Pesch, *Markus-Evangelium*, p. 435; D. Dormeyer, *Die Passion Jesu als Verhaltensmodell: Literarische und theologische Analyse der Traditions und Redaktionsgeschichte der Markus Passion* (Münster: Aschendorff, 1974), p. 110; R. Donahue, "Temple, Trial, and Royal Christology (Mk. 14:53-65)," in *The Passion in Mark: Studies in Mark 14-16*, ed. W. H. Kelber (Philadelphia: Fortress Press, 1976), pp. 68-69.

[10] Pesch, *Markus-Evangelium*, p. 435.

[11] This duplication of the saying is also typical for the evangelist Mark with the word σιωπᾶν; cf. Schenk, *Passionsbericht nach Markus*, p. 239; Klostermann, *Markus-Evangelium*, p. 155.

[12] Against Lührmann, "Markus 14.55-64", p. 459.

confession of Peter. A similar parallel can be seen between the silence of Jesus concerning these accusations and the charge for secrecy to the demons in Mark 1:24-25 and 3:12. The demons know Jesus, but they do not confess him. They attempt rather to use their knowledge of the person of Jesus to ward him off:

> They subject themselves to him in order to please him and at the same time tell his secret in order to free themselves from his power. They attempt to render his power useless by uncovering its source, an attempt which nonetheless fails.[13]

It is because the demons could not confess Jesus that they are given the command not to make known who he is: The Messiahship of Jesus could only become known after confession of him.

This prerequisite of confession seems to be fulfilled in Peter's confession in Mark 8:27-31. But even there Mark adds the command of secrecy.[14] This command of secrecy, despite Peter's confession, is probably related to the disciples' misunderstanding during the life of Jesus—a misunderstanding which is continually stressed by Mark (e.g., Mark 8:32-33; etc.). This misunderstanding of the disciples is, as with the statements of the demons, at first a denial or a failing to confess.[15] Mark thereby characterizes the situation of the earthly life of Jesus (as the studies of the "Messianic Secret" constantly make clearer).[16] Even if either command to secrecy was adopted by Mark from a previous tradition, Mark nevertheless emphasizes this command. He does this from the viewpoint that

> something fundamental about Jesus was first obvious only after his earthly activity. An actual Christological confession is only possible in the new situation which was established through the death and resurrection of Jesus, the situation in which Jesus works as exalted Lord.[17]

In this sense, according to Mark, the silence of Jesus against the accusations belongs to the earthly life of Jesus. The revelation to his enemies of who he is ushers in the new age which is understood in light of his exaltation.[18] Mark makes

---

[13] Grundmann, *Evangelium nach Markus*, p. 100 (here and below I have for the convenience of the reader provided translations of German texts); against Räisänen, *"Messiasgeheimnis" im Markus-Evangelium*, p. 93, who calls the words of the demons a "confession."

[14] Cf. Räisänen, *"Messiasgeheimnis" im Markus-Evangelium*, pp. 90-108.

[15] Jesus' saying, "Get behind me, Satan!" (vs. 33b), may point to this connection.

[16] On the entire problem of the Messianic Secret, see Räisänen's thorough work, *"Messiasgeheimnis" im Markus-Evangelium*.

[17] Räisänen, *"Messiasgeheimnis" im Markus-Evangelium*, p. 166; cf. also n. 1.

[18] That does not eliminate the fact that the revelation has already appeared in the words and

this clear by joining 14:60-61 and 14:62. During his earthly life Jesus deems it necessary to keep his Messiahship secret since it can only be understood after the resurrection event. In view of the future coming of the Son of Man, Jesus ends the secrecy at this time and reveals himself as the Coming, Exalted and Judging One. The disclosure of the coming Son of Man and the motif of the Messianic Secret are here very closely related.[19] For the entire Gospel of Mark, 14:61-62 indicate the bridge from the silence (in view of the way of suffering during his earthly life) to the revelation of the coming Son of Man.[20] At this point in 14:61a the secrecy of the Messiahship of Jesus depends upon confession to him. Through the fact that Jesus remains silent to the accusations against him (especially in his references to the Temple), Mark stresses that the relationship to Jesus requires not an accusation or denial but rather confession and acknowledgement.

II

The silence of Jesus in Mark 15:4-5 is thus to be understood as the silence against the accusers, the persons who think ill of him. The often-mentioned reversal (first Jesus' affirmation before Pilate to be the Messiah, then the silence before his accusers) has occasionally led some to change the order of the verses, in accordance with 14:61-62, so that vs. 2 follows vs. 5.[21] Usually Mark 15:1-5 is recognized as the older text, Mark 14:55-64 as a doublet.[22] Also promulgated, however, is the opposite view that Mark 14:61-62 is the older,[23] or it is claimed that both sections developed independently of each other though originating from the same pre-Markan tradition.[24] On this last assumption it is necessary to provide a reason for the changing of the text of Mark 15:1-5 itself.

---

actions of Jesus without reference to the exaltation (cf. Mark 2:10, 19-20, 28; 12:1-12). In these places the revelation is given to his enemies. These sayings are structurally comparable, but they can be understood only in light of the exaltation of Jesus.

[19] Cf. C. Colpe, "ὁ υἱὸς τοῦ ἀνθρώπου," in *TDNT*, VIII, p. 443.

[20] Cf. N. Perrin, "The High Priest's Question and Jesus' Answer," in *The Passion in Mark*, p. 81: "It is my concern in this essay to argue that 14:61-62, the High Priest's question and Jesus' answer, serves the combination of retrospective and prospective purpose." Perrin, however, does not include the motive of the silence of Jesus in his considerations.

[21] Cf. G. Braumann, "Markus 15.2-5 und Markus 14.55-64," *ZNW*, 52 (1961), p. 276, who says that the order of Mark 14 is "significant."

[22] Cf. Klostermann, *Markus-Evangelium*, p. 155.

[23] Cf. Linnemann, *Studien zur Passionsgeschichte*, p. 135; Schenk, *Passionsbericht nach Markus*, p. 245.

[24] Cf. Pesch, *Markus-Evangelium*, p. 428.

As in Mark 14:61-62, Jesus' response of self-revelation is again given to the one who questions him (at one time it is Pilate, at the other it is the High Priest) whereas the accusations of the group are answered by Jesus' silence. (The group referred to in Mark 14:55 is composed of "the chief priests and the whole council"; vs. 56 refers to "many" from among them; vs. 57 to "some." In Mark 15:1 the group is composed of "the chief priests with the elders and scribes and the whole council" and in vs. 3 only "the chief priests.") From its context the silence seems to be related to the accusations made against him, but in view of the fact that Jesus at one time answers first with silence and then with the revelation (14:60ff.) and at the other time first with the revelation and then with silence (15:1-5) it seems that his partner in dialogue plays an important role. To Pilate, a pagan, Jesus first gives the self-revelation (vs. 2); then Pilate experiences the silence of Jesus before the accusations. He experiences this as a silence which demands his own confession and his own comment (on the revelation). Therefore the silence of Jesus before Pilate serves somewhat of a "missionary" function—it provokes the pagan to respond by himself. But Pilate only "wonders": θαυμάζειν in this case has the meaning of failing to comprehend.[25] The appropriate reaction to Jesus' silence according to Mark is given only when in Mark 15:39 the centurion (who is also a pagan) confesses under the cross: "Truly this man was the Son of God."

The structure of Mark 15:1-5 shows, therefore, the missionary situation of the community after the resurrection: The revelation of the Messiah has taken place and now the silence requires each person to make his or her own comment. Likewise this structure is already found in the narrative of the transfiguration of Jesus in Mark 9:2-10, a narrative which is also to be understood from a post-resurrection point of view. In this text it is said that the revelation which was given to the three chosen disciples should be kept as a secret "until the Son of Man should have risen from the dead," or, in other words, only in light of the resurrection is it possible to confess to Jesus as the Christ. Even this "limited" command of secrecy belongs to the motif of the "Messianic Secret" in the Gospel of Mark[26] and (as is apparent from a comparison of the passages) it is taken up and confirmed in its requirement of a confession in the silence of Jesus in Mark 15:4-5.

---

[25] Cf. G. Bertram, "θαῦμα," etc., in *TDNT*, III, p. 38.
[26] Cf. Räisänen, *"Messiasgeheimnis" im Markus-Evangelium*, pp. 109-117.

III

In both Mark 14:60ff. and Mark 15:4-5 the silence of Jesus is brought into connection with the motif of secrecy which Mark stresses in the redaction of his Gospel.[27] In both cases Jesus' silence is in fact to be understood in connection with his self-revelation. In either case Jesus' silence requires an acknowledgement and a confession or it withholds the secret in the presence of unfaith and denial. In 14:60-61 Mark uses the motif of secrecy to give a retrospective representation of history: During his earthly activity, the Messiahship of Jesus has to be kept secret because it can only be revealed after the resurrection. This is substantiated by the following word of revelation in vss. 61b-62 which, in the form of question and answer, proclaims the faith of the community after the resurrection.[28] In Mark 15:4-5 the silence of Jesus is from the very first (through the reversal of the silence and revelation) prospectively related to the situation of the community: The silence is appropriate until the confession in the presence of the cross and the resurrection. Therefore the Mark 15:1-5 logically belongs to the situation of the community to which 14:61-62 refers: The silence has a missionary meaning based on the already given revelation.

On the other hand, Mark understands 15:1-5 also as a contribution within the scope of his representation of history: The silence of Jesus corresponds to that silence during the time between the transfiguration and the revelation of the Messiah through the resurrection (cf. Mark 9:9). The function of the silence of Jesus in Mark's passion narrative is, therefore, to signify the turning-point within the whole Gospel: Jesus' silence is the climax and conclusion of maintaining secrecy in view of his Messiahship. The command for the demons and disciples to be silent about who Jesus is and the silence of Jesus himself are closely related to the misunderstanding, the direct denial, and the accusations which Jesus experienced in his earthly life. The revelation and the confession, on the other hand, belong together with one's comprehension of the role of Jesus in light of the resurrection. The silence of Jesus and the passion of the Messiah are based on the misunderstanding and the denial of others. Only when the Suffering One reveals

---

[27] Cf. Räisänen, *"Messiasgeheimnis" im Markus-Evangelium*, p. 161.

[28] This is apparent from the combination of the three Christological Titles: Christ, Son of the Blessed, Son of Man; cf. M. Horstmann, *Studien zur vormarkinischen Christologie* (Münster: Aschendorff, 1973), p. 13; likewise F. Hahn, *Christologische Hoheitstitel: Ihre Geschichte im frühen Christentum*, second ed. (Göttingen: Vandenhoeck & Ruprecht, 1964), p. 289.

himself as the Coming One can the person who confesses to him begin to discover what the word δεῖ in Mark 8:31 signifies in light of the suffering role of Jesus and to understand also Jesus' Messiahship in light of the Bible. This ascertainment is only possible after the resurrection.

Mark 14:60ff. is therefore to be considered as a turning point of the whole Gospel. The Messianic Secret is not broken before the silence of Jesus even though, after Mark 9:9, no further command to keep the secret is given. Consequently, Mark appears even in this section of the passion narrative as a redactor and theologian who inserts the motif of the silence of Jesus into his entire framework,[29] and gives it a particular function in the transition from the secrecy to the revelation of Jesus as the Messiah.[30]

A comparison with the other Gospels provides corroboration for the great importance given by the evangelist Mark to the silence motif: For Matthew, who stays particularly close to the passion history of Mark, the motif is still maintained (Matt. 26:62-63.; 27:11-14). Through his striking of the typical Markan formulas,[31] however, as well as his stressing the question of the High Priest ("I *adjure* you by the living God. . . .") it has lost its importance. Luke says nothing about a silence of Jesus before the Sanhedrin or before Pilate. In place of that, however, one finds in the source peculiar to Luke a silence during the questioning of Jesus by Herod, Luke 23:6-12. To be sure, the silence has an entirely different meaning here: According to vs. 8 the question of Herod serves the purpose of his hope "to see some sign done by him," and so the silence of Jesus is to be understood in connection with his refusal to give a sign (cf. Luke 11:16, 29-31; 12:54-56).[32] In the Gospel of John the motif of the silence of Jesus is found only in his dialogue with Pilate before the condemnation, John 19:9b. Here it has, however, a typical Johannine meaning: Jesus is silent as the Sovereign who goes self-consciously on his way to suffering.[33]

---

[29] This implies no particular view of Mark as redactor; on the other hand, this Evangelist is also not to be seen simply as a collector.

[30] The simple historical question of whether Jesus had actually remained silent is, in this case, passed over in silence and is in fact no longer answerable.

[31] See n. 11, above.

[32] Cf. W. Grundmann, *Das Evangelium nach Lukas* (Berlin: Evangelische Verlagsanstalt, 1969), p. 425.

[33] Cf. A. Dauer, *Die Passionsgeschichte im Johannes-Evangelium* (Munich: Kosel, 1972), p. 118: "John had given a new interpretation to the traditional motif of the silence of Jesus in vs. 9. Jesus remains silent not as the Suffering Servant of God but as the Revealed Sovereign who refused to answer Pilate because he refused to accept the truth (18:38a)."

Concerning the silence motif in the passion marrative of Mark, it can be concluded that the silence of Jesus does in fact recall the Old Testament passages concerning the "Suffering Just One," but a direct connection to this is not given. Mark takes this motif much more from the Christian tradition, so that in the sequel of his Gospel his narrative of the Messianic Secret comes to its climax and conclusion, and, at the same time, Mark provides a bridge for the revelation of Jesus to be given to his enemies and the heathen. Only through a confession of Jesus as the Christ, the Son of God, the Coming Son of Man (14:61-62), and who is therefore seen in light of the cross and resurrection (cf. 15:39 and 9:9), is it possible to understand him as the One who brings the fulfillment of the Scriptures in the form of the Suffering Just One.

Creation in Johannine Theology

Abraham Terian

Professor of New Testament, Theological Seminary, Andrews University
Berrien Springs, Michigan

The marked similarity between the opening words of Genesis and those of the Gospel of John is readily recognizable. Not so readily recognizable is the sustained parallelism between John 1:1-5 and early Jewish interpretations of Gen. 1:1-5.[1] However one views the literary development of the Prologue of John (1:1-18), beneath the literary elements common to it and the first chapter of Genesis lies a vast difference in cosmological perceptions explicable by the Hellenistic Jewish background. As Thomas observes: "The physical categories of Gen. 1 have become the spiritual dimensions of John 1."[2] That the Evangelist made use of Hellenistic Jewish perceptions of creation is demonstrable by more than his use of the term λόγος. That he made use of a Christianized Jewish hymn to Wisdom/Torah is likely.[3] As we shall see, however, these early interpretations of certain elements from Gen. 1 have been reinterpreted at the outset of the Gospel and amplified in subsequent chapters—especially those that deal with the healing miracles on the Sabbath (chs. 5 and 9). Or, conversely, the Son's ability to grant life and light in

---

[1] For an appreciable study, see P. Borgen, *Philo, John and Paul: New Perspectives on Judaism and Early Christianity* (Atlanta: Scholars Press, 1987), pp. 76-85.

[2] R. W. Thomas, "'Life' and 'Death' in John and Paul," *SJT,* 21 (1968), p. 201.

[3] On the emerging scholarly consensus on this point, see R. Schnackenburg, *The Gospel According to St. John,* tr. K. Smyth *et al.* (New York: Seabury Press, 1968-82), I, pp. 224-225.

these chapters appears to have been summed up in the opening verses of the Prologue.[4]

Creation in Johannine theology is here discussed in three parts: (I) the theme of creation in the Prologue and the role of the Logos in particular; (II) the amplification of the theme through the notions of life and light expressed in conjunction with the healings on the Sabbath; and (III) a summary highlighting some of the observations made primarily in the light of Jewish sources from the Hellenistic period.

I. Creation and the Logos

Like all of God's acts and revelations recorded in the rest of the Pentateuch, creation in the Hellenistic Jewish interpretations of Genesis is attributed to the Logos who is at once the intermediary of God (Philo, *Opif.* 20. 24-25; *Leg.* III.96; *Deus* 57; *Migr.* 6; *Her.* 140) and God (Philo, *Somn.* I.229). The emanation of the Logos from God and their inseparable relation—if not their oneness or identity—appear to be theological derivations from an exegetical understanding of God's voice or his spoken word in Gen. 1 (vss. 3, 6, 9, 14, 20, 24; cf. Ps. 33:6). As for Philo's Logos doctrine, it may be deemed an amplification of an earlier tradition in Judaism where the Logos is seen more than literally as the "word" which God speaks ("And God said") before every creative act. A fragment of Aristobulus, for example, has this comment on the opening verses of Genesis:

> For it is necessary to take the divine "voice" not as a spoken word, but as the establishment of things. Just so has Moses called the whole Genesis of the world words of God in our Law. For he continually says in each case, "And God spoke and it came to pass." (Fr. 4:3; cf. Philo, *Q.G.* I.1-2)[5]

---

[4] I disagree with J. Painter's hypothesis: "Because the Prologue was one of the later strata added to the Gospel, the evangelist has not intoduced new motifs which appeared in his sources into the body of the gospel. Some of these, though suited to the theme of creation, were not readily applicable to the gospel story" (*The Quest for the Messiah: The History, Literature and Theology of the Johannine Community* [Edinburgh: Clark, 1991], p. 107).

[5] A comparable view on the instrumentality of God's voice is found in a fragment of Artapanus, according to whom God remains in the background when dealing with the patriarchs except for occasional miraculous manifestations in the "divine voice" (*apud* Eusebius, *Praep. Evang.* IX.27.21, 25-26, 36; cf. Philo, *Migr.* 47-49, on "seeing the voice" in Ex. 20:18, 22 and Deut. 4:12 LXX). An equally significant perspective is found in Irenaeus' denial of any intermediary role for the Logos who, as God, has no need of instruments to create (*Adv. Haer.* II.2.4-5, against the Gnostic view of the demiurge). On the latter, see P. Perkins, "Ordering the

Whether God's voice or his spoken word, Gen. 1 seems to have provided the Biblical grounds for the Hellenistic Jewish modified adoption of the Logos concept prevalent in Platonic and Stoic cosmology, a concept much elaborated upon in the Middle Platonism of New Testament times.[6]

As in Hellenistic Judaism, the intermediation of the Logos in the Prologue of John is perceived in terms of the self-extension or the outreach of a transcendent creator who is, nonetheless, immanently present. The Logos is more than the supreme intermediary of God in creation. Divine agency and divine presence are here equated, following an established tradition in Judaism, leading to the belief of beholding God in the Logos.[7]

From a common and conceivably early understanding of the role of God's spoken word in creation seems to derive the notion that the written word or the Torah, or personified Wisdom according to Prov. 8:22-31, had likewise been with God since the beginning, and that he employed Wisdom as an instrument of creation (1QH 1.14, 20; Wis. 9:1-4, 9; Odes Sol. 7:8; 2 Enoch 30:8; Hel. Syn. Pr. 3:19; 4:7, 38; 12:36; cf. Tg. Ps.-J. to Gen. 3:24; Gen. R. 1:1, 8; 8:2; M. Abot 3:14). The identification of Torah with Wisdom early in the post-exilic period is attested in Ezra 7:14 and 25 (cf. Sir. 24:8-9; T. Levi 13:1-9). The same conceptual relationships were dwelt upon in the apologetics for the universality of Jewish Law in the Hellenistic period.[8] Hengel observes: "An important preparation for the

---

Cosmos: Irenaeus and the Gnostics," *Nag Hammadi, Gnosticism, and Early Christianity,* ed. C. W. Hedrick and R. Hodgson, Jr. (Peabody, Mass.: Hendrickson, 1986), pp. 234-235.

[6] J. Dillon, *The Middle Platonists: A Study of Platonism, 80 B.C. to A.D. 220* (Ithaca, N. Y.: Cornell University Press, 1977), pp. 160-166; cf. such New Testament passages as Heb. 1:2; 11:3; Col. 1:16; 1 Cor. 8:6. A complex subject such as Philo's Logos cannot be treated fully in a short study, especially in one not fully devoted to the matter. Suffice it to say that Philo transmits several traditions regarding the Logos. Of special interest is his schematic understanding of God and his two principle powers: the creative power or God (ἡ ποιητική, called θεός, the power responsible for creation and bestowal of divine blessings) and the royal power or Lord (ἡ βασιλική, called κύριος, the ruling power). The schema recurs in several passages (e.g., *Q.G.* II.16, 51, 75; III.39; *Q.E.* II.62; *Leg.* I.95-96; III.73; *Her.* 166; *Mut.* 11-31; *Abr.* 107-132, on God's visit and apparition to Abraham—cf. *Q.G.* IV: 2, 8, 30; *Deo* 1-4; *Spec.* I.307). More elaborate descriptions of the two powers with the Logos situated in their midst are found in *Q.E.* II.68; *Cher.* 27-28; and *Fug.* 94-105. E. R. Goodenough has this preface to his remarks on these schemata: "We must bear in mind that Philo has definitely warned us against conceiving of these as anything but aspects of God's unity" (*By Light, Light* [New Haven, Conn.: Yale University Press, 1935], pp. 27-30). See also the brief survey in D. Winston, *Logos and Mystical Theology in Philo of Alexandria* (Cincinnati: Hebrew Union College Press, 1985), pp. 9-25, 59-64.

[7] Or, beholding the Father in Jesus (cf. 12:45; 14:9; 15:24; 17:24). For more on this subject, see below, n. 18.

[8] W. Gutbrod errs in thinking that the origin of these conceptual relationships lies in the

encounter of Jewish wisdom teaching with Greek thought was that it had become
more and more bound up with the doctrine of creation."[9] We see this in another
fragment of Aristobulus, where, after alluding to Wisdom in Prov. 8:22-31, he goes
on to relate it to the seventh day and the sevenfold principle (λόγος) of creation (Fr.
5:11-12). Commenting on the fragment, Yarbro Collins notes:

> Thus wisdom and Logos have similar functions. Wisdom is the source of light in
> which all things are contemplated. Through the sevenfold principle, we have
> knowledge of human and divine matters. . . . These reflections of Aristobulus are
> important for anyone seeking to understand the role of the Logos in Philo's
> thought or in the Gospel of John.[10]

The Biblical concept of God's word being inseparable from him has led to
a similar development in the Targums, the Aramaic paraphrases of the Hebrew
Scriptures, where the most common designation for God is "the Memra [i.e., Word]
of the Lord." The same is used synonymously with reference to God's name for
himself and alongside other rare names for God that are often left untranslated.[11]
Where the Hebrew has "the voice of God," for example, the Targums render "the
voice of the Memra of God," to safeguard divine transcendence and to avoid
anthropomorphic and anthropopathic suggestions. In addition to underscoring the
transcendence of God, his invisibility and inaudibility, the Memra is employed to
convey several other attributes of God: his power or omnipotence, his presence, his
omniscience, his ways and various activities.[12] The use of the word *memra* in the

Jewish apologetics of the Hellenistic period (cf. "νόμος" in *TDNT,* IV, p. 1049). His opinion
seems to be based on the often repeated assertion that the earliest identification of Torah with
Wisdom is found in Ben Sira (e.g., E. Schürer, *The History of the Jewish People in the Age of
Jesus Christ,* rev. and ed. G. Vermes *et al.* [Edinburgh: Clark, 1986], III, pp. 199-200; M.
Hengel, *Judaism and Hellenism: Studies in their Encounter in Palestine during the Early
Hellenistic Period,* tr. J. Bowden [Philadelphia: Fortress Press, 1974], I, pp. 157-162).
  [9] Hengel, *Judaism and Hellenism,* I, p. 156.
  [10] A. Yarbro Collins, "Aristobulus: A New Translation and Introduction," *The Old Testament
Pseudepigrapha,* ed. J. H. Charlesworth (Garden City, N.Y.: Doubleday, 1983-85), II, p. 835. For
more on this subject, see B. L. Mack, *Logos und Sophia: Untersuchungen zur Weisheitstheologie
im hellenistischen Judentum* (Göttingen: Vandenhoeck & Ruprecht, 1973), pp. 96-107, 141-154,
166-171. The two concepts are so closely intertwined in the history of ideas that it is difficult
to take the Logos as simply a later name for the earlier Wisdom.
  [11] C. T. R. Hayward, *Divine Name and Presence: The Memra* (Totowa, N.J.: Allanheld,
Osmun, 1981), esp. p. 24.
  [12] For more on these, see B. Grossfeld's introduction to *The Targum Onqelos to Genesis*
(Wilmington, Del.: Glazier, 1988), pp. 19-23; cf. D. Muñoz León, *Dios-Palabra: Memra en los
Targumim del Pentateuco* (Granada: Institución S. Jeronimo, 1974), pp. 117-125.

Targums is certainly more than a translational phenomenon. Hayward observes that the Memra conveys a distinctive theology of the Divine Name and Presence; "when He acts in or by means of His Memra, God is there, actively present with men."[13] Or, as Muñoz León suggests, the Memra doctrine seems to be directed against the widespread belief in angelic mediation, a belief current in first-century Jewish circles (the same could be said of the Johannine Logos doctrine; cf. 1:51).[14] Moreover, in a substantive study Hamp concludes that the Memra is not an entity apart from God and therefore not an intermediary, in a strict sense of the word, between God and his creation (it could likewise be said that the Johannine and the Philonic Logos is as indistinguishable from God himself as is the Memra in his relation to God in the Targums).[15] Although the Memra does not appear in the Targums to Gen. 1-2,[16] McNamara invites attention to the use of the term in Targum Neofiti to Ex. 12:42, which draws on the imagery of Gen. 1:1-3: "The first night when the Lord was revealed over the world to create it . . . and the Memra of the Lord was there, and there was light, and it shone. . . ."[17] There can be little or no doubt about the Evangelist's familiarity with the Memra theology which helps clarify the mediatory role of the Logos and his identity with God in the Johannine and Philonic writings. These three sources do not allow for a hypostasis,

---

[13] C. T. R. Hayward, "The Memra of YHWH and the Development of its Use in Targum Neofiti I," *JJS*, 25 (1974), p. 418.

[14] Muñoz León, *Dios-Palabra*, pp. 125-140. Cf. the polemic in Heb. 1-2, possibly aimed at such tendencies.

[15] V. Hamp, *Der Begriff "Wort" in den aramäischen Bibelübersetzungen: Ein exegetischer Beitrag zur Hypostasen-Frage und zur Geschichte der Logos-Spekulationen* (Munich: Neuer Filser-Verlag, 1938), p. 204; so also G. F. Moore, "Intermediaries in Jewish Theology: Memra, Shekinah, Metadron," *HTR*, 15 (1922), pp. 52-54. Moore, however, denies any connection of Memra with the Logos of Philo or that of Christian theology (pp. 54-55). Against Moore's latter position, see A. Díez Macho, "El Logos y el Espiritu Santo," *Atlántida*, 1 (1963), pp. 381-396; M. McNamara, "Logos of the Fourth Gospel and Memra of the Palestinian Targum, Exodus 12:42," *ET*, 79 (1968), pp. 115-117; P. Borgen, "Observations on the Targumic Character of the Prologue of John," *NTS*, 16 (1969-1970), pp. 288-295; C. T. R. Hayward, "The Holy Name of the God of Moses and the Prologue of St. John's Gospel," *NTS*, 25 (1978-79), pp. 16-32; and D. Muñoz León, *Palabra y Gloria: Excursus en la Biblia y en la Literatura Intertestamentaria* (Madrid: Institutio Francisco Suárez, 1983), pp. 27-33.

[16] The divine name *Elohim* in the first account of creation (Gen. 1:1-2:4a) and wherever it refers to God is rendered by the Tetragram *YHWH*, lest the plural connotation of *Elohim* should lead to acquiescence of polytheism; but when the divine names *YHWH Elohim* (usually translated "Lord God") appear in conjunction, such as in the second account of creation (Gen. 2:4b-25), they are left untranslated.

[17] McNamara, "Logos of the Fourth Gospel and Memra of the Palestinian Targum, Exodus 12:42," pp. 115-117. There is no need, however, for McNamara's emendation of the text; his point stands with the text as is (see Hayward, *Divine Name and Presence*, p. 135).

a distinct entity apart from God, such as formulated in early Christian apologetics.[18]

The Johannine statement, "All things came into being through him" (vs. 3a), like the corresponding statement, "the world came into being through him" (vs. 10), is an interpretation of "God created the heavens and the earth" (Gen. 1:1). The amplification that follows, "apart from him not one thing came into being" (vs. 3b), is a further interpretation of Gen. 1:1 and its sequel traditionally understood as referring to all things visible and invisible (e.g., Heb. 1:2; 11:3; Jos. Asen. 12:2). The Johannine verse also echoes a much debated issue within Judaism in general and Hellenistic Judaism in particular, where, in an attempt to absolve God from responsibility for evil, only the good things were attributed to him and, to some extent, to his Logos, and the rest was ascribed either to the Logos or to the lesser divine powers who stand hierarchically below the Logos and who are variously called λόγοι, ἄγγελοι or δυνάμεις (Philo, *Opif.* 72-75; *Leg.* III.177-178; *Conf.* 168-182; *Fug.* 65-76; *Mut.* 30-32).[19] The same sources, however, acknowledge that this does not altogether absolve God from responsibility for everything; he is still the creator of all, both the beneficial and the harmful (Philo, *Leg.* III.75-76; 1QS 3.25;

---

[18] The incarnation of the Logos (1:14) and his relation to God, creation, and humankind in the Prologue are best explained in terms of the post-Biblical Jewish circumlocutions for God and his manifestations in the Old Testament, such as his Presence or Glory; see L. Bouyer, *La Bible et l'Évangile. Le sens de l'Écriture: du Dieu qui parle au Dieu fait homme,* second ed. (Paris: Éditions du Cerf, 1958), pp. 202, 249; also Hayward, *Divine Name and Presence,* pp. 134-136 (his assessment of Philo's Logos, pp. 137-139, is dependent on H. A. Wolfson's unwarranted emphasis on Philo's originality in *Philo* [Cambridge, Mass.: Harvard University Press, 1962], I, pp. 226-289, 325-332; for a better treatment, see N. A. Dahl and A. F. Segal, "Philo and the Rabbis on the Names of God," *Journal for the Study of Judaism in the Persian, Hellenistic and Roman Period,* 9 [1978], pp. 1-28). In a profound study, L. W. Hurtado, *One God, One Lord: Early Christian Devotion and Ancient Jewish Monotheism* (Philadelphia: Fortress Press, 1988), underscores the common belief in Judaism of a divine mediator and goes on to show that the earliest Christian departure from Judaism came about as Christians began to worship the mediator. This came about, it seems, because the Logos was perceived as indistinguishable (or nearly indistinguishable) from God himself, and the Gospel of John may be viewed as the earliest Christian apology for this fundamental belief. On the continuity of these views in rabbinic Judaism, see H. Bietenhard, "Logos-Theologie im Rabbinat: Ein Beitrag zur Lehre vom Worte Gottes im rabbinischen Schriftentum," *Aufstieg und Niedergang der römischen Welt, II: Principat,* ed. H. Temporini and W. Haase (Berlin and New York: Walter de Gruyter, 1979), 19.2, pp. 580-618. The later dogmatic argument that the Word is distinct from the Father could be traced to Justin, *Dial.* 56.11; 62.2-3; 128.4; cf. *Apol.* 129.4.

[19] Cf. the Son's superiority over the angels in Heb. 1-2; also the task of the inferior agents in the creation according to Plato (*Tim.* 42D-E; *Rep.* 379A, 380D, 617E). Typical of the general attempt to absolve God from evil is Sir. 15:11: "That which he hateth made he not" (cf. Wis. 11:24: "If you had hated anything you would never have fashioned it").

cf. Plato, *Laws* 896D-F). The Johannine use of the singular Logos only and the equating of the Logos with God, implies that the Logos is more than an intermediary who is somewhat responsible for the lesser, inferior creation; he is, as noted above, the creator of "all things" or an extension of him (cf. vss. 1 and 18). By stressing "all things," the Evangelist seems to be adhering to the traditional Biblical view whereby God is perceived as being over and above all, both good and evil (e.g., Job 19:8; 30:26; Ps. 139:12; Isa. 45:7; Amos 3:6; cf. 4:13; 5:8; 9:3-4), a view later supported by adopting the teleological rationalizing of evil in Stoicism.[20]

The sovereignty of the Logos over the forces of evil is reaffirmed in vs. 5, in the inability of the acknowledged darkness to overpower the light; and this, in turn, is an interpretation of Gen. 1:2 LXX: ". . . darkness was over the deep, and the Spirit of God moved over the water" (cf. 6:16-21, Jesus walking over the stirred up sea in the dark).[21]

To the Logos is ascribed the best of the divine attributes: "In him was life," defined as "the light of all people" (vs. 4) and further explained as "the true light, which enlightens everyone, was coming into the world" (vs. 9; cf. 5:26a, the Father as life; 1 John 1:5, God as light; and 5:26b; 6:57; 11:25; 14:6; 1 John 5:11, 20, Jesus as life; 3:19; 8:12; 9:5; 12:35-36, 46, Jesus as light). The twin notions of life and light, as shall be demonstrated, owe more to the creation parlance of Gen. 1-2 than to passages beyond Genesis that speak of God as the giver of life (Job 10:12; 27:3; 32:8; 33:4) and light (Job 29:3; Ps 118:27), and others that speak of him as light (Ps. 84:11; Isa. 6:19-20; Mal. 4:2; cf. Rev. 21:23).[22] Of some interest are the Psalms where life and light appear in conjunction (27:1: "The Lord is my light and my salvation. . . . The Lord is the stronghold of my life"; 36:9: "For with you is the fountain of life; in your light we see light"; 56:13: "For you have delivered my soul from death, indeed my feet from stumbling, so that I may walk before God,

---

[20] See A. A. Long, "The Stoic Concept of Evil," *Philosophical Quarterly,* 18 (1968), pp. 329-343; cf. Philo, *Q.G.* IV.24: "Things which seem evil and deserving of condemnation are found through selective tests to be virtuous and very praiseworthy."

[21] The imagery of light and darkness is widespread in post-biblical Jewish literature; e.g., 1QH 9.26-27; 1QS 3.13-4.26; T. Jos. 19:3; Jos. Asen. 8:10; 15:13; T. Ab. B7; 3 Bar. 6:13; 2 Enoch 30:15; Odes Sol. 18:6; etc. Water as the habitat of demonic or evil powers is a consistent Biblical motif; e.g., Job 41:1-11; Ps. 74:12-17; 104:24-26; Isa. 27:1; etc. Of the Synoptic parallels to Jesus walking on the sea (Matt. 14:22-33; Mark 6:45-52), Matthew's account culminates with Peter's failed attempt to walk likewise.

[22] On creation in Biblical wisdom, see especially G. von Rad, *Wisdom in Israel* (Nashville: Abingdon Press, 1972), pp. 144-176.

in the light of life"; cf. Job 33:28; Prov. 6:23).

In a comprehensive article on the Biblical motif of light and darkness, Achtemeier observes:

> In the first chapter of Genesis, God creates the light *before* he creates the sun and moon and stars. This first light (Gen. 1:3) is the result of the creative word of God: it exists independently of the heavenly bodies, and of all the works of creation it alone is singled out as "good" (Gen. 1:4). The *order* of the creation is called "good" in Gen. 1:10, 12, 18, 21, 31—but the light itself, created by the word of God, is called good. In thinking of Jesus as the light of the world, it is with this original light that we have to deal.[23]

Consequently, Achtemeier goes on to relate "the true light" of John 1:9 to the original light of Gen. 1:3: "Jesus Christ is the incarnate Word of God, that creative Word through whom all things were made (John 1:3). He is the Word which was first spoken when God said, 'Let there be light' (Gen. 1:3)."[24] She then quotes 2 Cor. 4:6 as conveying the same thought: ". . . God, who said, 'Light shall shine out of darkness,' is the One who has shone in our hearts to give the light of the knowledge of the glory of God in the face of Christ." The Johannine and Pauline passages show clearly how both authors employ the language of Gen. 1:3: while they relate the Logos (or Christ) to that pre-celestial light, they hasten to equate him with the Word that preceded the creation of that light.

A closer look at the Hellenistic Jewish interpretations of Gen. 1:3 reveals a similar pattern of thought regarding the Logos. Following Aristobulus (Fr. 4:3, quoted above), Philo presents the Logos as the initial expression of divine creation, the noetic world or the pattern for subsequent material creation (*Opif.* 7-22). He then sums up his views, adding: "It was with a view to that original intellectual light, which I have mentioned as belonging to the order of the incorporeal world, that he created the heavenly bodies of which our senses are aware" (55; cf. *Migr.* 40: "Wisdom is God's archetypal luminary and the sun is a copy and image of it"). In another passage, significant for its clarification of relationships, he declares:

> He [God] is not only light, but the archetype of every other light, nay, prior to and high above every archetype, holding the position of the model of a model. For the model or pattern was the Word which contained all his fullness—light, in fact; for,

---

[23] E. R. Achtemeier, "Jesus Christ, the Light of the World: The Biblical Understanding of Light and Darkness," *Interpretation,* 17 (1963), p. 440.

[24] Achtemeier, "Jesus Christ, the Light of the World," p. 447.

as the lawgiver tells us, "God said, 'let light come into being.'" (*Somn.* I.75; cf. 238-241)

Colson notes on this passage: "The Logos *is* light, for if God *said* 'let there be light,' this was a λόγος in the sense of a saying."[25] There is, however, a deeper sense attached to the Logos in this passage than that indicated by Colson: as the model or the archetype for all subsequent light, the Logos is hardly distinguishable from the model of the model or the archetype above every archetype because of the commonality of light obtained between them and owing to the inseparability of the "saying" from the one who speaks. As Philo remarks elsewhere: "He himself is his own light. For the eye of the Absolutely Existent needs no other light to effect perception, but he himself is the archetypal essence of which myriads of rays are the effluence" (*Cher.* 96-97). Hence, the initial role of the Logos is to be seen in terms of the self-extension of the Absolutely Existent by way of light prior to that archetypal, pre-celestial light created by him or through his Logos. A strong parallel to the Johannine notion and one clearly reflective of a widespread understanding of primordial creation in first century Judaism is found in Odes Sol. 41:14: "And light dawned from the Word that was before time in him."

Time (χρόνος) began with the creation and the movement of the heavenly bodies on the fourth day of creation (Gen. 1:14-19). Before then there was eternity (αἰών), a synonym for "the beginning" (ἀρχή), in the light of which the opening words of the Prologue ought to be further interpreted (Philo, *Opif.* 13-16, 26-35; cf. *Leg.* I.20; *Deus* 31-32; *Her.* 165; *Mut.* 267; *Aet.* 52-54).

Without overlooking the dominant cosmological language in the rest of the Prologue and other specific elements suggestive of creation,[26] such as the ability of the Logos to bring forth children of God (vss. 12-13), elements to which we shall return, we shall trace the theme of creation as it unfolds through the notions of life and light (vs. 4).

II. Creation and the Sabbath

Taking the Prologue in its present form as reflecting summarily the theology of the

[25] F. H. Colson, *Philo* (Cambridge, Mass: Harvard University Press, 1934), V, p. 337. Elsewhere, Philo explains: the Logos is neither unbegotten like the Creator nor begotten like the creature, but stands midway between the two (*Her.* 205; cf. *Somn.* II.188).

[26] Of interest is Borgen's chiastic outline of the Prologue, demonstrating how vss. 6-18 constitute a regressive amplification of vss. 1-5 (*Philo, John and Paul,* pp. 93-96).

Gospel of John, we are compelled to consider the elaborations on creation in terms of life and light in the central passages devoted to these notions. It is noteworthy that the main discourses on life and light (chs. 5 and 9) are developed around the only two healing miracles in John that occur on the Sabbath—a further reminder of the creation week in Genesis.[27] These healings on the Sabbath with their emphases on life and light constitute a clear continuity of the theme of creation stressed in the Prologue, where the two notions are introduced in conjunction. Unlike the healings on the Sabbath in the Synoptics, those in the Gospel of John are peculiar to the Johannine tradition and are invariably related to the theme of creation.[28] Together with the Prologue, they furnish the most substantial Christological arguments to affirm not only the divinity of the Logos but also his identity with God, the giver of life and light (cf. 5:17-20; 10:30-38; 17:5, 11, 21-24 and the "I am" sayings, especially in ch. 8). The significance of the twin notions is underscored, though somewhat over-emphatically, by Bouyer: "Ces deux images associées, de la 'lumière' et de la 'vie,' sont comme les clefs de toute la pensée johannique."[29]

The healing miracles in these chapters are presented as divine acts of creation: the first is effected through the spoken word (5:8; cf. vs. 19, where this act is related to God's activity) and the second by handling the dust of the earth (9:6; cf. vs. 32, where another hint is given to relate this miracle to "the beginning of time"). The first is anticipated in 4:34: "My food is to do the will of him who sent me, and to accomplish his work" (cf. 5:30, 36) and the second is introduced in 9:3-5: ". . . in order that the works of God might be displayed. . . . We must work the works of him who sent me, as long as it is day; night is coming when no one can work. While I am in the world, I am the light of the world." The Son's

---

[27] These miracles are also set around two pools in Jerusalem, one to the north and the other to the south of the Temple area. J. Jeremias invites attention to the sick and the blind gathered at the Temple gates and, by analogy with Acts 3:1-10, assumes that the conversation between Jesus and the paralytic in ch. 5 was occasioned by a request for alms (cf. 9:8) (*Jerusalem in the Time of Jesus*, tr. F. H. and C. H. Cave [Philadelphia: Fortress Press, 1969], p. 118).

[28] In the Synoptics the Sabbath day is indicated before the healings, as a challenge for Jesus to heal on that day (Matt. 12:9-14 [and par. Mark 3:1-6, Luke 6:6-11] and Luke 13:10-17; 14:1-6); in John the day is indicated after the healings (5:9-10, 16; 9:14). Moreover, the two miracles in the Synoptics that resemble the two Johannine miracles under consideration (the healing of the paralytic in Matt. 9:1-8 [and par. Mark 2:1-12, Luke 5:17-26] and of the blind man in Mark 8:22-26) do not occur on the Sabbath. Those in John seem to illustrate, albeit unintentionally, the couplet in Ps. 146:8: "The Lord opens the eyes of the blind. The Lord lifts up those who are bowed down."

[29] Bouyer, *La Bible et l'Évangile*, p. 199.

ability to impart life to those who hear his voice is emphasized in both instances (5:19-29, to the opponents following the healing of the paralytic; 10:10-18, to the opponents following the healing of the blind). Together, these accounts pave the way for that ultimate miracle of giving life to the dead Lazarus (ch. 11), whose resurrection is only a sequel to the theme of the Son's ability to grant life (11:25; cf. 5:21, 25, 28-29) and light (11:9-11; cf. 8:12; 9:5), a theme both summed up and introduced in the Prologue (vs. 4). The sustained continuity of this theme allows the Evangelist to place the most elaborate discourse on the Son's ability to impart life following the miracle at Bethesda instead of after the miracle at Bethany. The first mention of a healing miracle on the Sabbath becomes a logical *locus* for the insertion of the main discourse. By way of further continuity, the raising of Lazarus is prefaced by similar statements as those introducing the healing of the man born blind: "This sickness is not unto death, but for the glory of God" (11:4); "Are there not twelve hours in the day? Those who walk during the day do not stumble, because they see the light of the world. But those who walk during the night stumble, because the light is not in them" (vss. 9-10; cf. 9:3-5). A further and direct connection between the healing of the blind man and the raising of Lazarus comes at 11:37: "Could not this man, who opened the eyes of him who was blind, have kept this man also from dying?" More importantly, the repeated admonition in the above passages to do God's work "as long as it is day" or to walk "during the day" or "while you have the light" (9:4; 11:9; 12:35) recalls the time of creation in Genesis, beginning with the calling forth of light.

In his defense for healing on the Sabbath, Jesus introduces two basic arguments: one propounded in 5:17, where he justifies his act in terms of the Father's working on the Sabbath, and the other in a later resumption of the debate over the same controversial healing in 7:19-24, where he refers to the law allowing circumcision on the Sabbath. Both of these arguments are explicable within the Judaism of Jesus' day.

In the first of these arguments the Johannine Jesus seems to be siding with a widespread apologetic movement within Judaism concerned with absolving God from charges of idleness or inactivity on the Sabbath lest it should be concluded that there is no divine providence at work on that day. We learn the following from Philo:

> And therefore Moses often in his laws calls the sabbath, which means 'rest,'
> God's sabbath (Ex. 20:10; etc.), not man's. . . . For in all truth there is but one

thing in the universe which rests, that is God. But Moses does not give the name of rest to mere inactivity. The cause of all things is by its nature active; it never ceases to work all that is best and most beautiful. God's rest is rather a working with absolute ease, without toil and suffering. (*Cher.* 87; cf. *Leg.* I.5-7)

Here Philo is elaborating on what seems to be a commonplace Alexandrian Jewish understanding of God's resting on the Sabbath, as attested in a fragment of Aristobulus:

It is plainly said by our legislation that God rested on the seventh day. This does not mean, as some interpret, that God no longer does anything. It means that, after he had finished ordering all things, he so orders them for all time. . . . For, having set all things in order, he maintains and alters them so [in accordance with that order]. (Fr. 5.11-12)[30]

God's providential care for his creation is described elsewhere by Philo as follows:

For it stands to reason that what has been brought into existence should be cared for by its Father and Maker. For, as we know, it is a father's aim in regard of his offspring and an artificer's in regard of his handiwork to preserve them, and by every means to fend off from them aught that may entail loss or harm. He keenly desires to provide for them in every way all that is beneficial and to their advantage. (*Opif.* 10; cf. 170-171; *Deus* 30; *Migr.* 186; *Spec.* III.189)

The Biblical grounds for the tradition about God working on the Sabbath could be traced to the inherent difficulties of Gen. 2:3, where the Hebrew text has God resting from all the work which "he created to make" (LXX: "he began to do"). As in Hellenistic Judaism, this progressive view of creation is well amplified in the Targums, where the Creator is said to have rested from all his work which "he had created and was to do" (Tg. Ps.-J. and Onq. to Gen. 2:3). The tradition about God working on the Sabbath persists in other early rabbinic speculations on this verse, and on the fourth commandment as well (Ex. 20:11 and 31:17). In a saying attributed to R. Akiba it is stated that God works on the Sabbath because the whole world is his domain and that he is not restricted in any way whatsoever: "He carries things on the sabbath anywhere throughout his worlds" (Pesikta Rabbati 23:8).[31]

---

[30] Cf. Ps-Aristotle, *Mundo* 398b23: "God does not take upon himself the toil of a creature that works and labors for itself, but uses an indefatigable power, by means of which he controls even things that seem a great way off."

[31] Later in the same section of the *piska* the following question is raised: "How could R.

In the resumption of the controversy at John 7:22-23 the issue of circumcision is introduced thus: "Moses has given you circumcision . . . and on the Sabbath you circumcise a man. If a man receives circumcision on the Sabbath in order that the Law of Moses may not be broken, are you angry with me because I made an entire man well on the Sabbath?" To be sure, rabbinic halakhah has ample provisions for circumcision on the Sabbath (M. Shabbat 18:3-19:4; M. Nedarim 3:11; B. T. Shabbat 131b, 132a, 133b; B. T. Yoma 85a-b; the rationale may be detected from Pesikta Rabbati 23:4: circumcision, like the Sabbath, was ordained before the Ten Commandments were given), though not for healing on that day (M. Shabbat 14:3-4). The response of Jesus is based on the Hellenistic jurisprudential argumentation *a minori ad maius,* the inference "from the lesser to the greater," later known as one of R. Hillel's seven *middot* or hermeneutical rules for the Torah.[32] The response implies a halakhic inconsistency which is well reiterated—if not rectified—in B. T. Yoma 85a: "If circumcision, which attaches [or, pertains] to one only of the 248 members of the human body suspends the Sabbath, how much more shall [the saving of] the whole body suspend the Sabbath!" The acknowledged inconsistency in rabbinic Judaism reflects the commonness of the argument—if not the obvious polemics in the Gospel of John.

In the second healing miracle on the Sabbath the reader is carried back to the most discussed notion in the Prologue, that of light, and on to the creation week in Genesis, which begins with the creation of light and culminates with the Sabbath. Jesus' spitting on the ground, making clay, and placing it on the eyes of the blind man (John 9:6) carry reminiscences from the creation of man in Gen. 2:7.[33] Following the heated polemic and the denunciations in John 8:31-59, Jesus is about to create a new entity as children of Abraham or children of God. The thought is not remote from the Baptist's declamation in the Synoptics: "Do not

---

Akiba have spoken as he did . . . ? Does not Scripture say, 'And on the seventh day he ceased from work and rested [Ex. 31:17]?'" R. Phinehas explained in the name of R. Hoshaia: "Even though it is written, 'Because that in it he rested from all his work [Gen. 2:3],' you must understand that the verse means he rested from the work of creating his world, but that he did not rest from [his concern about the] deeds of the righteous or the deeds of the wicked, and makes both the former and the latter see themselves for what they are."

[32] On the Hellenistic origin of this principle, see I. Heinemann, *Philons griechische und judische Bildung* (Breslau: Marcus, 1932), p. 493 and n. 6; also D. Daube, "Rabbinic Methods of Interpretation and Hellenistic Rhetoric," *Hebrew Union College Annual,* 22 (1949), pp. 239-264. On Philo's use of this principle, see F. H. Colson, *Philo* (Cambridge, Mass.: Harvard University Press, 1939), VIII, pp. 432-434.

[33] For a history of this interpretation, see Schnackenburg, *The Gospel According to St John,* II, p. 496 n. 13.

suppose that you can say to yourselves, 'We have Abraham for our father'; for I say to you that God is able from these stones to raise up children to Abraham" (Matt. 3:9; cf. Luke 3:8). Such an act of creation by Jesus is commensurate with his appeal in ch. 3 to be "born again" or "from above," that is "of the spirit," and his repeated "I am" declarations in ch. 8, especially vs. 12: "I am the light of the world; whoever follows me shall not walk in the darkness, but shall have the light of life" (cf. 12:36: "While you have the light, believe in the light, in order that you may become children of light"). The miracle, with the blind man's proclaiming his faith in the Son of Man (9:35-38), affirms the statements made in the Prologue, that "the true light, which enlightens everyone, was coming into the world" (vs. 9) and that "as many as received him, to them he gave the right to become children of God" (vs.12; cf. 17:1-9; 1 John 2:29; 3:9; 4:7; 5:1, 4, 18; also Philo, *Conf.* 41, 145-148; Odes Sol. 31:4). The notion of the Logos begetting "children of light" or "children of God" is stressed again near the end of the Gospel, with the risen Jesus breathing (ἐνεφύσησεν) on his disciples when imparting the Holy Spirit to them (20:22; cf. 1:33).[34] This final act of Jesus is related to God's breathing (ἐνεφύσησεν) the breath of life into the earthborn man whereby man becomes a living being (Gen. 2:7 LXX; the same verb is used in Ez. 37:9 and Wis. 15:11 to describe the creation of man). Commenting on 20:22, Dunn observes: "John presents the act of Jesus as a new creation: Jesus is the author of the new creation as he is of the old (1:3)."[35] In Hellenistic Judaism, following the Septuagint, the breath of life (πνοὴν ζωῆς) is synonymous with the life-giving Spirit of God (πνεῦμα θεοῦ) or the image of God (εἰκὼν θεοῦ) in humans, that divine light or the rational element (λόγος) in them whereby they resemble their maker.[36] The λόγος in humans

---

[34] Cf. the Pauline notion of children of God in the Spirit: Rom. 8:9-17; 1 Cor. 3:16-17; 6:12-20; Gal. 2:15-21; 4:1-7; Phil. 2:1-11; Col. 3:5-11.

[35] J. D. G. Dunn, *Baptism in the Holy Spirit* (Naperville, Ill.: Allenson, 1970), p. 180.

[36] The double account of the creation of humans in Gen. 1:26-31 and 2:4-7 receives ample and diverse treatment in Philo's works, especially in his *De Opificio,* where the first passage is variously taken to suggest the creation of the idea of man or a paradigmatic exemplar of man (24-25), the earthborn man with his rational and irrational faculties (69), and, more broadly, "an idea or type or seal, an object of thought, incorporeal, neither male nor female, by nature incorruptible," compared with the earthborn man contemplated in the second account (134-135). However, the two accounts in Philo's earlier commentaries on the opening chapters of Genesis are interpreted as two creations: one of the heavenly and the other of the earthly man (*Q.G.* I.4, 8; II.56, 59; *Leg.* I.31-32; III.96, 161); and in the passing references to these passages a single creation is seen in both accounts: that of the earthborn man with his rational and irrational faculties. In the interpretation of the double account as a single creation, the image of God (Gen. 1:27) and the inbreathed divine spirit (Gen. 2:7) are equated and taken for the human mind, that

is what distinguishes them from other creatures and draws them into the realm of the divine—a notion that owes much to certain other meanings of λόγος in Greek philosophy (cf. 10:34-36, quoting Ps. 82:6).³⁷ In this regard, the Johannine equation of Jesus with the indwelling Spirit or the Paraclete is noteworthy: it may be seen in its relation to the Logos doctrine. A similar interrelation is discernible in the words of Jesus which are said to be both spirit and life (6:63; cf. 12:50).³⁸

Moreover, the second instance of healing on the Sabbath is introduced by Jesus with a remark on his working "while it is day" (9:4). Here again we discern a common element with the first healing on the Sabbath, in the remark on his working as does the Father "until now" (5:17). The eschatological overtones of these remarks cannot be overlooked; they seem to be in keeping with the overall eschatology of the Gospel, where the end time expectations are perceived as ongoing realizations. Also, there is a certain emphasis on judgment in the sequel to these controversial healings on the Sabbath (5:22-30 and 9:39).

Of interest is the fifth fragment of Aristobulus where the Sabbath is explained in terms of cosmic significance: "According to the laws of nature, the seventh day might be called first also, as the genesis of light in which all things are contemplated" (Fr. 5:9; cf. Philo, according to whom the Sabbath marks "the birthday of the world": *Opif.* 89; *Mos.* I.207; II.210; 263-266; *Spec.* I.170; II.59, 70). Eschatological interpretations of the Sabbath as pointing to the Messianic Age owe somewhat to this traditional understanding of the seventh day as marking both an end as well as a beginning in Hellenistic Judaism. Besides, in Philo the Sabbath rest is symbolic of the rest in God, the uninterrupted peace of the soul that cannot be disturbed whether by war or by any other calamity (*Fug.* 174; *Abr.* 28; *Decal.* 96-105; *Spec.* II.56-70, cf. 71-139, his remarks on the sabbatical year and the year

---

divine, incorruptible element or the rational part of the soul whereby man is able to contemplate divine things and attain the virtues (especially wisdom) that bring the soul to happiness and immortality (*Det.* 80-86; *Plant.* 18-20; *Her.* 56, 164, 231; *Fug.* 71-72; *Somn.* I.74; *Spec.* I.81). T. H. Tobin (*The Creation of Man: Philo and the History of Interpretation* [Washington, D.C.: Catholic University Press, 1983], pp. 20-35) relegates to Philo's predecessors the traditional distinction between the heavenly man of Gen. 1:27 and the earthly man of Gen. 2:7 and attributes to Philo the more homogeneous understanding of these two accounts as a single creation.

³⁷ In Stoicism, e.g., see *Stoicorum Veterum Fragmenta,* ed. H. von Arnim (Leipzig: Teubner, 1903-24), II, secs. 528, 1127, 1208; III, secs. 333-339, 343. See also J. S. Ackerman, "The Rabbinic Interpretation of Psalm 82 and the Gospel of John: John 10:34," *HTR,* 59 (1966), pp. 186-191.

³⁸ R. E. Brown, *The Gospel according to John* (Garden City, N.Y.: Doubleday, 1960-70), II, pp. 1139-1141; F. Porsch, *Pneuma und Wort: Ein exegetischer Beitrag zur Pneumatologie des Johannesevangeliums* (Frankfurt/Main: Knecht, 1974).

of Jubilee; and Hel. Syn. Pr. 5).[39] The thought is reminiscent of the sayings of
Jesus in John 14:27 and 16:33 (cf. Matt. 11:28-29; Heb. 4:8).

Over against the constant obsession with the religious dictates for the
Sabbath, the Johannine Jesus translates Sabbath observance to a continuous concern
for humanity (as in the Synoptics; cf. Mark 2:27). Consequently, the miracles of
chs. 5 and 9 are conveyed as acts of philanthropy and come as a rebuke to those
who seemingly observe the Sabbath while being continually inconsiderate toward
the kind of people whom Jesus heals—thereby nullifying the very intent of Sabbath
observance (cf. 7:19, where Jesus accuses the opponents of not keeping the Law,
a charge based on their intention to kill him for—ironically—having broken the
Sabbath command as they perceived its observance to be). Here also the
apologetics of Hellenistic Judaism provide the theological backdrop. Because of
anti-Jewish slander from without and disenchantment with traditional religion from
within, Jewish Law in the Hellenistic period was interpreted apologetically, to show
that the end of the Law is philanthropy. The whole Law, from the least of the
commandments on what to do with a bird's nest (Deut. 22:6-7) to the Decalogue
(Ex. 20) and the precepts on *tephillin* and *mezuzot* (Ex. 13:9, 16; Deut. 6:8-9;
11:18-20), is said to teach humanity. Typical of this development are the Letter of
Aristeas, especially the central part of the document (128-171, Eleazar's apology
for the Law), and Philo's tractate on philanthropy (*Virt.* 51-174).[40]

III. Summary

Beyond the obvious similarities between the beginning of the Gospel of John and
that of the Book of Genesis, the theme of creation is sustained in the first five
verses of the Prologue and is discernible in the notion of the Logos as the divine
creator in whom there is life and light—two major motifs derived from the theme
of creation and conveying further reminiscences from Genesis. There is a further
unfolding of the theme, however, in John 5 and 9: one elaborating on life and the
other on light. Both chapters are developed around the only two healing miracles

---

[39] For more on Philo's understanding of the Sabbath, see H. Weiss, "Philo on the Sabbath,"
The Studia Philonica Annual, 3 (1991), pp. 83-105.

[40] Equally significant are the Synoptic sayings on "the least of these commandments" and
"the weightier provisions of the law" (Matt. 5:19; 23:23); see my essay, "Some Stock Arguments
for the Magnanimity of the Law in Hellenistic Jewish Apologetics," *Jewish Law Association
Studies I: The Touro Conference Volume,* ed. B. S. Jackson (Chico, Calif.: Scholars Press, 1985),
pp. 141-149.

done on the Sabbath—itself a reminder of creation. Moreover, both miracles are presented as divine acts of creation. The subsequent controversies are structured in terms of Hellenistic Jewish apologetics whereby creation is perceived as a process, with God still at work, and Sabbath observance, like all the laws of Torah, is shown to teach philanthropy.

Notwithstanding the essential differences between the Johannine, Philonic, and Targumic speculations on the Word, the former shares some common theological perceptions with the latter two. As regards creation, the Johannine Logos owes much to Hellenistic Jewish interpretations of Gen. 1. These were conditioned by the belief in a transcendent and yet immanent God whose remoteness and nearness—both of which are attested in numerous scriptural passages—constantly called for explanation. The belief necessitated various circumlocutions for God's presence and activity and the eventual removal of anthropomorphisms and anthropopathisms from the Scriptures when translating first the Septuagint and then the Targums. The history of the doctrine of the Word within Judaism shows a decisive influence of Greek philosophy on Jewish theology in the Hellenistic period—whether in Alexandria or in the land of Israel.

The overriding burden of the Johannine Prologue, like the Christology of the rest of the Gospel, is to affirm not only the divinity of the Logos but also his identity with God, the giver of life and light. This is accomplished for the most part in the treatment of the healing miracles on the Sabbath and the ensuing discourses on life and light. The theology of chs. 5 and 9 and their sequel is summed up in the Johannine affirmation that God had made all things through his Logos, regarding whom it is said: "In him was life, and the life was the light of all people" (1:4).

In the polemical discourses following the two miracles, those who claim to observe the Sabbath and who advocate its observance are rebuked for their indifference and even hostility toward the kind of people whom Jesus heals. They are nullifying the philanthropic purpose for the Sabbath command by their misanthropy—even toward needy coreligionists just outside the Temple gates. They do not have the love of God (5:42); they do not see (9:39-41). Conversely, those who show concern for afflicted humanity and help alleviate human suffering are deemed true observers of the Sabbath because they fulfill its intent. Their acts of mercy extend life and light and are commensurate with God's ongoing, creative and restorative work.

"The True Light Which Illumines Every Person"

Ed. L. Miller
Professor of Philosophy/Religious Studies, University of Colorado
Boulder, Colorado

We examine here an oft-cited verse in the Prologue of John's Gospel: John 1:9. The Greek text, unpunctuated, reads,

ἦν τὸ φῶς τὸ ἀληθινὸν ὃ φωτίζει πάντα ἄνθρωπον ἐρχόμενον εἰς τὸν κόσμον.

which is rendered in the New Revised Standard Version (NRSV) as,

The true light, which enlightens everyone, was coming into the world.

That we encounter in this verse the idea of the illumination of every individual by the true light is clear. Beyond that, however, the situation is exceedingly complicated. There are four questions involved here: what I shall call the three "little" questions and the one "big" one. The little questions concern notorious and vexing exegetical points which, for all their technicality, must be addressed if the verse is to receive a full exposition, though it would be possible for the less technically inclined to pass over these and proceed directly to the big question. The big question addresses the central idea of the verse, and asks exactly what is meant by the claim that the true light "illumines every person,"[1] and, specifically,

---

[1] I am persuaded that while the NRSV avoids the gender-exclusive translation "man" for

whether this claim may be enlisted as Biblical evidence for a "general revelation."

I. Three Little Questions

The relevant and various angles on our three little questions may be found in the standard commentaries and articles,[2] and our purpose here is only to reflect these angles and to indicate some preferences, while avoiding an extended and tedious treatment. At the same time, it is necessary to state at the outset that my brief discussion of these points, as well as the larger discussion, presupposes two convictions about the Prologue (John 1:1-18), which, though controversial, I maintain nonetheless: (1) The Prologue was originally compounded from various short pieces of varying length and type, including hymnic material, narrative material, memorable lines, and probably secondary interpolations; (2) the substance of the Prologue material was composed by the same hand as the remainder of the Gospel, including ch. 21.

The first little question is, *Who is coming into the world?* The unpunctuated Greek text (bearing in mind that punctuation was not introduced until about 200 C.E.) is utterly ambiguous as to the subject of the participial phrase, "coming into the world," as was noted at least as early as Origen. From a purely grammatical standpoint the participle ἐρχόμενον, "coming," can be taken as neuter, agreeing with φῶς, "light," which then would be the subject, as in

1-A: He was the true light coming into the world, which illumines

---

ἄνθρωπος, its "everyone" does not do justice to the phrase πάντα ἄνθρωπον. Recurringly in the Gospel of John, "everyone" is rendered by the simple word πᾶς (accusative = πάντα). That we have here πᾶς + ἄνθρωπος is, as in 2:10, conspicuous and suggests a somewhat stronger translation. Though I am not altogether happy with "person" as a rendering of ἄνθρωπος it is possible and certainly preferable to "human."

[2] A sampling of relevant discussions: R. E. Brown, The Gospel according to John (Garden City, N.Y.: Doubleday, 1966-70), I, pp. 9-10.; L. Morris, *The Gospel according to John* (Grand Rapids, Mich.: Eerdmans, 1971), pp. 92-95; C. K. Barrett, *The Gospel according to St. John*, second ed. (Philadelphia: Westminster Press, 1978), pp. 160-161.; R. Schnackenburg, *The Gospel according to St. John*, tr. K. Smyth (New York: Seabury Press, 1968-82), I, pp. 253-255; K. Barth, *Witness to the Word: A Commentary on John 1*, ed. W. Fürst, tr. G. W. Bromiley (Grand Rapids, Mich: Eerdmans, 1986), pp. 59-62; A. Feuillet, *Le Prologue du Quatrième Évangile: Étude de Théologie Johannique* (Paris: Desclée de Brouwer, 1968), pp. 62ff.; M. E. Boismard, *St. John's Prologue*, tr. Carisbrooke Dominicans (Westminster, Maryland: Newman Press, 1957), pp. 27-32; B. Prete, "La Concordanza del Participio *erchomenon* in Giov. 1:9," *Bibbia e Oriente*, 17 (1975), pp. 195-208.

every person.

or as in

> *1-B*: The true light was coming into the world, which illumines every person.

or as masculine, modifying ἄνθρωπον, "person," as in

> 2: He was the true light, which illumines every person coming into the world.

Notwithstanding the ambiguity, *2* was the interpretation adopted by the Latin, Syriac, and Coptic versions and by the rank and file of commentators throughout the tradition. Those who opt for *2* usually do so, with Rudolf Bultmann, on the grounds that *1-B* involves the grammatically troublesome interposition of a relative clause between a modal verb and its participle, and/or that the complete expression, "every person coming into the world," reflects a standard rabbinic locution for "person."[3] With most recent scholars I reject these appeals and am inclined toward *1-A* or *1-B*, half on intuition and half on critical considerations. The critical considerations involve three points. First, *1-A* or *1-B* is strongly suggested by the general Johannine context wherein frequently the Logos, the Prophet, the Son, the Christ, etc., is represented in one way or another as coming into the world (e.g., 1:14; 6:14; 4:39; 11:27; 15:22; 16:28; 18:37), and light, specifically, is represented as coming into the world in that very way, as in 3:19 ". . . the light has come into the world. . . ," and in 12:46, "I have come, a light, into the world." On the other hand, outside the debatable case of 1:9, one never encounters the expression "person coming into the world," which in any case does not conform to the rabbinic locution actually cited—the actual formula, "everyone coming into the world," would most naturally have been rendered in Greek as πάντα ἐρχόμενον εἰς τὸν κόσμον, forcing Bultmann to the rather arbitrary claim that ἄνθρωπον was "an explanatory gloss" introduced by the translator of an Aramaic original.[4] Second,

---

[3] R. Bultmann, *The Gospel of John*, tr. G. R. Beasley-Murray *et al.* (Oxford, England: Blackwell, 1971), p. 52, n. 2.

[4] Bultmann, *Gospel of John*, p. 52, n. 2. He also believed that bracketing ἄνθρωπον resulted in a better (shorter) length of the poetic line. We leave aside the problematic and now almost

suggested by the character of the Prologue in which 1:9 finds itself and wherein the Logos' advent into the world is a recurring idea, implicitly or explicitly, as in 1:4,[5] 10, 11, 14, 15, 17, and 18.[6] It may be especially relevant that 1:9 is followed *immediately* by the incarnational reference in 1:10, "He was in the world. . . ." One might object, of course, that even on our own view the material in the Prologue is a mosaic of originally independent pieces and there is, thus, no certainty that in their original form vss. 9 and 10 were connected. But even so, it may have been precisely a *formal* connection (a continuity of ideas) that dictated, eventually, that these pieces should be *materially* connected. The third consideration involves the grammatical point about the interposition of the relative clause between the subject and the participial phrase, and brings us to the second little question.

The second little question is, *How do we decide between "He was the true light" and "The true light was coming into the world"?* We thus come to the difference between *1-A* and *1-B*, which concerns the placing of the imperfect ἦν, "was." Some take it as connecting the unexpressed subject with the participial phrase, as in *1-B*. Certainly it is no problem for *1-A* that the unexpressed subject is implicit in the verb, and its defenders almost always opt for it on the grounds that though the imperfect ἦν ("was") may be taken together with a participle—the "periphrastic" participle[7]—in the Greek text before us ἦν ("was") is separated from the participle ἐρχόμενον ("coming") by an intervening relative clause, ὃ φωτίζει πάντα ἄνθρωπον ("which illumines every person"); in fact, ἦν is the *first* word in the sentence, thus removed as far as possible from the participial phrase that it allegedly connects with. Such a construction, as is involved in *1-B*, is deemed by many to be a grossly improbable one, and has even been regarded as impossible, as by W. Eltester: "ἦν mit ἐρχόμενον verbinden zu wollen, ist philologisch zulässig, da die coniugatio preiphrastica nicht so zerrissen werden darf."[8] Further, and more

---

in a better (shorter) length of the poetic line. We leave aside the problematic and now almost universally discarded argument for an Aramaic original of the Prologue.

[5] On this controversial instance, see E. L. Miller, *Salvation-History in the Prologue of John: The Significance of 1:3/4* (Leiden: Brill, 1989), *passim*.

[6] Reading with the best witnesses, θεός: "the unique *God*, who is in the bosom of the Father." This reading, rather than the traditional υἱός ("son"), more obviously gives the verse at least an implicitly incarnational meaning.

[7] Cf. M. Zerwick, *Biblical Greek*, fourth ed., tr. J. Smith (Rome: Pontifical Biblical Institute, 1963), p. 126: The periphrastic construction, wherein a participle employs as an auxiliary some form of the verb "to be," was "a favored expression in Hellenistic Greek by the general tendency to greater expressiveness," and in the New Testament the frequency of the imperfect periphrastic in particular reflects, no doubt, a Semitic influence.

[8] W. Eltester, "Der Logos und sein Prophet: Fragen zur heutigen Erklärung des Johanneischen

theologically, it has been asked what could be the significance of the claim in *1-B*, and signalled by the imperfect ἦν, that the light *was coming* into the world; was not the advent into the world of the incarnate light a singular and "punctiliar" event? Against the rejection of *1-B* and in favor of *1-A* however, and again in agreement with most recent scholars, I would make two points. (1) John has, in fact, something of a penchant for periphrastic participial constructions employing the imperfect modal, as in 1:28, 2:6, 3:23, 10:40, 11:1, 13:23, 18:18, 18:25, and 18:30. Many of these involve several intervening words between the imperfect modal and the participle, but especially important are 2:6 and 18:18 each of which include a prepositional phrase within the intervening words.[9] It is true that in 1:9 the intrusion of a relative clause renders the construction more strained than in these other instances, but it would seem to be nonetheless grammatically and structurally possible. (2) It remains to ask about the odd-sounding claim that the light *was coming* into the world. It should be noted, first, that even with its present participle *1-B* sounds odd itself inasmuch as it claims that he, the Logos, was the light *coming* into the world. In the case of either *1-A* or *1-B* a continuing activity is suggested, but at least *1-B* with its imperfect tense casts this, more appropriately, into the past. Some have seen theological significance in the expression, suggesting as it seemed to Westcott, for example, the ways in which the light has come to people continuously through the ages "in type and prophecy and judgment."[10] I think, though, that in the end 1:9 must refer to the incarnation and that the odd-sounding imperfect should be understood as an instance of John's inconsistent and perhaps imaginative use of language. In 3:24, 19:20, and 19:41, the imperfect ἦν is used with the perfect participle, though the action in each case is clearly a punctiliar one, and in 6:50 the bread from heaven is represented as "coming" (present participle) from heaven whereas in 6:51, immediately following, it is represented as the bread which "came" (aorist participle) from heaven.

We come, then, to the third little question: *What is meant by "true" light?* Many (such as St. Augustine and St. Thomas Aquinas) have seen great metaphysical significance in the adjective ἀληθινόν in 1:9. One recent example is Dodd who took the expression "true light" as an equivalent to the Platonic-Philonic

---

Prolog," in *Apophoreta* (Berlin: Topelmann, 1964), p. 128.

[9] It is possible in 18:18, taken alone, to construe the imperfect verb with the prepositional phrase, but a comparison with 18:25 makes this extremely unlikely.

[10] B. F. Westcott, *The Gospel according to St. John* (Grand Rapids, Mich: Eerdmans, 1978 [orig. 1880]), p. 7.

φωτὸς ἀρχέτυπον, "archetypal light," or "the eternal 'idea' or light, of which all empirical lights are transient copies."[11] But attempts to interpret the relevant Johannine complex of words (ἀλήθεια ["truth"] and the two adjectives ἀληθής and ἀληθινόν ["true"]) along Hellenistic metaphysical-speculative lines are out of step with what is now generally regarded as a thoroughly Jewish document. Even Calvin's less extreme interpretation, according to which the adjective signifies *veram lucem, cui natura proprium est lucre*, "the true light, whose own nature is to be light,"[12] strikes me as too philosophical a sentiment for this Gospel. In contrast to any speculative or Hellenistic slant, what we encounter in the Johannine documents is the *practical* though semantically odd ideas of *doing* the truth (John 3:21), *walking in* the truth (2 John 4), and of a person *being* the truth (John 14:6).

But we must look more carefully at the expression before us. The adjective ἀληθινόν, "true," bears two closely related senses:[13] (1) the sense in which a conformity to reality is affirmed, and (2) the sense in which authenticity is affirmed in contrast to something spurious or falsely conceived. The adjective ἀληθινόν occurs nine times in John. When used in reference to propositions, etc., it bears, naturally, the first sense, as in a true saying (4:37), true judgment (8:16), and true testimony (19:35). When, however, it is used of *things* or *persons*, it appears always to bear the second sense, as in the *real* worshipers as opposed to idolaters (4:23), the *real* bread as opposed to the Old Testament manna (6:32), the *real* vine as opposed to the Old Testament vine, Israel (15:1), and the *real* God as opposed to idols (17:3). This leaves 7:28, with its representation of the one who sent Jesus as being, oddly, ἀληθινόν. If this is an exceptional usage of ἀληθινόν it is the exception that proves the rule, and it is noteworthy that in this instance the different adjective ἀληθής is given in a few manuscript witnesses, including P[66] and Sinaiticus. Especially in view of the connection between vs. 8 and vs. 9 (remembering that the connection may not be original) a contrast similar to those just mentioned is suggested here also: John was indeed a light (5:35) but not *the* light (1:8)—the Logos was the *real* light (1:9). And this particular contrast coheres, of course, with the interest throughout the Fourth Gospel in placing the Baptist in

---

[11] C. H. Dodd, *The Interpretation of the Fourth Gospel* (Cambridge, England: Cambridge University Press, 1953), p. 203.

[12] John Calvin, *Commentarius in Quatuor Evangelia, ad loc.*

[13] This will do for our present needs though the issue is no doubt more complex. Cf. Barth (*Witness to the Word*, pp. 60-61), who delineates four meanings of ἀληθινός (and finally rejects the one we espouse), and R. Bultmann, "ἀληθινός," in *TDNT*, I, pp. 249-250.

a proper, indeed subordinate, position relative to Christ, as in 1:19ff. and 3:30. If the contrast is not between the Logos and the Baptist (remembering, again, that the connection between vs. 8 and vs. 9 may not be original) then surely, in view of the aforementioned contrasts involving a literal, sensible vine, bread, etc., the contrast in 1:9 must be between the literal, sensible sunlight and the authentic, spiritual light of the Logos—without the Alexandrian or metaphysical overtones often attached to this contrast. All of this yields, for me at least, a cumulative impression that ἀληθινόν in 1:9 means "true" in the second sense: "genuine" or "authentic."

We are then, somewhat tentatively, left with the following rendering of 1:9:

The true light, which illumines every person, was coming into the world.

This agrees essentially with the NRSV translation, cited at the start, except, it will be noted, that we have translated φωτίζει as "illumines" rather than "enlightens," and this brings us, finally, to the big question.

II. The Big Question

What does it mean to say that the Logos was "the true light which φωτίζει every person"? An ambiguity pertaining to the verb φωτίζω[14]—which encompasses a great breadth of meaning including "shine upon," "illuminate," "enlighten," "give light to," "bring to light," and "reveal"—leads to two radically different interpretations.

I will call these the "positive" and "negative" interpretations, and will consider them now in turn. The first, the positive interpretation, understands the verb, φωτίζω to mean, as it certainly may, "to illumine" or "to enlighten" with the agreeable sense of providing intellectual and/or moral awareness. On this view, the Logos is the source of universal enlightenment and, thus, an enlightenment which is in some way *natural*, or by nature present to or in all. The essential features of this interpretation are vividly expressed by the nineteenth-century French commentator Godet, who insisted on seeing in vs. 9 the same idea which, he thought, has already been expressed in vs. 4, namely, "the Logos, as the internal

---

[14] On φωτίζει see the numerous relevant comments in H. Conzelmann, "φως" etc., in *TDNT*, IX, pp. 310-358, esp. 349-355. Also, in H.-C. Hahn and C. Brown, "*phōs*," in DNTT, II, pp. 490-496, esp. pp. 493-495.

light, enlightening all people, illuminating them by the sublime intuition of the good, the beautiful and the true,"[15] and it is not for nothing that John 1:9, with its alleged doctrine of an "inner light," has been dubbed "the great Quaker text."

It is, of course, not feasible to provide here a whole history of the interpretation of John 1:9. It is possible, however, to provide at least some evidence that the internal-enlightenment interpretation of φωτίζει was probably a very early one, and certainly that it has dominated the history of the exegesis of this verse. What is especially significant about the following sample is that it reflects different periods in the Christian tradition and, to some degree, different theological perspectives.

Origen is often called the greatest theologian and scholar of the early Fathers. His knowledge of Scripture was unparalleled for this period, he was the first great textual critic of the church, and his commentaries on John are the earliest extant exegetical works of the Christian tradition. He was born and reared theologically in Alexandria where he succeeded Clement as head of the school. It is hardly surprising, then, that his interpretation of John 1:9 reflects the intellectualist stamp of Clement who taught that even certain strains of pagan Greek philosophy were a divine gift, as the Law was to the Hebrews, preparing Greek culture for the advent of the Gospel. The portion of Origen's commentary on John which includes his discussion of 1:9 is lost, but his interpretation of this verse is clear from the commentary's introductory remarks:

> He is called the true light: "The true light which enlightens every man, was coming into the world." In Isaiah, He is the light of the Gentiles. . . . "Behold, I have set Thee for a light of the Gentiles, that thou shouldst be for salvation to the end of the earth." Now the sensible light of the world is the sun, and after it comes very worthily the moon, and the same title may be applied to the stars; but those lights of the world are said in Moses to have come into existence on the fourth day, and as they shed light on the things on the earth, they are not the true light. But the Saviour shines on creatures which have intellect and sovereign reason, that their minds may behold their proper objects of vision, and so he is the light of the intellectual world, that is to say, of the reasonable souls. . . .[16]

In some ways the high-water mark of the internal-enlightenment

---

[15] F. L. Godet, *Commentary on the Gospel of John*, third ed., tr. T. Dwight (New York: Funk & Wagnalls, 1893), p. 259.

[16] Origen, *Commentary on the Gospel of John*, I, 24, tr. A. Menzies, in *ANF*, Supplemental Vol. X.

interpretation of John 1:9 is found in St. Augustine for whom John's characterization of the Logos as the "the true light which illumines every person" is a Scriptural proof-text for his own theory of divine illumination. Though laboring throughout his life under the spell of Platonist philosophy, he was constrained by his Christian theological orientation eventually to displace the Platonic theory of knowledge as recollection (with its implication for pre-existence of the soul) with a theory of a God-given inner illumination, possessed by all, and by virtue of which we are all enabled to grasp the same eternal truths—intelligible, absolute, immutable, etc. Echoing Plato's famous Analogy of the Sun (though Augustine himself knew the analogy from Plotinus), he thought that as the sun is the source of the sensible light which illuminates sensible objects which are grasped by the senses, so God is the source of the intelligible light which illumines eternal truths which are grasped by the intellect. Such a view is especially agreeable to Augustine because it is, as he says, *consonans evangelio*, "in harmony with the Gospel," and certainly the Gospel of John, and most certainly John 1:9. It is not from his *Homilies on John* that we have Augustine's best expression of the illumination interpretation of "the true light which illumines every person," but from the *City of God*. Speaking of Plotinus and the Neo-Platonists, "these more estimable philosophers," he says:

> . . . they perceived, and in various forms abundantly expressed in their writings, that the spirits have the same source of happiness as ourselves,—a certain intelligible light, which is their God, and is different from themselves, and illumines them that they may be penetrated with light, and enjoy perfect happiness in the participation of God. . . . That great Platonist, therefore, says that the rational soul or rather the intellectual soul—in which class he comprehends the souls of the lesser immortals who inhabit heaven,—has no nature superior to it save God, the Creator of the world and the soul itself, and that these heavenly spirits derive their blessed life, and the light of truth, from the same source as ourselves, agreeing with the gospel where we read, "There was a man sent from God whose name was John; the same came for a witness to bear witness of the Light, that through Him all might believe. He was not that Light, but that he might bear witness of the Light. That was the true Light which lighteth every man that cometh into the world."[17]

We come next to St. Thomas. Setting aside his more technical but not unrelated conception (inspired by Aristotle) of natural illumination as the agent

---

[17] St. Augustine, *City of God*, X, 2, tr. M. Dods, in *NPNF*, II.

intellect which abstracts universal concepts from particular sensibles, St. Thomas also speaks of illumination in a more religious vein. And we are now hardly surprised by an appeal yet again to the Sun-Analogy in St. Thomas' exposition of John 1:9 in the *Summa Theologica*:

> . . . we must consider that God is the universal cause of the illumination of souls, according to John 1:9: "That was the true light which enlighteneth every man that cometh into this world," even as the sun is the universal cause of the illumination of bodies, though not in the same way. For the sun illumines by necessity of nature, whereas God works freely through the order of his wisdom.[18]

In a more extended discussion in his commentary on John, St. Thomas interprets the light which shines on every person as the light of natural reason which everyone possesses by virtue of a participation in the true light, the source of all creation, and, by appealing to the immediately following vs. 10, appeals to the creative immanence of the light:

> . . . when the Evangelist says, he "enlightens every man," this seems to be false, because there are still many in darkness in the world. However, if we bear in mind these distinctions and take "world" from the standpoint of its creation, and "enlighten" as referring to the light of natural reason, the statement of the Evangelist is beyond reproach. For all men coming into this visible world are enlightened by the light of natural knowledge through participating in this true light, which is the source of natural knowledge participated in by men.
> . . . it is clear, from the efficacy of the divine Word, that the lack of knowledge in men is not due to the Word, because he is effective in enlightening all, being "the true light, which enlightens every man coming into this world."
> But so you do not suppose this lack arose form the withdrawal or absence of the true light, the Evangelist rules this out adding, "He was in the world." A comparable statement is found in "He is not far from any one of us," that is, God, "for in him we live, and move, and are" (Acts 17:28). It is as though the Evangelist were saying: The divine Word is effective and is at hand in order to enlighten us.
> . . . the true light was in the world, as an efficient and preserving cause: "I fill heaven and earth" as said in Jeremiah (23:24).[19]

It is not surprising that the interpreters considered thus far adopt the

---

[18] St. Thomas, *Summa Theologica*, Part I of Part II, Qu. 79, Art. 3, tr. in *Basic Writings of St. Thomas Aquinas*, ed. A. C. Pegis (New York: Random House, 1945).
[19] St. Thomas Aquinas, *Commentary on the Gospel of John*, tr. James A. Weisheipl and Fabian R. Larcher (Albany, N.Y.: Magi Books, 1980), I, pp. 71-73.

enlightenment interpretation of John 1:9. They all belong loosely to the *rationalist* tradition with respect to the question of faith's relation to reason. While not denying the priority of faith, they nonetheless pursue and embrace the contribution of reason wherever it may be found, even adapting in various ways pagan philosophies in the interest of a more articulate and compelling Christian faith. Not so with our final example, John Calvin, one of the starkest representatives of the *fideist* tradition with its suspicions of reason's intrusion into the domain and mysteries of faith, and which extends all the way from Tertullian to Barth. It is thus somewhat unexpected that in Calvin too we encounter the enlightenment interpretation of John 1:9. In his discussion of "the true light which illumines every person," Calvin distinguishes this light as the great "light of nature" in contrast to faith, explaining that

> rays from this light are diffused in all of mankind. . . . We know that men, above all other living beings, have been endowed with reason and intelligence, and that they have engraved in their consciences the ability to discriminate between right and wrong. There is therefore no one who is without some intuition of the eternal light.[20]

Calvin's harsh doctrine of the Fall is well known. But even though at times he speaks of the complete "obliteration" of the *imago Dei,* at other times he softens the blow by stressing that the originally given light of the understanding and moral awareness yet shines (or at least flickers) amidst the ruins of fallen human nature. This, indeed is exactly his interpretation of John 1:5 which is, of course, part of the immediate context of the passage before us:

> Since reason, therefore, by which man distinguishes between good and evil, and by which he understands and judges, is a natural gift, it could not be completely wiped out; but it was partly weakened and partly corrupted, so that its misshapen ruins appear. John speaks in this sense: "The light still shines in the darkness, but the darkness comprehends it not" [John 1:5]. In these words both facts are clearly expressed. First, in man's perverted and degenerate nature some sparks still gleam. These show him to be a rational being, differing from brute beasts, because he is endowed with understanding. Yet, secondly, they show this light choked with dense ignorance, so that it cannot come forth effectively.[21]

---

[20] John Calvin, *Commentaries,* tr. J. Haroutunian, in *LCC,* XXIII (Philadelphia: Westminster Press, 1958), p. 133.

[21] John Calvin, *Institutes of the Christian Religion,* II, 11, ed. J. T. McNeill, tr. F. L. Battles, in *LCC,* XX and XXI (Philadelphia: Westminster Press, 1960).

As was said earlier, this general interpretation—the internal-enlightenment interpretation—has held sway throughout the tradition, but in the context of contemporary exegesis the situation becomes somewhat more complicated.

That the positive, internal-enlightenment view has its advocates among recent interpreters is apparent, for example, from Dodd who reads the verse as a Philonic sentiment:

> [The true light] enlightens every man (since in every man there dwells essential humanity . . . which is . . . the offspring of "the Father of all who is life and light." The majority of mankind however are not aware of the presence of the light (they do not rise from contemplation of phenomena to recognition of their archetypes), but those who "receive" the light, the "enlightened" minority, have that knowledge of God which makes them sons of God and sharers in his life.[22]

Other recent interpreters, however, hold to the positive view while shifting from the idea of internal light to *external* light: The light which illumines every person is not a light that shines *in* but *on* him or her, not a subjective light but an objective light, a light that illuminates from without. There are variations on this positive but external-enlightenment view. Brown, for example, sees in the verse an echo of Messianic expectations, particularly as expressed in Is. 9:2, 42:6, and 60:1-2.[23] For example, Isaiah 9:2:

> The people who walked in darkness
>   have seen a great light;
> those who dwelt in a land of deep darkness,
>   on them has a light shined.

As the fulfillment of this the incarnate Logos of John 1:9 is, thus, a light shining from without and upon a people who otherwise are in darkness. Bultmann takes the verse to refer to existential enlightenment, the self-understanding accessible in the Christ-event:

> . . . only in the revelation which occurred in Jesus can man receive the proper understanding of his existence which he constantly seeks and fails to find . . . life in its authenticity is possible only in the clarity in the self-understanding which is given through revelation.[24]

---

[22] C. H. Dodd, *Interpretation of the Fourth Gospel*, pp. 204-205.

[23] Brown, *Gospel according to John*, I, p. 28.

[24] Bultmann, *Gospel of John*, p. 53.

Here too it is not a matter of some innate or natural power or faculty but of an encounter with something "out there," God's revelation in Christ. This type of interpretation of John 1:9, both positive (in that it stresses the desirable deliverances of the revelatory light) and external (in that it stresses the source of the deliverance as lying outside the individual) is otherwise preferred by the majority of recent commentators, sometimes construing the light with the incarnate Word and/or sometimes with a general revelation. Examples: Sanders/Mastin speaks of "the general revelation available at all times, if only men could see it";[25] Morris: "There is a general illumination of mankind. . . . John attributes this general illumination to the activity of the Word";[26] Schnackenburg: ". . . the reader is meant to think at once of the incarnate Logos whose 'illumination' . . . has been bestowed in a special manner since the Incarnation on men, that is, on those who believe";[27] Bernard: ". . . it speaks only of the universal enlightenment which was shed upon mankind *after* the Advent of Christ."[28]

Here, however, a few scholars, such as Barrett, go against the grain of the standard interpretation. We said earlier that the positive-subjective interpretation of John 1:9 dominated through the centuries, and we have now seen that this has given way, largely, to the more recent positive-objective interpretation, but both strongly emphasizing the agreeable deliverances of the Light. Is it possible, against so great a cloud of witnesses, that this interpretation, if not wrong, at least fails to do justice to the passage? The answer, is, Yes—in a way. And this brings us to what we may call the *negative* interpretation.

We have seen that most modern interpreters take the true light to represent an objective, rather than subjective, illumination and in this they are surely correct. They also take the illuminating activity of the true light to be an activity of the incarnate (rather than pre-existent) Logos, and in this too they are surely correct. A positive view of the light shining on everyone is almost always adopted when in fact what is involved here, says Barrett, is the altogether different and negative view of φωτίζει as signifying the illuminating, exposing light of *judgment*.[29]

The evidence for this negative interpretation is, in fact, relevant. It consists

[25] J. N. Sanders and B. A. Mastin, *The Gospel according to St. John* (London: Black, 1968), p. 76.

[26] Morris, *Gospel according to John*, p. 95.

[27] R. Schnackenburg, *Gospel according to St. John*, I, p. 254.

[28] J. H. Bernard, *A Critical and Exegetical Commentary on the Gospel According to St. John*, ed. A. H. McNeile (Edinburgh: Clark, 1928), p. 12.

[29] Barrett, *Gospel according to John*, p. 161.

simply in the observation that not only does John recurringly represent the coming of the Logos into the world as bringing judgment (e.g., 9:39), but in 3:19 employs identical language as 1:9 but further and unambiguously represents the function of the light as effecting judgment. The linguistic parallels between 1:9 and 3:19-21 are as obvious in English as in Greek:

> 1:9: The true light, which illumines every person, was coming into the world.

> 3:19-21: This is the judgment, that the light has come into the world, and people loved the darkness more than the light because their deeds were evil. For everyone practicing evil hates the light and does not come to the light lest one's deeds be exposed. But the one doing the truth comes to the light in order that one's deeds may be revealed, that they have been done in God.

Brown comments on 3:19-21: "Jesus is a penetrating light that provokes judgment by making it apparent what man is."[30] This would seem to be an exactly right interpretation of that passage and of a strain that runs throughout John's Gospel. It might be, therefore, incautious for any interpretation of φωτίζει, "illumines," in 1:9 to exclude utterly this judging, revealing, exposing, condemning function of the light, and in this respect most of the interpreters, advocating as they do an exclusively positive interpretation, are probably mistaken.

But neither does it seem to me possible to give to the φωτίζει of 1:9 a wholly negative or even primarily negative interpretation. This would seem impossible from a consideration of the Gospel as a whole, wherein Jesus' role as the light is also cast into a distinctively positive mode, as in 8:12, "I am the light of the world. The one following me will not walk in darkness but will have the light of life," and, more specifically, where the light is represented as *having come into the world* (cf. 1:9), as in 12:46, "I, a light, have come into the world, in order that the one believing in me may not remain in darkness." The negative-judgment interpretation of 1:9 is thrown into further doubt by the more immediate context of the Prologue in which it occurs. The flavor and feel—one might say, "texture"—of the Prologue presents, by and large, a jarring contrast to the judgment interpretation of vs. 9.

---

[30] Brown, *Gospel according to John*, I, pp. 148-149.

Throughout, the accent falls on the positive: The Logos was in the beginning, was with God, was God, created all things, overcomes the darkness, became incarnate, we saw his glory, John the Baptist accorded him a superior position, in him was fullness, he brings grace and truth, and he reveals the Father.[31] Alongside all this, a reference to the judging, exposing, condemning activity of the Logos strikes an intrusive and dissonant note. The case for the negative interpretation is even more difficult to sustain in view, specifically, of the (no doubt) hymnic lines of vs. 4:[32]

> What has appeared in him was Life,
> And the Life was the Light of people.

I take the first line to refer to the spiritual and salvific life that enters the world in the Logos[33]—a positive idea if there ever was one. But life here is immediately identified with "light"; in fact, the construction renders the terms interchangeable. It would be extremely odd, from a literary-aesthetic standpoint, if "light" here were intended to bring to mind an idea involving a quite different texture from the "life" with which it is identified. That "light" in vs. 4 bears an essentially positive sense is further evident from vs. 5:

> And the Light shines in the Darkness,
> And the Darkness has not overcome it.[34]

Here we have the image not of the darkness fleeing from or cowering before the exposing light but rather struggling (unsuccessfully) against it. Here the light is, then, not the light that exposes evil deeds, but rather vanquishes and dispels the darkness, as in, once again, 8:12: "I am the light of the world. The one following me will not walk in darkness but will have the light of life."[35] "Light" in vs. 4

---

[31] It would appear that the only really "negative" note in the Prologue is in vs. 10c and vs. 11b, which, in any event, do not bear on the activity of the Logos (the put-down of John the Baptist in vs. 8, belongs, I think, to the original opening of the Gospel: 1:6-8, 19ff.).

[32] Taking the phrase ὃ γέγονεν as beginning vs. 4 (cf. Miller, *Salvation-History in the Prologue of John, passim*, esp. Ch. 1).

[33] For this "incarnational" interpretation of John 1:4a, see Miller, *Salvation-History in the Prologue of John, passim*, esp. pp. 76-89.

[34] This is an attempt to reproduce what I take to be a gnomic aorist, representing here a punctiliar act repeated over and over.

[35] I take this as a genitive of definition wherein the light is identified with the life, as it is elsewhere in John.

thus bears the positive sense of the happy presence of the Logos which illumines everyone with respect to the grace and truth of God (cf. vs. 17), thereby dispelling "darkness."

The question thus becomes: Can "light" in vs. 4 bear this positive and happy sense, and in vs. 9 bear a negative and condemnatory sense? Of course it *could*, but I think it extremely unlikely. Even though we understand the Prologue to be, as mentioned previously more than once, a mosaic of originally independent pieces and bearing the marks of literary "seams," we think that as collected in this particular "anthology" they display, nevertheless, continuities of *ideas*.

Where does this leave us? It is important to appreciate that the negative and positive functions are functions of the same light, and that in John sometimes the one function is stressed and at other times the other. In the Prologue, certainly in vs. 4, it is the positive sense that is exclusively intended. In the case of vs. 9, however, we cannot be so sure. We are dealing here with a verse the original setting of which we do not know and involving the different verb, φωτίζω (φαίνω is employed in vs. 5). It is even possible that in the original setting of vs. 9 the light that shines bore an entirely negative meaning. Nonetheless, as adapted to its present position in the Prologue it would seem to be intended to bear primarily, at least, a positive sense, though overtones of the negative sense need not be excluded utterly.

However, one problem yet remains. We saw above that while most contemporary scholars who opt for the positive interpretation of the light which shines in 1:9 have rejected the traditional "inner"-light conception, they are nonetheless divided on the nature of the "outer" light. Is this external illumination to be conceived (1) as a kind of *general* revelation naturally bestowed on all peoples by the pre-incarnate Logos, or supernaturally if it is bestowed as prevenient grace? Or is it to be conceived (2) as a general revelation radiating specifically from the incarnate Logos and benefiting, nonetheless, everyone? Or is it to be conceived (3) as a special revelation radiating specifically from the incarnate Logos and holding benefits only for those whose lives are touched by him? Of the examples of recent and contemporary scholars mentioned above, the first of these interpretations is embraced by Sanders/Mastin and Morris, the second is embraced by Bernard, and the third by Brown, Bultmann, and Schnackenburg.

The second of these interpretations seems to involve a certain conceptual incoherence: How could a general revelation radiating from the specifically *incarnate* Logos hold illuminating power for *all* people in *all* places and *all* times?

Against the first, in our consideration of the first "little" question, above, we concluded that according to 1:9 it is in all likelihood the light that was coming into the world (not every person) and that the verse thus bears a clear incarnational teaching. It seems to me, further, that the most natural interpretation, in view of many other Johannine passages, would construe the shining of the light with the *advent* of the light. If so, we have here a light that radiates from the incarnate Logos rather than the pre-existent Logos. Nevertheless, it would be possible to interpret the verse as teaching that the light which has always shone on people—providing a general revelation—was *now* coming into the world. Even so, if one takes the first interpretation in this way *or* adopts the second interpretation according to which a general revelation originates with the *incarnate* Logos, there remains an insuperable problem: The idea of a universal revelation by which people in general are illuminated with respect to some basic knowledge of God or spiritual truths is otherwise utterly inimical to the Johannine literature. On the contrary, what we encounter repeatedly in this literature is, on the one side, the idea that any real knowledge of God has been made accessible in, and only in, the revelatory activity of the incarnate Logos—it is not for nothing that he is called the "Word"—and, on the other side, the recurring and unmistakable Johannine judgment that apart from the revelatory activity of the Logos all is *darkness* and that "the whole world lies in sin" (1 John 5:19). Even limiting ourselves to specifically light-references, is not this two-sided claim that the world lies in darkness and can be illuminated only by the incarnate Logos apparent from the following?

> "I am the light of the world. The one who follows me will not walk in darkness" (John 8:12).

> "The light is yet with you for a little while. Walk while you have the light. . . ." (John 12:35).

> "I, a light, have come into the world, in order that the one who believes in me may not remain in darkness" (John 12:46).

> " . . . the darkness is passing away, and the true light is already shining" (1 John 2:8).

That John 1:9 teaches a universal enlightenment strikes me, by its contrast to the tenor of the whole of the Johannine literature, as an unjustifiable bolt out of the blue. It might be responded, of course, that bolt or no bolt, the text does not say that the light illumines only those it illumines, but that it illumines *every person*. I, in turn, would respond that the light does *in principle* illumine every person, and that this coheres with Johannine expression elsewhere, such as 12:32 where it is asserted that Jesus, when "lifted up," will draw everyone to himself, which, of course, is factually false though true in principle.

We are, then, left with the third interpretation: The "light" of 1:9 is to be conceived as providing a *special* revelation, radiating specifically from the incarnate Logos and holding consequences and benefits only for those whose lives are touched by it. This interpretation will seem to many to involve a jarring exclusivism. They are, of course, right. But this can hardly stand as an indictment of the interpretation inasmuch as such an exclusivism is encountered throughout the Johannine literature; in fact, the exclusivism of 1:9 only enhances our interpretation.

From all of this it follows that the appropriation of John 1:9 in support of a Biblically justified idea of general revelation is misguided. We have seen that this employment of John 1:9 has characterized the traditional interpretation, it has been advanced by a few recent and contemporary exegetes, and, we now add, it has played a central role among contemporary Christian apologists, usually of an Evangelical stamp. A good example of the latter may be found in Bruce A. Demarest's prize-winning book, *General Revelation*.[36] Here, recurringly, John 1:9 is cited (along with other passages) as Biblical evidence for an *a priori* or innate *sensus divinitas*, general revelation, or natural theology[37]—Demarest does not systematically distinguish these terms, and we use them here, as he does, as roughly synonymous in affirming that at least some rudimentary knowledge of God is accessible apart from a special, active self-disclosure by God. A clear instance of this is:

> John, in the fourth Gospel, describes the Logos as "the true light that gives light
> to every man who comes into the world" (John 1:9 NIV margin). The Logos, who
> is "the truth" (John 14:6), may be regarded as the principles of reason that enables
> the sinner to function as the rational creature God intended him to be. Through the
> common operation of Logos, man qua man is endowed with the capability to think

---

[36] B. A. Demarest, *General Revelation: Historical Views and Contemporary Issues* (Grand Rapids, Mich.: Zondervan, 1982).

[37] Cf. Demarest, *General Revelation*, pp. 138, 228, 242.

God's thoughts after Him. . . . Effable intuition, as one aspect of reason, may be
regarded as the eye of the soul that perceives first principles with immediacy.
Upon reflection before the self, the mind enabled by a general illumination intuits
eternal, changeless truths, including the reality of God, from the first moment of
mental and moral self-consciousness.[38]

Obviously, I believe that this is a misappropriation of John 1:9. Not only is it, as
we have seen, exegetically wrongheaded and incompatible with the teaching of the
Johannine literature generally, it is also—we would now stress—out of step not
only with the teaching of the rest of the New Testament (note especially the
function specifically of light/darkness in Luke 1:79, Acts 26:18, Rom. 2:19, Eph.
5:8, Col. 1:13, 1 Thess. 5:4, and 1 Pet. 2:9) but with the whole of the Biblical
tradition. With many other apologists, Demarest enlists a rather standard list of
passages, in addition to John 1:9, as Biblical proof-texts for general revelation: Ps.
19:1-6, Job 36:24-37 and ch. 24, Rom. 1:18-21, Rom. 2:14ff., Acts 13 and 17.

I cannot here consider these passages as I have done in the case of John 1:9.
I only say that, in my view, they cannot bear the burden that is so often claimed
for them. First, one must be struck by how *few* the proof-texts are. Second, in
several instances we are not persuaded that they say what is often asserted of them.
One example. Demarest rightfully calls Rom. 1:18ff. the *locus classicus*. Certainly
it has been cited more often than any other passage in support of general
revelation, as by St. Thomas:

The falsity of this opinion [that the existence of God cannot be demonstrated
through reason alone] is shown to us by the truth in the words of the Apostle
Paul: "For the invisible things of God . . . are clearly seen, being understood by
the things that are made" (Rom. 1:20).[39]

But is this not to miss the point? The point of the passage when read in its entire
context is not the Good News that God may be known through a reflection on the
natural world, but rather the Bad News that, apart from a gracious, special
revelation from God, people in their sinful state *don't* and *won't* see the God that
is there apparent.

Surely the situation is not as simple as I have represented it here. There are
many strands and strains that constitute the Biblical tradition, and, not surprisingly,

---

[38] Demarest, *General Revelation*, p. 228.
[39] St. Thomas Aquinas, *Summa Contra Gentiles*, I, 12, 6, tr. A. C. Pegis (Notre Dame, Ind.:
University of Notre Dame Press, 1955).

some of these are more amenable to the idea of general revelation than others—one thinks, for example, of the Wisdom literature which at many points suggests a kind of cosmological speculation, and Rom. 2:14ff. does, in fact, seem to teach a kind of moral a priority. But the broad thrust of the Biblical tradition on the question is unmistakable. In New Testament, and specifically Johannine, language, it is that "the true light, which illumines every person, was coming into the world."

Speeches in Acts and Hellenistic Canons of Historiography and Rhetoric

Earle Hilgert

Professor of New Testament, McCormick Theological Seminary
Chicago, Illinois

Several of Professor Bo Reicke's contributions to New Testament scholarship have dealt with aspects of the Acts of the Apostles.[1] A notable feature of these significant studies is their characteristic grounding in the history and culture of the Hellenistic-Roman world. In honoring him, therefore, it may not be inappropriate to turn once again to the issue of Luke's[2] intention and method in the speeches he incorporates into his narrative and to consider these both in light of Hellenistic historiography and rhetoric and of his particular theological-historical point of view.

---

[1] Among Reicke's writings on the Acts are: "Die Mahlzeit mit Paulus auf den Wellen des Mittelmeers: Act. 27: 33-38," *TZ*, 4 (1948), pp. 401-410; "Der geschichtliche Hintergrund des Apostelkonzils und der Antiochia-Episode, Gal. 2:1-14," in *Studia Paulina in Honorem De Zwaan* (Haarlem: Bohn, 1953), pp. 172-187; "A Synopsis of Early Christian Preaching" in *The Root of the Vine*, ed. A. Fridrichsen (London: Dacre, 1953), pp. 128-160; "Die Verfassung der Urgemeinde im Lichte jüdischer Dokumente," *TZ*, 10 (1954), pp. 95-112; *Glaube und Leben der Urgemeinde*: *Bemerkungen zu Apg. 1-7* (Zürich: Zwingli, 1957). Quotations from the English Bible in the present article follow the Revised Standard Version unless otherwise indicated.

[2] We use the name of Luke, the traditional author of the Acts, as a convenient cipher, without prejudice as to whether "Luke the Physician" and member of the Pauline circle was the actual author or not.

Good News in History

I

In seeking to evaluate Luke's use of speeches in the Acts, it has been common to take Thucydides' familiar statement (I.22.1) on his use of speeches as a point of reference.

> As to the speeches that were made by different men . . . it has been difficult to recall with strict accuracy the words actually spoken, both for me as regards that which I myself heard, and for those who from various other sources have brought me reports. Therefore the speeches are given in the language in which, as it seemed to me, the several speakers would express, on the subjects under consideration, the sentiments most befitting the occasion [τὰ δέοντα μάλιστ' εἰπεῖν], though at the same time I have adhered as closely as possible to the general sense of what was actually said [ἐχομένῳ ὅτι ἐγγύτατα τῆς ξυμπάσης γνώμης τῶν ἀληθῶς λεχθέντων, οὕτως εἴρηται].[3]

This passage has proved to be a frustrating one, however, because it appears to be, in a certain measure, contradictory.[4] As a consequence, all too often its interpretation by students of Acts has been shadowed by prior commitments in regard to the inerrancy, or at least the historical "trustworthiness," of the New Testament documents, with the more critical scholars emphasizing the first part of the statement, conservatives the second.[5]

Recently K. S. Sacks, in a study of "Rhetorical Approaches to Greek History Writing in the Hellenistic Period,"[6] has offered insights on the use of speeches in

---

[3] *Thucydides*, tr. C. F. Smith (Cambridge, Mass.: Harvard University Press, 1928), I, p. 39. See, for instance, P. W. Schmiedel, "Acts of the Apostles," *Encyclopaedia Biblica*, ed. T. K. Cheyne and J. Sutherland (London: Black, 1899-1903), I, p. 47; J. Moffatt, *An Introduction to the Literature of the New Testament* (New York: Scribner, 1918), p. 43; F. F. Bruce, *The Acts of the Apostles*, second ed. (London: Tyndale, 1952), p. 18; M. Dibelius, *Studies in the Acts of the Apostles*, ed. H. Greeven (New York: Scribner, 1956), pp. 110-142; H. J. Cadbury, *The Making of Luke-Acts* (London: SPCK, 1958), pp. 185-186; T. F. Glasson, "The Speeches in Acts and Thucydides," *ET*, 76 (1965), p. 165; D. Guthrie, *The Gospels and the Acts: New Testament Introduction* (Chicago: Intervarsity Press, 1965), p. 327; W. Gasque, *A History of the Criticism of the Acts of the Apostles* (Tübingen: Mohr, 1975), pp. 225-228.

[4] See the extensive discussion of its interpretation by O. Luschnat, "Thukydides," *RE, Suppl.* 12 (1970), cols. 1162-1183.

[5] Contrast, for instance, the evaluations of Dibelius and Gasque, cited in n. 3 above.

[6] K. S. Sacks, "Rhetorical Approaches to Greek History Writing in the Hellenistic Period," presented at the Annual Meeting of the Society of Biblical Literature, Chicago, December 10, 1984, and published in *Society of Biblical Literature 1984 Seminar Papers*, ed. K. H. Richards (Chico, Calif.: Scholars Press, 1984), pp. 123-133. I owe many of the classical references in this section to Sacks' article.

Hellenistic historiography which appear to be significant for an understanding of Luke, for as N. Dahl has reminded us, Luke was himself "a minor Hellenistic historian."[7] Sacks addresses the question of how Thucydides' seemingly ambiguous statement on the use of speeches in the writing of history was understood in the Hellenistic world. He focuses attention particularly on Dionysius of Halicarnassus (fl. 30-38 B.C.E) and Lucian of Samosata (ca. 120-180 C.E.), the two writers of the period who concern themselves with Thucydides' principles of history writing. In discussing their work I shall follow Sacks' argument.

Dionysius is particularly significant for our investigation as the major ancient literary critic of Thucydides. As a rhetorician, he concerns himself with the speeches as possible models for rhetorical study and imitation. In *Thuc.* 41, Dionysius calls Thucydides' declaration in I.22.1 specifically to witness against him, and in such a way as to reveal his own understanding of the passage. Criticizing the Melian Dialogue (Thucydides, V.58-113), Dionysius declares:

> That the historian was not present on that occasion at the meeting . . . may readily be seen from what the author writes about himself in the present book. . . . So it remains to be examined whether he has made the dialogue appropriate to the circumstances and befitting the persons who came together at the conference [εἰ τοῖς τε πράγμασι προσήκοντα καὶ τοῖς συνεληλυθόσιν εἰς τὸν σύλλογον προσώποις ἁρμόττοντα πέπλακε τὸν διάλογον], "adhering as closely as possible to the overall purpose of what was actually said" [ἐχόμενος ὡς ἔγγιστα τῆς συμπάσης γνώμης τῶν ἀληθῶς λεχθέντων], as he himself stated in the proem of his history. . . . I for my part do not believe that such words were appropriate [προσήκειν λέγεσθαι] for commanders who were sent from a city that enjoyed the very best of laws to foreign cities. . . . I believe that even if any other people attempted to say such things in the presence of the Athenians, they who have exercised such a humanizing influence on everyday life would have grown indignant. For these reasons I do not approve this dialogue.[8]

In light of this statement, it appears that for Dionysius, Thucydides' principle of "adhering as closely as possible to what was actually said" means, first and foremost, that the speech be "appropriate to the circumstances and befitting the persons" involved. Thus in the case of the *Melian Dialogue*, Dionysius' argument

[7] N. A. Dahl, "The Purpose of Luke-Acts," in *Jesus in the Memory of the Early Church: Essays* (Minneapolis: Augsburg Press, 1976), p. 88.

[8] W. K. Pritchett (ed.), *Dionysius of Halicarnassus: On Thucydides* (Berkeley: University of California Press, 1975), pp. 33-34; *Dionysii Halicarnasei Opuscula*, ed. H. Usener and L. Radermacher, (Leipzig: Teubner, 1899), I, pp. 395-396.

is that Thucydides has been untrue to his own announced principle in I.22.1 by offering a speech that is out of moral character for Athenians.[9]

To express this criterion of appropriateness, Dionysius repeatedly uses the term πρέπον, and this concept is indeed basic to his critical thinking. In *Ep. ad Pompeium* 3 he declares: πασῶν ἐν λόγοις ἀρετῶν ἡ κυριώτατη τὸ πρέπον: "In speeches, of all the virtues the most important is appropriateness."[10]

That Dionysius could understand not only Thucydides' τὰ δέοντα, "the sentiments befitting the occasion," but also and more importantly his τὰ ἀληθῶς λεχθέντα as subsumed under the rubric of τὸ πρέπον, that which was "appropriate" to characters and situation, is made more understandable by a second and closely related criterion that he advances: Worthy speeches are those which are presented as ἀληθινοὶ ἀγῶνες, "genuine contests," in contrast to epideictic orations intended more for reading than for public delivery in a situation of tension.[11] Regarding

---

[9] Cf. *Thuc.* 39, also regarding the *Melian Dialogue*: "Words like these were appropriate [ἔρμοττε λέγειν] to oriental monarchs addressing Greeks, but unfit [οὐκ ἦν προσήκοντα εἰρῆσθαι] to be spoken by Athenians to Greeks whom they liberated from the Medes" (Pritchett, *Dionysius*, p. 31; Usener-Radermacher, *Opuscula*, I, p. 391), and again ch. 40: "These words . . . are not fit to be spoken [οὐ πρέποντα εἰρῆσθαι] by either Athenians or [any other] Greeks" (Pritchett, *Dionysius*, p. 33; Usener-Radermacher, *Opuscula*, I, p. 394). Similarly in *Ep. ad Pompeium* 5 regarding Philistus: "He is trivial and commonplace. . . . Moreover, he does not write speeches worthy of the greatness of the speakers" (W. R. Roberts [ed.], *Dionysius of Halicarnassus: The Three Literary Letters* [Cambridge, England: Cambridge University Press, 1901], pp. 120-121).

[10] Roberts, *Dionysius*, p. 114 (my translation); cf. the discussion of Dionysius' sense of τὸ πρέπον, Pritchett, *Dionysius*, pp. xxvi-xxvii, and his own statement, *Thuc.* 40, quoted in n. 9 above. Dionysius was not alone in this sentiment; in fact it was probably a generally recognized rhetorical principle: Cf. Theon of Alexandria's (first century C.E.) rhetorical handbook, the *Progymnasmata* (ed. L. Spengel [Leipzig: Teubner, 1854], II.115.11-116.14); in describing how students of rhetoric are to practice *prosopopoeia*, "character delineation," through the representation of a person not now present as speaking, he says: "*Prosopopoeia* is the presentation of a character [προσώπου] described through speeches that are indisputably appropriate [οἰκείους] both to himself and to the basic circumstances [πράγμασιν]. . . . Under this type of [rhetorical] exercise fall the panegyric form of speech, the hortatory and the epistolary. First of all, one must attend to the rule that the person of the speaker and that of the one to whom the speech is directed are in character [ὅμοιον]: their ages at that time, the time and place, their stations in life and the subject matter with which the intended speeches are to deal. Then one should try to compose speeches that are appropriate. For in age one group should be fittingly related [πρέπουσι] to another; those things appropriate to an older person and those to a youth are not the same. . . . By nature, different speeches would be appropriate to women and men; by station in life, to slaves and freemen; by vocation, to soldiers and peasants; and in accord with disposition, to the passionate and to the self-controlled. . . . Speech and place should be appropriate [πρέπουσι] to the time. For [speeches] should not be the same in the army camp as in the assembly, nor in peace as in war, nor in victory as in defeat, and whatever else dogs the steps of human beings. And as well, each and every circumstance [πράγματα] has its appropriate [mode of] expression [πρέπουσαν ἑρμηνείαν]" (my translation).

[11] This is based on a division found already in Aristotle, *Rhet.* 1421b: "Public speeches are

speeches in Thucydides of which he approves, Dionysius refers to them as "addresses . . . that are characterized by purity and perspicuity and are suitable for actual contests [εἰς τοὺς ἀληθινοὺς ἀγῶνας ἐπιτήδειοι]." He then goes on to say of such speeches that "the figures are appropriate to the matter" (τὰ σχήματα τῶν πραγμάτων ἴδια).[12] Again, in regard to Demosthenes, he notes that he "omitted the far-fetched part of Thucydides' diction . . . as unsuited to genuine contests [οὐχ ἡγησάμενος ἐπιτήδεια τοῖς ἀληθινοῖς ἀγῶσι]."[13] Similarly, comparing Philistus with Thucydides, Dionysius declares: "He is a better model for genuine contests [ἀληθινοῦ ἀγῶνας] than Thucydides."[14]

As Sacks has pointed out, Dionysius also refers to ἀληθινοὶ ἀγῶνες as ἐναγώνιοι λόγοι and as ἀληθινοὶ λόγοι.[15] From these terms it was but a short step linguistically to Thucydides' ἀληθῶς λεχθέντα, particularly if the adverb ἀληθῶς, in the attributive position, is understood to be functioning as an adjective.[16] In light of this, it is understandable that Dionysius could interpret both Thucydides' τὰ δέοντα and his ἀληθῶς λεχθέντα on rhetorical rather than historical grounds:[17] Speeches were to be judged by the criterion of appropriateness to speaker and circumstance, and they should reflect the tension of debate and deliberation; in this sense they were ἀληθῶς λεχθέντα.

That Dionysius was not alone in such an understanding of Thucydides is

of three kinds, parliamentary, ceremonial and forensic [τὸ μὲν δημηγορικόν, τὸ δ' ἐπιδεικτικόν, τὸ δὲ δικανικόν]" (Aristotle, *Rhet. ad Alexandrum*, tr. H. Rackham [Cambridge, Mass.: Harvard University Press, 1957], p. 275). In Dionysius' rhetorical parlance ἀληθινοὶ ἀγῶνες were understood to include forensic and deliberative speeches, but not epideictic. Note his *First Letter to Ammaeus* 3, where he refers to Demosthenes' speeches as "his ἀγῶνες, both forensic and deliberative" (τοὺς . . . ἀγῶνας τούς τε δικανικοὺς καὶ τοὺς δημηγορικούς) (Roberts, *Dionysius*, p. 56, my translation). Similarly in *Ant. Rom.* I.8.3, Dionysius assures his readers he will not bore them with simply an annalistic account, but will vary his presentation with a combination of all kinds of materials, "agonistic, theoretical and narrative" (ἐναγωνίου τε καὶ θεωρητικῆς καὶ διηγηματικῆς) (*The Roman Antiquities*, tr. E. Cary [Cambridge, Mass.: Harvard University Press, 1937-50], I, p. 26); and again *Demosthenes* 45: ". . . his agonistic speeches [ἐναγώνιοι], those that were given in a court of law or in governing assemblies. . . ." (Usener-Radermacher, *Opuscula*, I, p. 229, my translation).
[12] *Thuc.* 42 (Pritchett, *Dionysius*, pp. 34-35; Usener-Radermacher, *Opuscula*, I, p. 398).
[13] *Thuc.* 53 (Usener-Radermacher, *Opuscula*, I, p. 413).
[14] *Ep. ad Pompeium* 5 (Roberts, *Dionysius*, I, p. 120, my translation).
[15] *Demosthenes* 45 (Usener-Radermacher, *Opuscula*, I, p. 229.); *Ant. Rom.* I.8.3 (Cary, *Roman Antiquities*, I, p. 27); *Isaios* 20 (Usener-Radermacher, *Opuscula*, I, p. 123).
[16] Sacks, "Rhetorical Approaches," p. 131, n. 37.
[17] Note Pritchett's judgment, *Dionysius*, p. xxxi: "Dionysius' criticisms of the speeches of Thucydides are regarded almost exclusively from the point of view of contemporary rhetoric, not at all from the historian's."

highly probable. As Plümacher has noted in another connection, "Dionys ist nun alles andere als eine originelle schriftstellerische Persönlichkeit gewesen, eher ein Spiegel von zu seiner Zeit weitverbreiteten literarischen Anschauungen."[18] It is therefore no surprise that Lucian appears to have had a similar understanding of Thucydides' criteria for speeches. In his discussion of how history should be written, Lucian declares:

> If a person has to be introduced to make a speech, above all let his language suit his person and his subject [ἐοικότα τῷ προσώπῳ καὶ τῷ πράγματι οἰκεῖα] and next let these [words] also be as clear as possible. It is then, however, that you can play the orator and show your eloquence.[19]

Here, as with Dionysius, Lucian's particular concern is not that the speeches be those actually delivered, but that they "suit his person and his subject." Lucian has just paraphrased another part of the same discussion where the great Athenian historian sets out his criteria for collecting and judging data (Thucydides, I.22.2-4). Since Lucian clearly is following Thucydides in his discussion of historiographical principles and methods, it is logical to conclude that in his instruction on speeches we also have his understanding of Thucydides. He seems to take the first principle, that speeches should accord with τὰ δέοντα—should reflect the circumstances—as normative and as allowing the historian a certain freedom in composition. He goes no further than this in regard to the second principle, τῆς ξυμπάσης γνώμης τῶν ἀληθῶς λεχθέντων. Thus he appears to subordinate the second to the first and understands it in light of that. Sacks can therefore conclude:

> Whereas modern interpretation creates a troublesome dichotomy between the allowance for τὰ δέοντα and yet a concern for faithfulness to actual speeches, there are now two promises for appropriateness: first, that the speeches will fit the characters and circumstances [that is, τὰ δέοντα]; and second, that they will reflect the agonistic style. . . . Of course Dionysius' understanding of Thucydides is certainly not consistent with our own, and we need not feel bound by it. . . . Nevertheless, we can say that Dionysius quite clearly, and Lucian more than

[18] E. Plümacher, *Lukas als hellenistischer Schriftsteller: Studien zur Apostelgeschichte* (Göttingen: Vandenhoeck & Ruprecht 1972), p. 36; see also n. 10 above.

[19] Lucian, *Quomodo historia conscribenda sit* 58 (*Lucian*, tr. K. Kilburn [Cambridge Mass.: Harvard University Press, 1959], VI, pp. 70-71); *Luciani Opera*, ed. M. D. Macleod (Oxford: Clarendon Press, 1980), III, p. 318; cf. the opening sentence of the quotation from Theon, n. 10 above.

likely, understood all of Thucydides I.22.1 as a call for appropriateness.[20]

An important insight which emerges from these considerations is that for an understanding of Luke the question of what Thucydides meant to say is not as important as what later Hellenistic writers understood him to have said.

II

We shall now attempt to evaluate several of Luke's speeches in Acts in light of the two principles regarding speeches that we have observed in Hellenistic historiography: τὸ πρέπον and ἀληθινοὶ ἀγῶνες. That Luke was aware of Hellenistic canons of historiography, and that such a comparison is therefore legitimate, is apparent from the prologue to his Gospel—which I take to be valid for both of his volumes[21]—where, like Lucian, he speaks of πράγματα, and, as with Lucian, takes the πράγματα as focal. Like Lucian also, he indicates the importance of eyewitnesses.[22]

Luke adheres unwaveringly to the principle that his speeches should be ἀληθινοὶ ἀγῶνες. All of the more than twenty[23] large and small compositions addressed to bodies of people in Acts reflect "genuine contests," i.e., situations of tension in the sense that the speaker seeks to move or sharpen the viewpoint of his audience. This is true of both the "missionary sermons" in the earlier chapters as well as the speeches in the latter. There are no epideictic speeches, no panegyric orations.

Furthermore, not only are all his speeches ἀγῶνες, but Luke places the major ones at crucial turning points in his unfolding narrative of the history of salvation: at Pentecost, where the kerygma is first proclaimed to Jews from the whole world; to Cornelius, the first Gentile convert; in the synagogue at Antioch, where Paul declares, "Behold, we turn to the Gentiles" (Acts 13:45); at Troas, where (in Luke's scenario) Paul's work as a freely itinerant missionary ends; and Paul's final speeches to the Jews: successively to the people (ch. 22), to the Sanhedrin (ch. 23)

---

[20] Sacks, "Rhetorical Approaches," p. 132.

[21] So, e.g., H. J. Cadbury, "Commentary on the Preface of Luke," in *The Beginnings of Christianity*, ed. F. J. F. Jackson and K. Lake (New York: Macmillan, 1922), Part I, Vol. II, p. 492; *contra*, H. Conzelmann, *The Theology of St. Luke* (New York: Harper & Row, 1961), p. 16, n. 1; E. Haenchen, *Die Apostelgeschichte* (Göttingen: Vandenhoeck & Ruprecht, 1965), p. 106, n. 3.

[22] Cf. Thucydides, I.22.2-4.

[23] Dibelius (*Acts of the Apostles*, p. 150), counts "about twenty-four."

and to the Jewish king Agrippa (ch. 26). At each major turning point Luke has
inserted a speech that is an ἀληθινὸς ἀγών.

Such speeches are more than artistic embellishments intended to heighten the
profile of significant moments in the story. As Plümacher has made clear, they are
intended to be in themselves a motivating factor of major movements in the
story.[24] For Luke the Spirit, through the speeches, moves the history of salvation
forward on its appointed way (cf. Luke 21:12-15). Plümacher remarks,

> Lk will also . . . Predigt darstellen . . . als das, was den Fortgang der Kirchen-
> (bzw. Heils-) geschichte bewirkt hat; und darin wird nun doch auch in diesen
> Reden etwas von dem historischen κτῆμ᾿ ἐς ἀεί [Thucydides 1.22.4] sichtbar.[25]

This dynamic, motivating function of the speeches is thoroughly in accord
with Dionysius' announced intention in his *Antiquitates Romanae*. Writing of the
granting of rights to the plebeians in the early Republic, he says:

> I thought it necessary above all things to report the speeches which the heads of
> both parties made upon that occasion. I might express my surprise that some
> historians . . . do not consider it necessary to report the speeches by which the
> extraordinary and remarkable events were brought to pass.[26]

Thus it seems reasonable to conclude that on Hellenistic terms, Luke's
speeches in Acts reflect the ἀληθῶς λεχθέντα in the first instance because of the
dynamic role they play as ἀληθινοὶ ἀγῶνες in the developing course of sacred
history. Embodying τὰ δέοντα, "the sentiments most befitting the occasion," they are
eminently examples of τὸ πρέπον.

It remains to consider other techniques Luke employs in order to establish
the appropriateness of his speeches. In particular I would draw attention to
instances where he has constructed inner thematic ties between the narrative that
provides the setting for the speech, and the content of the speech itself. Among
studies of the speeches in Acts made over the last quarter century, that of Ulrich
Wilckens, *Die Missionsreden der Apostelgeschichte*,[27] has been one of the most

---

[24] Plümacher, *Lukas als hellenistischer Schiftsteller*, pp. 35-38.

[25] Plümacher, *Lukas als hellenistischer Schriftsteller*, p. 35.

[26] Dionysius, *Ant. Rom.* VII.66.3 (Cary, *Roman Antiquities*, IV, pp. 344-347); cf. Plümacher,
Lukas als hellenistischer Schriftsteller, p. 36.

[27] U. Wilckens, *Die Missionsreden der Apostelgeschichte*, third ed. (Neukirchen-Vluyn:
Neukirchener Verlag, 1974).

provocative. As a result of his minute analysis, Wilckens finds that the mission sermons in chs. 2-13 are all smoothly coherent with their contexts: "Nähte oder Risse werden nirgends sichtbar."[28] This leads him to conclude against the idea that the sermons as a whole are secondary insertions into the narrative materials. He finds that they reflect the same theological viewpoint as do the narratives, and declares: "Im jetzigen Zusammenhang der Apostelgeschichte sind die Reden gerade auch in ihrer Form, in dem zugrunde gelegten Schema, durchgehend von der theologischen Gesamtkonzeption des Lukas her verständlich."[29] Wilckens has demonstrated that, from a literary standpoint, the sermons are of a piece with their contexts. Like Wilckens we are impressed with the lack of gaps or seams between the sermons and their narrative settings. We have been struck with the fact that each of the sermons of Peter and Paul which were preached to Jews (chs. 2, 3, 4, 5, 10, 13) follows on and is related to a "story,"[30] a narrative containing an encounter with the supernatural. The questions we would pose are these: If such an arrangement was not accidental—and it occurs regularly enough to constitute a pattern—did Luke tie the stories and the sermons together in more than obviously situational ways? Are there internal theological relationships between them which enhance the appropriateness of the speeches to their contexts, their quality of being πρέπον?

In pursuit of these questions, we shall consider four of the missionary sermons preached by Peter and Paul to Jews, together with the stories to which they are related in the course of the book. These are the coming of the Spirit and the gift of tongues and Peter's ensuing discourse at Pentecost (ch. 2), the healing of the lame man and Peter's sermon in Solomon's Portico (ch. 3), Peter's address to the Council, which relates also to the healing of the lame man (ch. 4), and Paul's encounter with the sorcerer Bar-Jesus and his sermon in the synagogue at Pisidian Antioch (ch. 13). In each case we shall seek to determine what inner thematic ties may exist between story and sermon, what their significance may be for an under-

---

[28] Wilckens, *Missionsreden der Apostelgeschichte*, p. 71.

[29] Wilckens, *Missionsreden der Apostelgeschichte*, p. 100.

[30] We use "story" here in the sense of R. Bultmann (*History of the Synoptic Tradition*, tr. J. Marsh [Oxford, England: Blackwell, 1963], pp. 307ff.) as indicating a general category of narrative material, including among other forms, both miracle stories and legends. With the exception of the healing of the lame man (Acts 3), which is clearly in the form of a miracle story, the narratives under consideration may all be classified as legends—narratives not in precise miracle story form, but which "instead of being historical in character are religious and edifying. For the most part they include something miraculous" (pp. 241-245). The encounter with Bar-Jesus (Acts 13) also exhibits some elements of a miracle story.

standing of Luke's major concerns, and how he thus uses the canon of appropriateness for his theological purposes.

The Day of Pentecost (Acts 2)

Certain obvious relationships exist between the story of the coming of the
Spirit and Peter's sermon at Pentecost. The word πνοή (vs. 2) is used to describe
the wind-like sound of the Spirit's approach. It probably is Luke's play on πνεῦμα,
which is mentioned first in vs. 4 and repeatedly in the sermon, vss. 17, 18, 33, 38.

The list of nations[31] clearly illustrates both vs. 5, "all nations under
heaven," and also the phrase in Peter's quotation from Joel 2:28, "upon all flesh"
(vs. 17), as well as "the whole house of Israel" (vs. 36) and "all who are far off"
(vs. 39).[32] Finally, the use by "others" (vs. 13) of the accusation of drunkenness
as a point of departure for Peter's address (vs. 15) provides a situational tie
between the story and the sermon.

Beyond these obvious relationships, there appear to be other motifs common
to both the story and the sermon that deserve investigation.[33] The first of these is
the figure of Elijah. The initial words of ch. 2, καὶ ἐν τῷ συμπληροῦσθαι τὴν ἡμέραν
τῆς πεντηκοστῆς, are strikingly reminiscent of the opening clause of Luke's Travel
Narrative (9:51): ἐγένετο δὲ ἐν τῷ συμπληροῦσθαι τὰς ἡμέρας τῆς ἀναλήμψεως αὐτοῦ.[34]
It is universally recognized that Luke 9:15 opens a major new section of the
Gospel, for here it is in Luke's design to indicate that the time had come for Jesus'
ἀνάλημψις, his "ascent," not only geographically to Jerusalem but also, and more

---

[31] Evidence indicates that the list of nations in vss. 9-11 relates in some way to geographical
and/or astrological lists current in the Hellenistic world (for the literature see H. Conzelmann, *Die
Apostelgeschichte* [Tübingen: Mohr, 1963], p. 26); cf. Reicke, *Glaube und Leben*, pp. 34-36.

[32] Cf. J. Thomas, "Formgesetze des Begriffs-Katalogs im N.T.," *TZ*, 24 (1968), p. 16:
"*Kataloge* nicht, wie man aus der Behandlung in der wissenschaftlichen Literatur annehmen
könnte, eine paränetische Angelegenheit, sondern eine allegmeine *rhetorische Form*. . . . [Ihre
Strukturlosigkeit] dient nicht dazu, dem Leser eine ungeordnete Summe zu seinem Gebrauch und
zur beliebigen Aufteilung und Auswahl anzubieten. Vielmehr soll sie eine in sich *geschlossene
Fülle* demonstrieren: Die Fülle des Judentums, das zerstreut ist über die Völker, wird erreicht
vom Wehen des Geistes Gottes nach Act. 2: 1-11."

[33] Since this study was written, L. O'Reilly, in a doctoral dissertation presented to the
Gregorian University (*Word and Sign in the Acts of the Apostles* [Rome: Gregorian University,
1987]), has also considered the relationships between Peter's speeches and their narrative settings.

[34] Cf. also 4 Kingd. 2:9 LXX, where ἀναλημφθῆναι refers to Elijah's ascension. M. Miyoshi
(*Der Anfang des Reiseberichts Lk 9: 51-10, 24* [Rome: Biblical Institute, 1974], pp. 55-57),
points to the strong Elijah imagery behind Luke 9:61-62 and cites further literature.

importantly, to those events that would culminate in his crucifixion, resurrection and ascension. Thus Luke 9:51 encapsulates the theme of the entire remainder of the Gospel. In a similar way the story of Pentecost which is opened by Acts 2:1 also constitutes a summary forecast of the theme of the entire book of Acts—the proclamation of the Gospel to the world.

It does not seem unreasonable to suggest, therefore, that in Luke's extended view of the history of salvation, Luke 9:51ff. and Acts 2:1ff. are interrelated, major turning points in his design. In Luke 9:64, James' and John's plea to call "fire to come down from heaven and destroy" the Samaritans is a quotation from 2 Kings 1:10, 12, where Elijah brings fire from heaven to consume the soldiers of Ahaziah, "king of Samaria" (vs. 3). But in Luke 9:55, Jesus rebukes his disciples for desiring to bring down fire from heaven on the Samaritans,[35] and in Acts 1:8 Samaria is, after Jerusalem, the point of departure for the mission to the whole world, symbolized in the Pentecost experience.[36] When, then, "the day of Pentecost had come" (Acts 2:1), fire did come from heaven and the mission to the world began. Rather than in Samaria and when the disciples wished, it was in Jerusalem (Luke 24:47) and in the time "which the Father has fixed by his own authority" (Acts 1:7) that the fire from heaven descended. For Luke this also fulfills the declaration of the Baptist, "He will baptize you with the Holy Spirit and with fire" (Luke 3:16).

Considered from this point of view, the motif of fire as it appears in Peter's sermon also reflects the Elijah theme. The quotation from Joel 2:30-31 (Acts 2:19-20) declares: "And I will show wonders in the heaven above and signs on the earth beneath, blood, and fire, and vapor of smoke . . . before the day of the Lord comes, the great and manifest day." Of all the "wonders" listed in the passage from Joel, only fire is characteristic of Pentecost. Furthermore, while Elijah does not appear as a figure in Joel, the words, "before the day of the Lord comes, the great and manifest day" are identical with Malachi 4:5, the passage *par excellence* regarding the eschatological appearance of Elijah. Luke seems to be saying, then, that in the

---

[35] Something similar seems to be implied in Luke 12:49-50 where the casting of fire upon the earth is paired with the Passion, for both of which the time has not yet come. L. Gaston, *No Stone on Another* (Leiden: Brill, 1970), p. 289, sees Luke 9:51-56 as an anti-Elijah polemic: "The whole point of the story is Jesus' rebuke of his followers who want to see him in the role of Elijah." We would suggest that Luke does indeed see Jesus in an Elijah role, but that for him the question is one of when in the divine plan this role becomes effective.

[36] Note also the remark of F. V. Filson ("The Journey Motif in Luke-Acts," in *Apostolic History and the Gospel*, ed. W. W. Gasque and R. P. Martin [Grand Rapids: Eerdmans, 1970], p. 72): "His [Luke's] travel section in his gospel (Luke 9:51-19:44) prepares for but does not begin the ministry to the Samaritans."

gift of the Spirit the risen Lord finally fulfills one aspect of the eschatological role of Elijah: He sends fire from Heaven, fire which had been denied his disciples at an earlier point because, in the divine economy, the time had not yet come. This is one of Luke's ways of indicating that the proclamation of the Gospel to the world begins at a specific, divinely appointed time in the history of salvation.

Closely related to the motif of Elijah is that of Moses. These two eschatological figures are already paired in the Transfiguration story (Matt. 17:3; Mark 9:4; Luke 9:30), which apparently draws on a Jewish tradition reflected in Deut. R. 3 (201c), where R. Jochanan ben Zakkai is said to have declared: "God said to Moses, 'When I send the prophet Elijah, you will both come together.'"[37] A similar tradition is probably behind Rev. 11:3-13, where the "two witnesses" are possessed of powers characteristic of Elijah and Moses in that they can destroy their enemies with fire, prevent rain and call down plagues.

In chapter 2, the figure of fire probably relates to Moses as well as to Elijah. Fire plays a significant role in the stories of Moses, particularly in those of the burning bush (Ex. 3:2) and the giving of the law on Sinai (Ex. 19:18; Deut. 4:11, 12, 15, 33, etc.). In the story of Pentecost, it is the Sinai motif that appears to be in view. Philo declares of the giving of the law on Sinai:

> I should suppose that God wrought on this occasion a miracle of a truly holy kind by bidding an invisible sound to be created in the air more marvelous than all instruments . . . which giving shape and tension to the air and changing it to flaming fire, sounded forth like the breath through a trumpet an articulate voice so loud that it appeared to be equally audible to the farthest as well as the nearest.[38]

Even should this allusion to fire be nothing more than Philo's own elaboration of the passages in Exodus and Deuteronomy which describe the fire on Sinai at the giving of the Law, it demonstrates the fact that the fire theme could be associated with the divine voice at Sinai and indeed in such a way as to declare that all, no matter how distant they were, could perceive without difficulty what was said. Later Rabbinic tradition attests to the idea that God's voice at Sinai was

---

[37] H. L. Strack and P. Billerbeck, *Kommentar zum Neuen Testament aus Talmud und Midrasch* (Munich: Beck, 1924-61), I, pp. 756-757 (on Matt. 17:3); E. Lohmeyer, *Das Evangelium des Markus* (Göttingen: Vandenhoeck & Ruprecht, 1963), p. 175, n. 4; H. M. Teeple, *The Mosaic Eschatological Prophet* (Philadelphia: SBL, 1957), pp. 43-44.

[38] Philo, *Decal.* 33-35, tr. F. H. Colson, in *Philo*, VIII (Cambridge: Mass.: Harvard University Press, 1937). O'Reilly, *Word and Sign*, pp. 42-53.

heard in a multitude of languages, though whether such a notion existed in the late first century we cannot say. A *baraitha* preserved in B. Shabbat 88b and attributed to the school of R. Ishmael (d. *c.* 135 C.E.), if authentic, comes sufficiently close to Luke's time to provide a probable parallel: "Every single word that went forth from the Holy One, blessed be He, split up into seventy languages."[39]

All this suggests that a further implication of Luke's story of the tongues of fire and the accompanying gift of tongues with which the Gospel is proclaimed to all nations is that Christ is the new Moses and Pentecost is a new Sinai at which is initiated the proclamation of the new Law.[40]

In Peter's sermon, the motif of Moses seems to reappear in the declaration that Christ has been "exalted at the right hand of God" (vs. 33), which is then juxtaposed with a quotation from Ps. 110:1. Behind this theme of Christ's exaltation and the ensuing outpouring of the Spirit also seems to lie Ps. 68:19 (68:18 LXX): ἀνέβης εἰς ὕψος, ἠχμαλώτευσας αἰχμαλωσίαν, ἔλαβες δόματα ἐν ἀνθρώπῳ ("Having ascended on high, thou hast led captivity captive, thou hast received gifts for man"), a clear allusion to Moses on Sinai (note the previous verse) which is applied to Christ in Eph. 4:8 and related there to gifts of the spirit.[41] Similarly, Philo says of Moses: "There are still others, whom God has advanced even higher, and has trained them to soar above species and genus alike and stationed them beside himself. Such is Moses to whom He says 'stand here with me' [σὺ δὲ αὐτοῦ στῆθι μετ' ἐμοῦ, Deut. 5:31 LXX]."[42] The probability that vs. 33 contains an allusion to Moses is strengthened by the recurrence of the exaltation theme in 5:31, where as we shall see, the figure of Moses is even more clearly apparent.

It seems evident then, that the story and the sermon in ch. 2 are tied together not only by a situational framework, but also by the themes of Elijah and Moses, both of whom are seen as figures fulfilled in Christ.

---

[39] *The Babylonian Talmud*, tr. I. Epstein (London: Soncino, 1938), II, p. 420.

[40] Cf. R. Le Déaut, "Targumic Literature and New Testament Interpretation," *BTB*, 4 (1974), pp. 269-360.

[41] Cf. J. Dupont, "Les discours missionaires des Actes des Apôtres," *RB*, 69 (1962), p. 48; Dupont, however, understands τῇ δεξιᾷ in vs. 33 (and also 5:31) as instrumental rather than locative, which makes it possible for him to see a connection also with Ps. 117 (118):16: δεξιὰ κυρίου ὕψωσέμε. On the basis of Ps. 110:1 and Acts 7:55-56, as well as the analogy cited from Philo, we prefer to understand τῇ δεξιᾷ as locative, as does Wilckens, *Missionsreden der Apostelgeschichte*, p. 152.

[42] Philo, *Sac.* 8, tr. F. H. Colson, in *Philo*, II (Cambridge, Mass.: Harvard University Press, 1929); cf. *Post.* 28-31; *Deus* 23-26; *Gig.* 56-57.

The Healing of the Lame Man and Peter's Sermon in Solomon's Portico (Acts 3)

The story of Peter's healing the lame man (Acts 3:1-10) is, in form, a miracle story. Luke provides an obvious structural tie with Peter's sermon (ch. 3:12-26) by making the healing the occasion of the sermon (vs. 11). Thematically, however, the significant tie between story and sermon is found in vs. 16, where Peter is made to refer back to his words at the performance of the miracle ("in the name of Jesus Christ of Nazareth, walk," 3:6) by now declaring that the miracle was effected "by faith in his name."[43] Vs. 16 is given prominence in that it breaks the flow of thought, which otherwise would move logically from vs. 15 directly to vs. 17.

This theme of "the name" has important implications for the figure of Moses, which is alluded to directly in vs. 22 and implied repeatedly elsewhere throughout the sermon. The quotation in vs. 22-23; "The Lord God will raise up for you a prophet from your brethren as he raised me up. You shall listen to him in whatever he says. . . ." is taken from Deut. 18:15, and as applied by Luke clearly designates Christ as a second Moses. A Jewish or Christian reader familiar with this Messianic passage[44] could scarcely have avoided being reminded of the verses (Deut. 18:20-22)[45] which follow, in which Moses speaks of true and false prophets: The sign of the true prophet is that he speaks "in my name" only what the Lord has given him to speak; if what he says "in the name of the Lord" does not come to pass, he

---

[43] Cf. Wilckens, *Missionsreden der Apostelgeschichte*, p. 60. The efficacy of "the name of the Lord" has already been declared, however, in Peter's "programmatic" sermon at Pentecost, where the quotation from Joel 2:28-32 climaxes with the declaration, καὶ ἔσται πᾶς ὃς ἐὰν ἐπικαλέσηται τὸ ὄνομα κυρίου σωθήσεται (Acts 2:21; cf. Rom. 10:13). The expression τοῖς ἐπικαλουμένοις τὸ ὄνομα κυρίου appears at 1 Cor. 1:2; cf. James 2:7, and also in the speeches of Acts 9:14, 21; 15:17; 22:16. It is thus pre-Lukan (if not pre-Pauline) and had wide currency in the early church, being almost a synonym for "Christians" (C. H. Dodd, *According to the Scriptures* [London: Nisbet, 1953], p. 47, n. 2; M. Wilcox, *The Semitisms of Acts* [Oxford, England: Clarendon Press, 1966], p. 77). Hence already in this "keynote address," which anticipates so much of the theological development throughout the book of Acts, Luke lifts "the name" above the level of thaumaturgy.

[44] Deut. 18:18-19 is part of a collection of Messianic testimonia in 4QTest.; cf. J. M. Allegro, "Further Messianic References in Qumran Literature," *JBL*, 75 (1956), pp. 182-187; J. A. Fitzmyer, "'4QTestimonia' and the New Testament," *TS*, 18 (1957) pp. 513-537. On the "prophet" as an eschatological figure, cf. Teeple, *Eschatological Prophet*, pp. 29-73, 84-94, and R. C. Zehnle, *Peter's Pentecost Discourse* (Nashville: Abingdon Press, 1971), pp. 79-82.

[45] C. H. Dodd argues that early Christian apologetic method included the "selection of certain large sections of Old Testament scriptures" which "were understood as wholes, and particular verses or sentences were quoted from them rather as pointers to the whole context than as constituting testimonies in and for themselves" (*According to the Scriptures*, p. 126).

is a false prophet. This principle seems to be reflected in Acts 3:16 where Peter offers the fact of the man's being healed as evidence for the efficacy of "faith in his name."

Luke is careful to emphasize that in the healing miracle, Christ is at work, his name is efficacious (vss. 12-16). Thus the Moses typology can oscillate between Christ himself and his apostle, Peter, who in this instance seems to fulfill the role of the true prophet who speaks "in the name of the Lord." This is possible because whatever the apostle does or says, it is in fact Christ working and speaking through him. Behind this probably lies the theme of Moses' having received the divine name at Horeb (Ex. 3:13-14). Thus when Peter speaks "in the name of Jesus" and heals the lame man, he can disclaim that it is by "our own power or piety we have made him walk" (vs. 12); rather, it is "the faith which is through Jesus" that effected the cure (vs. 16). While at this point the imagery of Moses focuses on Peter rather than on Jesus, this shift is possible because in reality the words and deeds of Peter are those of his Lord.[46] The extension of Jesus' power to his disciples makes possible this refocusing of the imagery of Moses upon the disciples.[47]

At the same time, it is clear that for Luke there is more here than simply the story of a θεῖος ἀνήρ, despite the fact that taken in the context of the miracle story, Peter's words, "in the name of Jesus Christ of Nazareth, walk" (vs. 6), appear to

---

[46] Cf. Josephus' depiction of Moses' encounter with Pharaoh's magicians: When they transform their staves into "pythons," Moses declares, "O king, I too disdain not the cunning of the Egyptians, but I assert that the deeds wrought by me so far surpass their magic and their art as things divine are remote from what is human. And I will show that it is from no witchcraft or deception of true judgment, but from God's providence and power that my miracles proceed" (*Ant.* II. 286; in *Josephus*, ed. H. St. J. Thackeray [Cambridge, Mass.: Harvard University Press, 1930], IV). An alternative way of viewing this oscillation in focus between Christ and his disciples would be to understand the Moses typology here in terms of a "corporate Christ" (cf. the words to Paul on the Damascus Road, where the risen Christ is identified with the church ["I am Jesus whom you are persecuting"; see Acts 9:4-5; 27:8; 26:15]). So understood, this would be an exception to the rule suggested by C. F. D. Moule ("The Christology of Acts," in *Studies in Luke-Acts*, ed. L. E. Keck and J. L. Martin [Nashville: Abingdon Press, 1966], pp. 159-185) that in Acts only statements associated with Paul approach the "corporate conception of Christ found in the Pauline epistles" (p. 181). See also O'Reilly, *Word and Sign*, pp. 152-156.

[47] On the extension of Jesus' power as θεῖος ἀνήρ to Peter and Paul, cf. N. Perrin and D. C. Duling, *The New Testament: An Introduction*, second ed. (New York: Harcourt, Brace, Jovanovich, 1982), pp. 84-85. On Moses as a divine man and miracle worker by virtue of his possession of the divine name, see Artapanus in Eusebius, *Praep. Evang.* IX.27; Josephus, *Ant.* III.179-180; and discussion in J. G. Gager, *Moses in Greco-Roman Paganism* (Nashville: Abingdon Press, 1972), pp. 280-281; D. L. Tiede, *The Charismatic Figure as Miracle Worker* (Missoula, Mont.: SBL, 1972), p. 169, nn. 118, 170.

be virtually a magical formula, invoking a divine name to produce a miraculous effect in a manner familiar to us from the magical papyri. The disclaimer that Luke enters for Peter as the real source of the miracle (vs. 12) is doubtless a defense against the accusation that Christian miracle-workers were magicians. The degree to which magic was common in the Hellenistic-Roman world and flourished in Jewish circles is well known. O. Betz has pointed to several early rabbis who, noted for their miracle-working, made efforts to avoid the charge of magic by insisting, as Luke does, that the success of the miracles was not due to themselves, but to God, that no fame or honor should be given them.[48] Similarly, in the sermon Luke lifts the significance of the phrase "in the name" to a higher level and reveals that what is really meant is faith in Jesus Christ (vs. 16). Here for the first time in the Acts Luke introduces the theme of faith.[49]

Scholars repeatedly have pointed out that the sermon of Acts 3 is replete with other allusions to Moses which refer directly to Christ. As Zehnle shows, this is apparent particularly in a comparison of parallel motifs in chs. 3 and 7; he finds no less than ten such parallels between Moses and Jesus in these two chapters.[50] It has also been argued that the παῖς-Christology of 3:13, 26, 4:25, 27, 30, which draws on the Suffering Servant figure of Isa. 42:1, 52:13, 53:11, is in reality a Moses typology: A. Bentzen and others have seen in the Suffering Servant a New Moses or a Moses *redivivus*.[51] While these all relate not to the miracle story but only to the sermon, they suggest how strongly the Moses figure is embedded there.

The Healing of the Lame Man and Peter's Sermon Before the Council (Acts 4)

Peter's first sermon before the Council (Acts 4:8-12, 19-20) presupposes his sermon in the previous chapter and summarizes its contents.[52] Similarly the two sermons relate to the same miracle story, the healing of the lame man (3:1-10). The

---

[48] O. Betz, "Das Problem des Wunders bei Flavius Josephus im Vergleich zum Wunderproblem bei den Rabbinen und im Johannesevangelium," in *Josephus-Studien*, ed. O. Betz et al. (Göttingen: Vandenhoeck & Ruprecht, 1974), pp. 23-24. Betz cites Honi (d. 65 B.C.E.), Abba Hilkia (*c.* 50 C.E.), and Hanina ben Dosa (*c.* 70 C.E.).

[49] However, in a vignette of primitive Christian life he has already referred to the community as οἱ πιστεύσαντες (2:44).

[50] Zehnle, *Peter's Pentecost Discourse*, pp. 76-78.

[51] A. Bentzen, *King and Messiah* (London: Lutterworth, 1955), pp. 56-57. Note also Isa. 52:13 LXX (ὑψωθήσεται) and Acts 2:33, 5:31. See the discussion in Teeple, *Eschatological Prophet*, pp. 56-58, 92.

[52] Wilckens, *Missionsreden der Apostelgeschichte*, pp. 61-62.

tie between this sermon and the miracle story is clear from the outset (4:7), where the rulers ask, "By what power or by what name did you do this?" and this tie continues throughout the short narrative that follows the sermon (vss. 14, 16, 21, 22). In fact, the miracle is more at issue in ch. 4 than in ch. 3.

This question, which Luke uses as a link between the miracle story and this sermon, is reminiscent of Ex. 3:13-14, where Moses is equipped with the divine name and told to say to Israel as a sign of his commission, "'I am' has sent me to you." It may also be compared with the Hellenistic tale regarding Moses told by Artapanus, where Pharaoh "ordered Moses to declare the name of the god who had sent him,"[53] which also doubtless derives from Ex. 3:13-14. The rulers' question also seems to echo Deut. 18:20, where the issue as to the name in which a prophet speaks is a test of his truth or falsity. In either case, the figure of Moses is in view.

We already have seen that in the sermon in Solomon's Portico Luke lifts the implication of "the name" to a new level by coupling it with faith (3:16). Similarly, in the present sermon, while he says nothing of faith, he accomplishes much the same movement by tying "the name" to a play on the word σῴζειν. Thus the question in vs. 9, ἐν τίνι [ὀνόματι] οὗτος σέσωσται;, refers to healing by a name, but in vs. 12, at the climax of the sermon, the declaration, οὐδὲ γὰρ ὄνομά ἐστιν ἕτερον . . . ἐν ᾧ δεῖ σωθῆναι ἡμᾶς, shifts the meaning of σῴζειν to focus on salvation from final judgment; with it the efficacy of the "name" once more transcends the figure of a miracle-working θεῖος ἀνήρ.[54] That for Luke the healing "by faith in his name" in 3:16 and the coupling of "name" with the verb σωθῆναι in the sense of spiritual salvation in 4:12 are closely related, is also suggested by certain passages in his Gospel. The combination of σῴζειν, in the sense of healing, with "faith" is common to the Synoptic tradition (ἡ πίστις σου σέσωκέν σε: Matt. 9:22 = Mark 5:34 = Luke 8:48; Mark 10:52 = Luke 18:42; cf. Mark 5:26, 36), but in the Lukan *Sondergut* it is lifted to the level of salvation from future judgment (Luke 7:50; cf. Luke 8:12).[55] As Haenchen remarks, "For Luke there is no sharp line between

---

[53] Artapanus in Eusebius, *Praep. Evang.* IX.27; also quoted by Clement of Alexandria, *Strom.* I. 23.; text and translation in C. R. Holladay, *Fragments from Hellenistic Jewish Authors* (Chico, Calif.: Scholars Press, 1983), pp. 218-219.

[54] Haenchen, *Apostelgeschichte*, p. 176, remarks on 2:12: "Das heilungspendende ὄνομα, das die christlichen Exorzisten gebrauchen, und das im göttlichen Gericht rettende ὄνομα treten nicht auseinander." While the "name" remains the same, the level of its efficacy changes with the shift in the meaning of σῴζειν from vs. 9 to vs. 12.

[55] Cf. W. C. van Unnik, "L'usage de ΣΩZEIN 'sauver' et des dérivés dans les évangiles synoptiques," in *La formation des évangiles*, ed. J. Cambier *et al.* (Louvain: Desclée de Brouwer, 1957), pp. 180, 186, 188, 190.

healing and exorcism (cf. Luke 4:39)"[56]; freedom from disease, from demons and from judgment to come are a continuum because they all are accomplished in the name of the Lord who has triumphed in all of these spheres.

Another theme common to the miracle story of ch. 3 and the sermon of ch. 4 is that of the Temple. A number of things suggest that Luke has more than simply a literal story in mind in recounting the healing of the lame man, or indeed in his depiction of the Temple as the locus of primitive Christian worship and preaching (2:45; 3:1, 11; 5:12, 20, 21, 25, 42). Gerhardsson has pointed out that Luke's view of the Temple in the early chapters of Acts is based on a series of pericopes in Luke 19:45-20:19.[57] The opening sentence of Acts 3, "Now Peter and John were going up to the temple at the hour of prayer," is reminiscent of a tradition common to the Synoptics where Jesus declares, in cleansing the temple, "My house shall be a house of prayer" (Luke 19:46 = Mark 11:17 = Matt. 21:13). Another Synoptic tradition, which Luke unites more closely with the foregoing pericope than do Matthew or Mark, is that in which Jesus, when challenged by the priests and scribes as to his authority to teach in the Temple, which he has been doing "daily" since he cleansed it (Luke 19:47; cf. Acts 2:46), refuses to answer (Luke 20:1-8; cf. Matt. 21:23-27; Mark 11:27-33). For Luke, at least, this refusal seems to reflect the early Christian conviction that Christ, in cleansing the Temple, made it his house, and that they therefore needed offer no apology for their presence or activity. In Luke, as in the other Synoptics, Jesus' refusal to answer regarding his authority to teach in the Temple is followed closely by the parable of the Wicked Husbandmen, which climaxes with the declaration, "He will come and destroy those tenants, and give the vineyard to others" (Luke 20:16 = Mark 12:9 = Matt. 21:41). Jeremias has demonstrated that in all three Synoptics, but especially in Luke and Matthew, this parable, as understood by the primitive church, is an allegory of the rejection of Jesus by the Jews.[58] Matthew, at least, interprets the giving of the vineyard to "others" (21:41) as meaning that "the kingdom of God will be taken away from you and given to a nation producing the fruits of it" (vs. 43). While Luke offers no such explicit interpretation of the "others" to whom the vineyard will be given (20:16), in view of the allegorical nature of his presentation of the parable and of his view of the history of salvation,

---

[56] Haenchen, *Apostelgeschichte*, p. 176, n. 6.

[57] B. Gerhardsson, *Memory and Manuscript* (Lund: Gleerup, 1961), pp. 217-220.

[58] J. Jeremias, *The Parables of Jesus*, revised ed., tr. S. H. Hooke (New York: Scribner, 1963), pp. 70-77.

it is difficult to escape the conclusion that he too intends to imply that the church now has been given custody of the "vineyard."

That Luke's understanding of the Temple in Acts 3 and 4 is rooted in these pericopes in his Gospel is further indicated by the fact that the quotation from Ps. 117 (118):22 regarding the rejected cornerstone (or keystone) appears both at the end of the parable of the Husbandmen (Luke 20:17) and in Peter's sermon to the Council (Acts 1:11).[59] This familiar Christological proof-text (cf. Matt. 21:42; Mark 12:10; 1 Pet. 2:7) in each case vindicates Jesus against his rejection by the Jewish leaders, and sees him become "the keystone in God's new Temple."[60] In Acts 4:11 it also constitutes a tie between Peter's sermon and the miracle story of the healing of the lame man, both in that it reflects the temple theme and because it comes immediately after a reference to the healing (vs. 10). Further, the assertion that Christ is the cornerstone of the Temple implies once more that the Temple is indeed his and that his people have a right to be there. This distinction *vis-à-vis* the Jewish leaders is heightened by Luke's nuance of adding ὑμῶν to the quotation from Ps. 117 (118):22, so as to accuse his hearers of being themselves the rejecters (4:11).

All of this suggests, then, that in the story of the healing of the lame man we may see a Temple imagery which reflects Luke's familiar view of salvation history. We propose that the story may be understood somewhat along these lines. The apostles, in entering the Temple at the hour of prayer (3:1), are indeed entering the house which their Lord has cleansed (Luke 19:45) and which is now his and, therefore, theirs. Accordingly, when like Jesus (Luke 20:1-8) their authority to teach and work there is questioned by the Jewish leaders (Acts 4:7; cf. vss. 18-20), the only answer they need give is to invoke his name (Acts 4:10). The miracle of healing, interpreted as it is in Peter's sermon both in a physical and in a spiritual sense (4:9, 12), suggests the conversion of new believers in Christ. Such details of the miracle story as that Peter "took him by the right hand and raised him up" (3:7) and that the man "entered the temple with them, walking and leaping and praising God" (vs. 8) seem to fit this interpretation. Hitherto the man had only sat at the

---

[59] A further connection is the theme of the rulers being unable to destroy Jesus when teaching in the Temple because of "the people" (Luke 19:17-48); this theme is repeated of the apostles in Acts 4:21.

[60] E. E. Ellis, "Midrashic Features in the Speeches of Acts," *Mélanges Bibliques en Hommage au R. P. Béda Rigaux*, ed., A. Descamps and A. de Halleux (Gembloux: Duculot, 1969), p. 310. Ellis investigates the possibility that the quotations of Ps. 117 (118):22 in the Gospels and in Acts 4:11 originated in early Christian *midrashim*.

gate; now "saved," he enters the Temple on the same terms as the apostles. At this point Luke may have had in mind the passage immediately preceding the one regarding the cornerstone:[61] "Open to me the gates of righteousness; entering through them I will give thanks to the Lord. This is the gate of the Lord; the righteous shall enter through it. I will thank thee that thou hast answered me and hast become for me salvation [σωτηρίαν]." (Ps. 117 [118]: 19-21 LXX).

That the gate at which the lame man sat is called the "Beautiful Gate" (τὴν θύραν τοῦ ἱεροῦ τὴν λεγομένην Ὡραίαν) (3:2) and the man himself is characterized in terms of it (ὁ . . . καθήμενος ἐπὶ τῇ Ὡραίᾳ Πύλῃ τοῦ ἱεροῦ) (3:10) may rest on Psalm 67 (68):11-12 LXX. Rabbinic tradition (B. Shabbat 88b) relates this passage, in its Hebrew form, to the Law at Sinai having been heard in seventy languages, a theme that, as we have seen, surely lies behind the Pentecost story and relates in Christian thought to the proclamation of the Gospel as the new Torah.[62] Although the Hebrew of the passage is notoriously difficult, the Greek translation, while badly garbled,[63] might well have served Christian apologetic interests and have been included in a book of *testimonia* known to Luke; it reads: κύριος δώσει ῥῆμα τοῖς εὐαγγελιζομένοις δυνάμει πολλῇ, ὁ βασιλεὺς τῶν δυνάμεων τοῦ ἀγαπητοῦ, καὶ ὡραιότητι τοῦ οἴκου διελέσθαι σκῦλα. Without reference to the Hebrew and from a Christian point of view, this could be understood to mean: "The Lord will give a word [cf. Luke 21:15; Acts 5:20] to those who preach the Gospel [cf. Luke 20:1] with much power [or, to a great host], the king of the hosts of the beloved [cf. Luke 3:22; Eph 1:6], to divide the spoils even for the beauty of the house." So understood, these verses bring together the notions of proclaiming the Gospel and of winning "spoils" for the beautification of the "Temple," themes consonant with Luke's presentation of the story of the healing of the lame man.[64]

---

[61] The possibility that a book of *testimonia* lies behind some of Luke's quotations and allusions is heightened by the fact that his quotation of Ps. 117 (118):22 in 4:11, while unmistakable, is quite at variance with the Septuagint (which he quotes verbatim in Luke 20:17); cf. Haenchen, *Apostelgeschichte*, p. 176, n. 5.

[62] "R. Johanan [bar Napaha, d. 279 C.E.] said: 'What is meant by the verse, The Lord giveth the word: They that publish the tidings are a great host?'—Every single word that went forth from the Omnipotent was split up into seventy languages" (*Babylonian Talmud*, II, pp. 419-420). This dictum, offered in exposition of Jer. 23:29, is found already in a *baraitha* attributed to the school of R. Ishmael.

[63] The real meaning of the Hebrew, using archaic vocabulary only now made intelligible by comparison with Ugaritic (see W. F. Albright, "A Catalogue of Early Hebrew Lyric Poems," *Hebrew Union College Annual*, 23 [1950-51], pp. 21-22; M. Dahood, *Psalms II* [Garden City, N.Y.: Doubleday, 1968], pp. 140-141), was lost not only to the Rabbis, but also to the translator of the Septuagint, who struggled to make sense out of something he could not have understood.

[64] If this understanding of the miracle story is correct, it may well follow that the reason no

The Episode with Bar-Jesus and Paul's Sermon at Antioch in Pisidia (Acts 13)

At first sight, the story of Paul's encounter with Bar-Jesus and his sermon in the synagogue of Antioch seem to have no particular relationship with each other. Closer consideration, however, suggests that this quasi-miracle story and the sermon that follows, though separated in setting, do indeed have much in common, as we have seen to be the case with other story-sermon complexes in the early chapters of Acts.

Long ago A. Loisy threw out the suggestion—without developing it—that the Bar-Jesus story is symbolic: "La conversion de Sergius Paulus est un symbole, comme l'opposition et la cécité de Bariésous."[65] Concerning this, Haenchen remarks, "Weshalb Lukas aber eigentlich solche Symbolik auf die Szene stellt, verrät uns Loisy leider nicht."[66] We would suggest that in this instance Loisy is correct, and that Luke did indeed have good reason for using symbolism at this point.

It is generally recognized that ch. 13 constitutes the major turning point in the book of Acts. Here Paul, under the direction of the Holy Spirit, is commissioned by the church at Antioch as an apostle to the Gentiles (vss. 1-3). This is followed immediately by his first witness to a Gentile, the Cypriot proconsul, Sergius Paulus (vss. 6-12). The remainder of the chapter is given over to Paul's and Barnabas' experience at Pisidian Antioch: Paul's "Musterpredigt"[67] in the synagogue (vss. 26-41), which ends in a warning to the Jews if they reject the Gospel, is followed by the Jews' actual rejection of his message and the enthusiastic reception of it by Gentiles.

The story of Paul's encounter with Bar-Jesus, then, should be seen in the context of the whole movement of ch. 13. It is part of Luke's stage setting for his narrative of the shift in focus from the Jews to the Gentiles; this setting, in fact, consists of the three segments noted above: the commission, the encounter with Bar-Jesus, and the sermon at Antioch.

Set as this story is in the context of the beginning of the Gentile mission, the encounter it presents with a Jewish magician who opposes the Gospel and a Gentile official who favors it portrays in miniature a dialectical situation which characteriz-

---

one has yet fixed the location of the "Beautiful Gate" is that it existed only in Luke's symbolism.

[65] A. Loisy, *Les Actes des Apôtres* (Paris: Nourry, 1920), p. 518.

[66] Haenchen, *Apostelgeschichte*, p. 346.

[67] P. Zingg, *Das Wachsen der Kirche* (Freiburg/Schweiz: Universitätsverlag, 1974), p. 231.

es the rest of the book of Acts. Almost without exception, wherever Paul will encounter opposition it is the result of Jewish reaction against his preaching. In contrast, Gentile response will be favorable. (Note that the first instance of this follows directly on Paul's preaching at Antioch [vss. 45-50].)

Not only does the general outline of the story reflect the rejection of the Gospel by the Jews and the initiation of the Gentile mission, but certain aspects of Paul's rebuke of Bar-Jesus (vss. 10-11a) suggest this as well. The characterization of Bar-Jesus as "enemy of all righteousness" (ἐχθρὲ πάσης δικαιοσύνης) (vs. 10) is the only instance in Luke's writing where he applies the term ἐχθρός specifically to a Jewish opponent of the Gospel. In Rom. 11:28, however, Paul declares of the Jews: "As regards the gospel they are enemies [ἐχθροί] of God." We appear to have here an attempt by Luke to couch his words in Pauline language and thought particularly reminiscent of the apostle's anguished discussion of the Jews in Rom. 9-11. Similarly, references to "righteousness" (δικαιοσύνη) are not frequent in Luke (elsewhere only at Luke 1:75; Acts 10:35; 17:31; 24:25), who never uses the word in a characteristically Pauline sense. In ch. 13, however, he seems purposely to introduce the term to give his writing a Pauline cast, both here and in the sermon at Antioch, where he has Paul declare: "By him everyone that believes is freed [δικαιοῦται] from everything from which you could not be freed [δικαιωθῆναι] by the law of Moses" (vss. 38-39).[68]

The expression, "the hand of the Lord" (χεὶρ κυρίου) (vs. 11) is peculiar to Luke in the New Testament and appears in his writing elsewhere only at Luke 1:66 and Acts 11:21, in both instances in the expression, "The hand of the Lord was with him/them." It implies the action of divine power in a sustaining way (cf. 2 Kingd. 3:12 LXX). In Luke 3:17 "his [Christ's] hand" refers to eschatological divine judgment in separating the righteous from the wicked. In Acts 4:28 "your [God's] hand" is a figure for divine predestination of the death of Jesus; in vs. 30 the same phrase represents the power of God to "heal," in the face of threats to the church from the Jews. In every instance in the Lucan writings, the hand of God represents a divine action by which the plan of redemptive history is brought a step further

---

[68] Ph. Vielhauer, "On the 'Paulinism' of Acts," in *Studies in Luke-Acts,* ed. L. E. Keck and J. L. Martyn (Nashville: Abingdon Press, 1966), pp. 41-42; cf. Haenchen, *Apostelgeschichte,* p. 354, n. 4. Note also that this is the only instance of the verb δικαιόω in Acts. In Luke's Gospel it appears only at 7:29, 35; 10:29; 16:15; 18:14, and never in a "Pauline" sense. Nor does Luke carry through his "Paulinizing" in Acts 13 with any thoroughness; e.g., υἱὲ διαβόλου (vs. 10), ἄνδρες ἀδελφοί (vs. 26), λόγος τῆς σωτηρίας ταύτης (vs. 26) never appear in Paul's writings.

on its way. Thus "the hand of the Lord" on Bar-Jesus is not simply a display of divine power; it implies rather a significant moment in Luke's view of the history of salvation.

In Paul's words to Bar-Jesus, the clearest indication both of Luke's concern with the shift in focus from Jews to Gentiles and of his "Paulinizing" is found in the declaration: "You shall be blind and unable to see the sun for a time" (vs. 11). Of the Synoptic evangelists, it is Luke who is most conscious of the spiritual implications of blindness (Luke 4:18; 6:39). In the present instance he seems to reflect the sentiment of Rom. 11:25: "A hardening [πώρωσις] has come upon part of Israel, until the full number of the Gentiles come in." While πώρωσις means "hardening" in a general medical sense, as applied to mental and spiritual perception it is connected repeatedly with the notion of blindness. Thus in regard to the Jews, at 2 Cor. 3:14 Paul parallels the declaration, "their minds were hardened" (ἐπωρώθη) with "a veil upon their hearts" (vs. 15). The antithesis is to behold the glory of the Lord "with unveiled face" (vs. 18). Similarly in John 12:40, "he has blinded their eyes" is paralleled with "hardened [ἐπώρωσεν] their heart." Mark 8:17-18 and Job 17:17 LXX, where πορούν refers to a weakened condition of the eyes, may also be compared with this.

Returning to Rom. 11, it is clear that the figure of blindness is in Paul's mind. In vss. 7-8 he follows the declaration regarding Israel that "the rest were hardened [ἐπωρώθησαν]" with a composite quotation from Deut. 29:4 and Isa 29:10, "God gave them a spirit of stupor, eyes that should not see and ears that should not hear," and then follows from Ps. 68:24 LXX with "Let their eyes be darkened so that they cannot see." In view of this it seems reasonable to conclude that at least one implication of Rom. 11:25, "a hardening has come upon part of Israel," is spiritual blindness (so NEB: "This partial blindness has come upon Israel.").[69]

For Paul, this blind insensitivity is a "mystery," a chapter in the divine plan not unlike that implied by the phrase, "the hand of the Lord," in Acts 13:11. It is both an act of God (Rom. 11:7-10) and also the result of Israel's choice (ch. 9:30-

---

[69] Certain ancient versions also understand the reference here to be to blindness: vg and some of the it read *caecitas*, sy^p reads *'wyrwt*. It is possible, however, that these translations rest on a confusion of πώρωσις and πήρωσις; while there are no variants of πώρωσις in the Greek text of Rom. 11:25, πηρόω is a variant of πωρόω at Mark 8:17 in D*, and at John 12:40 in P⁶⁶, S, W, pc. At the same time, direct analogies to the translation of Rom. 11:25 are offered by Mark 6:52, in which there also are no known Greek variants for πωρόω but in which vg reads *obcaecatum* and the sy^s *'wyr*; similarly sy^p at 2 Cor. 3:14 reads *'t'wrw*, "were blinded" (see K. L. Schmidt and M. A. Schmidt, "πωρόω," *TDNT*, V, p. 1027).

10:3). Similarly the blindness of Bar-Jesus is an act of God, but only in view of his opposition to the Gospel. Finally, in each case the blindness is temporary: For Paul it is only "until the full number of the Gentiles come in" (vs. 25); for Luke it is ἄχρι καιροῦ (Acts 13:11). This phrase is unique to Luke in the New Testament and appears only here and at Luke 4:13, where he declares that when Jesus' temptation was ended, the devil "departed from him until an opportune time [ἄχρι καιροῦ]." Conzelmann understands this verse to signal the beginning of the central period in Luke's "story of salvation"—the period of Jesus' ministry which terminates with the return of Satan and his entry into Judas Iscariot preparatory to the Passion (Luke 22:3).[70] This terminal point in a major segment of the *Heilsgeschichte* is indicated by the phrase ἄχρι καιροῦ. In the same way, then, ἄχρι καιροῦ in Paul's rebuke of Bar-Jesus can be seen to mark off another major segment in the ongoing story of salvation: the time of the Gentile mission and the "blindness" of the Jews, the period introduced by Luke in Acts 13.

If, as we have tried to show, the narrative of Paul's encounter with Bar-Jesus is symbolic of the rejection of the Gospel by the Jews and the beginning of the Gentile mission, do correspondences exist between it and the missionary sermon that follows in the Antioch synagogue?

These themes are nowhere explicit in the sermon. Implicitly, however, they permeate it and constitute the ideological presupposition of the entire address. Luke places Paul's remarks in the setting of a synagogue service on the Sabbath.[71] The apostle speaks in response to the reading of Torah and Haphtarah and at the invitation of the officials of the Jewish community (vs. 15). Much of his sermon is a recounting of the mighty acts of God for the salvation of Israel. When Christ is introduced, he is declared to be of the seed of David and a savior for Israel (vs. 23). Even his crucifixion is laid simply to the fact that the Jews of Jerusalem "did not recognize him nor understand the utterances of the prophets" (vs. 27). Their action was, in fact, a fulfillment of prophecy (vss. 27, 29). Thus for Luke, the crucial rejection of Jesus by the Jews, and the beginning of a new period in salvation history, is not at the cross, but now, as the Gentile mission is about to begin. The new situation finally comes out clearly in the climax of the sermon (vss. 38-41) with the declaration: "By him everyone that believes is freed [πᾶς ὁ πιστεύων

---

[70] H. Conzelmann, *Theology of St Luke*, pp. 16, 27-28.

[71] Cf. J. Bowker, "Speeches in Acts: A Study in Proem and Yelammedenu Form," *NTS*, 14 (1967), pp. 101-104, who analyzes this sermon in terms of typical homiletic form in the synagogue.

δικαιοῦνται] from everything from which you could not be freed by the law of Moses." Here "everyone that believes" in Christ is suddenly shown to be the beneficiary of the "holy and sure blessings of David" (vs. 34) through him. The repeated reference to the presence of god-fearing Gentiles in the congregation (vss. 16, 26) probably is intended to strengthen this point.

The final warning words of the sermon (vs. 41) are a quotation from Hab. 1:5. Luke's Jewish and Christian readers could hardly have missed the implication of its context,[72] for in the verse that immediately follows, the Lord declares: "For behold, I am arousing upon you the warlike Chaldeans, that bitter and hasty nation [ἔθνος], which marches the breadth of the earth to inherit [κατακληρονομῆσαι; cf. Acts 13:19] habitations that are not theirs" (Hab. 1:6 LXX). Translated into the life situation of the early Church, this "deed you will never believe, if one declares it to you" (Acts 13:41) is the awakening of the Gentiles across "the breadth of the earth" to an inheritance that is not originally theirs (cf. Rom. 11:17-24). By climaxing Paul's sermon with the words of Hab. 1:5, Luke leaves unspoken the real nature of the divine "deed" and allows his readers' minds to run on to the following verse and thus to grasp the true implication of the warning. That such is his intent can hardly be doubted in view of the epilogue to the sermon: On the following Sabbath Paul's preaching is rejected by the Jews, whereupon the apostles declare, "It was necessary that the word of God should be spoken first to you. Since you thrust it first from you, and judge yourselves unworthy of eternal life, behold, we turn to the Gentiles" (Acts 13:46).

III

When Luke's speeches are evaluated in terms of the Hellenistic canons of "appropriateness" (τὸ πρέπον) and "genuine contests" (ἀληθινοὶ ἀγῶνες), it is clear that they meet both standards. Luke presents speeches reflective of situations of tension and is concerned to relate his speeches to their contexts both in terms of general situation and of inner thematic ties. At the same time, he may be both compared and contrasted with Dionysius in his understanding of what "appropriateness" means.

For Dionysius this criterion is a rhetorical, not a historical one. As Pritchett says,

---

[72] See above, n. 44.

Dioynsius' criticisms of the speeches in Thucydides are regarded almost
exclusively from the point of view of contemporary rhetoric, not at all from the
historian's. . . . Speech and narrative are two rigidly separated categories, and it
never occurs to Dionysius to examine the narrative surrounding a speech which
shocks his notion of τὸ πρέπον to see if it supplies some justification for the
speech.[73]

Thus for Dionysius as a critic, a speech is inappropriate not because of a
disjunction with its historical context but because it is implausible in terms of what
one would, in general terms, expect of the character of the speaker. He considers
the Melian Dialogue inappropriate because his idealized Athenians simply would
not make such despotic demands. When, however, he turns from the rhetorical
criticism of other historians' speeches to become a writer of history himself, he
then emphasizes a dynamic interaction between speech and history, as we have
seen.[74]

Luke, of course, nowhere undertakes rhetorical criticism of speeches, so we
can only infer from his practice what his understanding may have been. His
concern for appropriateness is comparable with that of Dionysius in that he offers
speeches that (within the limited resources we have for comparison) apparently
were intended to be credible in terms of what he knew of Peter and Paul. While
the speeches are certainly his own composition and are intended to advance his
own theological point of view, yet in chs. 2 and 3 he uses a number of primitive,
though not always thoroughly integrated, Christian understandings, some of which
may indeed reflect authentic Petrine traditions;[75] and in ch. 13, as we have seen,
he is at pains to employ certain Pauline terms and ideas, again without fully
understanding them. The point, however, is that within the limits of his knowledge
he makes an obvious effort to present a believable "Peter" and "Paul."

Also, as with Dionysius, Luke has a sense of the dynamic significance of his
speeches in moving history forward. This is evident in his placing of them at key
turning points in his scenario.[76]

---

[73] Pritchett, *Dionysius,* p. xxxi. On the way in which Thucydides does in fact tie together his
speeches and their contexts, see H. D. Westlake, "The Settings of Thucydidean Speeches" in *The
Speeches in Thucydides,* ed. P. A. Stadter (Chapel Hill, N.C.: University of North Carolina Press,
1973), pp. 90-108. Westlake shows that with few exceptions Thucydides prefaces his speeches
with only a short statement of the situation under which the speech is made, and these "are
normally brief, straightforward, and factual, in striking contrast to the complexity of the
speeches" (p. 91).
[74] *Ant. Rom.* VII.66.3
[75] Reicke, *Glaube und Leben,* pp. 39-41, 50-51; Zehnle, *Peter's Pentecost Discourse,* p. 17.
[76] Note Dionysius' sense of a Roman *"Heilsgeschichte"*: Immediately after the statement cited

Above all, however, Luke's sense of appropriateness is governed by his theological concerns. It is at this point that the inner thematic ties we have seen are particularly significant. As vehicles of the Spirit, they tie speech to narrative and so strengthen Luke's message that his story is indeed a history of salvation.

---

above (n. 26) regarding "the speeches by which the extraordinary and remarkable events were brought to pass," he continues, "for if there is anything about the Roman commonwealth that is . . . deserving of imitation by all mankind . . . it is in my opinion . . . that neither the plebeians in contempt of the patricians took up arms against them . . . nor, on the other hand, the men in positions of dignity . . . destroyed all the plebeians . . . but conferring together about what was fair and just . . . they settled their controversies" (*Ant. Rom* VII.66.4-5; Cary, *Roman Antiquities*, IV, p. 347).

Paul and His Opponents in Corinth:
2 Corinthians 6:14-7:1

Bruce N. Kaye

Master, New College, University of New South Wales
Kensington, NSW, Australia

2 Cor. 6:14-7:1 has attracted quite an amount of consideration by scholars as well as having a considerable use, in more modern times, and at a popular level, in regard to the appropriate limits to a Christian's involvements with unbelievers. It has sometimes been used as the basis for a view that Christians ought not to marry unbelievers on the understanding that being "unequally yoked" is a reference to marriage.

At the scholarly level two questions have often dominated the discussion:[1] the question of whether Paul actually wrote the passage and, along with this, the character of the connection between this passage and its present context.[2] It has sometimes been suggested that this is part of the severe letter which Paul wrote to the Corinthians and which has not otherwise survived, and it has also been argued

---

[1] See M. E. Thrall,"The Problem of II Corinthians 6:14-7:1 in some Recent Discussion," *NTS*, 24 (1977), pp. 132-148.

[2] See B. Gärtner, *The Temple and the Community in Qumran and The New Testament* (Cambridge, England: Cambridge University Press, 1965), p. 50 n. 1.; D. Georgi, *Die Gegner des Paulus in 2 Korintherbrief*, (Neukirken-Vluyn: Neukirkener Verlag, 1964), p. 21, n. 3. For the view that the passage reflects the thought of the Qumran documents, see J. A. Fitzmyer, "Qumran and the Interpolated Paragraph in 2 Cor. 6:14-7:1," in *Essays on the Semitic Background to the New Testament* (London: Chapman, 1971), pp. 205-217.

that the views of this passage are those of Paul's opponents or, at least, are non-Pauline and that they have been accidentally or wrongly inserted into his letter at this point.[3]

The arguments which are deployed in relation to these two questions are usually linguistic in character and have to do, as well, with the meaning of the passage in relation to the rest of 2 Corinthians and Paul's thought generally, and the meaning of other proposed backgrounds from which the passage might be thought to have come. That discussion, naturally, implies a certain understanding of what the passage means, although this aspect is not always treated as fully as the discussion of background material.

In this essay I wish to propose that the passage refers to Paul's opponents in Corinth, that it was written by Paul, and that it is an integral part of 2 Corinthians. I shall try to support this point of view by reference to the passage and its terms, the Scriptural material in the passage, and its connection with the immediate context. This interpretation has certain implications of more general interest in regard to Paul's use of scripture and also as to the nature of apostolic authority as conceived by Paul.

A. The Passage and Its Terms

The passage we are considering falls naturally into three sections. There are the opening and closing exhortations in 6:14 and 7:1 and then, between these, is the Scriptural material of 6:16a to 6:18. The opening exhortation is supported by a series of rhetorical questions which lead to the introduction of the Scriptural material. The concluding exhortations are connected with this Scriptural material syntactically, and the main verb for the exhortations is drawn from the Scriptural material. The general orderliness of this passage can be seen from the way in which it has been set out below.

6:14: μὴ γίνεσθε ἑτεροζυγοῦντες ἀπίστοις· τίς γὰρ μετοχὴ δικαιοσύνῃ καὶ ἀνομίᾳ; ἢ τίς κοινωνία φωτὶ πρὸς σκότος;

6:15: τίς δὲ συμφώνησις Χριστοῦ πρὸς Βελιάρ, ἢ τίς μερὶς πιστῷ μετὰ ἀπίστου;

---

[3] J. J. Gunther, *St. Paul's Opponents and Their Background* (Leiden: Brill, 1973), pp. 308-313; and H. D. Betz, "2 Cor. 6:14-7:1: An Anti-Pauline Fragment?" *JBL,* 92 (1973), pp. 88-108.

6:16: τίς δὲ συγκατάθεσις ναῷ θεοῦ μετὰ εἰδώλων; ἡμεῖς γὰρ ναὸς θεοῦ ἐσμεν ζῶντος. καθὼς εἶπεν ὁ θεὸς ὅτι ἐνοικήσω ἐν αὐτοῖς καὶ ἐμπεριπατήσω, καὶ ἔσομαι αὐτῶν θεός, καὶ αὐτοὶ ἔσονταί μου λαός.

6:17: διὸ ἐξέλθατε ἐκ μέσου αὐτῶν καὶ ἀφορίσθητε, λέγει κύριος, καὶ ἀκαθάρτου μὴ ἅπτεσθε· κἀγὼ εἰσδέξομαι ὑμᾶς. . . .

6:18: καὶ ἔσομαι ὑμῖν εἰς πατέρα, καὶ ὑμεῖς ἔσεσθέ μοι εἰς υἱοὺς καὶ θυγατέρας, λέγει κύριος παντοκράτωρ.

7:1: ταύτας οὖν ἔχοντες τὰς ἐπαγγελίας ἀγαπητοί, καθαρίσωμεν ἑαυτοὺς ἀπὸ παντὸς μολυσμοῦ σαρκὸς καὶ πνεύματος, ἐπιτελοῦντες ἁγιωσύνην ἐν φόβῳ θεοῦ.

It will be seen from the text that the exhortations are expressed by means of the imperatives that appear in 6:14 and 7:1. In the structure of the passage, there are three important connectives, γάρ at 6:14, καθώς at 6:16b and οὖν at 7:1. These connectives provide a significant syntactical shape to the passage as a whole. The first exhortation, "Do not become unequally yoked," is explicated by the material introduced by the γάρ at 6:14. That is to say, the series of rhetorical questions in parallel form in 6:14 to 6:16 constitute the supporting explication for the initial exhortation not to be unequally yoked with unbelievers. This rhetorical support for the exhortation is confirmed by a second argument in support, namely, the Scriptural material which is introduced at 6:16 by καθώς. Οὖν at 7:1, in turn, illustrates that the second exhortation in 7:1 is, itself, based upon the Scriptural material in the preceding verses.

There is in the passage, therefore, a degree of coherence and even, perhaps, symmetry. However, this is not so symmetrical or so highly refined a piece of prose construction that it requires us to regard it as some separate piece. There are many passages in Paul's letters which show a similar degree of structural care in the manner in which they are assembled. What is apparent in this case, however, is that the Scriptural material and the rhetorical questions in the passage are important in holding together the two exhortations at the beginning and end of the passage. More than this, it is important as well to recognize that the rhetorical questions in 14 to 16 are, in fact, rhetorical. Their force derives from their pithy statement of alternatives rather than from their delineation of absolute exclusions.[4]

---

[4] See, in general terms, J. Weiss, "Beiträge zur Paulinischen Rhetorik," in *Theologische*

The Scriptural material has an important place as a different kind of support argument from that contained in the rhetorical questions just preceding it.

This is so, not only because it is a different kind of motivation that is being appealed to, but also because it is being expressed in a way which is quite different. There is not, here, a rhetorical argument. It is a straight application of material drawn from Scripture. So we have here, in fact, a passage which begins and ends with exhortations which have certain similarities about them and which are supported by two different kinds of motivations which are differently expressed.

A1. The Opening Exhortation

The passage begins with the exhortation, "Do not be unequally yoked with unbelievers" (γίνεσθε ἑτεροζυγοῦντες). The term ἑτεροζυγεῖν is used here only in the New Testament, and it is not used in the Septuagint, although a noun form ἑτερόζυγος is used in the Septuagint at Lev. 19:19.[5] The various forms of this compound word, in general terms, mean "out of balance" an image associated with the scale being unbalanced to one side. The term, itself, does not appear to have been used before the time of the New Testament and, in that sense, might be regarded as a new word. Hence, its meaning can still be taken as under the influence of the substantive, ζύγος, meaning a "yoke" or "balance." One needs to be careful about placing too much weight on this argument from silence since it might have more to do with our surviving evidence than actual usage. The compound συνζύγος occurs at Phil. 4:3 in the vocative and is generally translated something like "yoke fellow." The word is not listed in Liddell, Scott, and Jones, and Westcott and Hort print it as if it were a name. The term is used as a balance in Rev. 6:5, and it is used as a weight, in a metaphorical sense, in regard to slavery at 1 Tim. 6:1, or some kind of spiritual or moral burden or constraint in Gal. 5:1 and Acts 15:10.

In Matt. 11:29ff., Jesus is reported as having used the image of a yoke to characterize discipleship to himself.[6] It is more likely, in the context of Matt. 11:28ff., that ζύγος here probably has the more extended sense of weight or burden and that Jesus is using it in a very figurative way. His exhortation begins as an

---

Studien, ed. C. R. Gregory (Göttingen: Vandenhoeck & Ruprecht, 1897).

[5] See *TDNT*, II, p. 901.

[6] See M. Maher, "Take my yoke upon you: Matt. 11:29," *NTS*, 22 (1975), pp. 97-103.

appeal to those who are laboring and are heavy-laden (πεφορτισμένοι), and he assures them that he will give them rest, contrary to their present experience of being heavy-laden. If they undertake his burden or weight then they will find that as they learn from him, they will be better off because he is meek and lowly of heart and they will find rest for their souls. In other words, the imagery is taken from that of the stated situation of Jesus' listeners and he is saying that, in contrast to their present situation, if they become his disciples, their burdens will be less because of his own humility. Thus, in Matt. 11:30, he says "My burden is light [χρηστός] and my burden is easy [ἐλαφρόν]." The φορτίον here, almost certainly echoing the participle of the same word in vs. 28 of the same word by which Jesus described his hearers. In other words, Jesus is using the image of a yoke in the extended sense of a burden, somewhat similarly to the way in which it is used in Gal. 5:1 and Acts 15:10, and he is doing so in the context of drawing that image from the present situation of his hearers and saying that their present religious affiliation is to them burdensome.[7] If, however, they come to him and become his disciples and learn from him, then that burdensomeness of their present religious affiliation will be eased because he is a meek and lowly leader. In that sense, by comparison, the burden of discipleship with Jesus will be light. One might characterize this by saying that the present religious affiliation of Jesus' listeners leads to their being morally and spiritually overburdened but, if they change that religious affiliation and become his disciples, then they will be unburdened. This is because Jesus' character of humility and meekness will change not only the form but the real substance of their religious allegiance. It is important to notice that, in this context, the crucial question in the application of the imagery of "yoke" or "burden" is a change in the religious allegiance of Jesus' hearers. This point stands, also, for the usages in Galatians and Acts since, in both cases, the point of reference is the religious affiliation of the people involved. In the one case it is an allegiance to the Law, and in the other case it is an allegiance to a common Christian fellowship which gives rise to requirements laid upon Christian people by the so-called Jerusalem Council. In passing, one might note that the image is not

---

[7] E. Haenchen, *The Acts of the Apostles*, ed. R. McL. Wilson (Oxford, England: 1921 p. 446, n. 3, regards this use of "yoke" in relation to the law as Lukan and neither Pauline nor Jewish. He refers to H. L. Strack and P. Billerbeck, *Kommentar zum Neuem Testament aus Talmud und Midrash* (Munich: 1928-61), I, pp. 608ff., and says that the idea of "yoke" (of the law) "denoted the religious duties and contained no complaint that the law was hard or intolerable." One might contrast Matt. 23:15. See also J. B. Lightfoot, *Galatians* (London, Macmillan: 1876), pp. 172ff.

used anywhere in the Biblical material in reference to marriage.[8]

The second substantial term in the exhortation in 6:14 is the term "unbelievers" (ἀπίστοις). This, and its related terms, have occurred on a number of occasions in 1 Corinthians as follows:

> 6:6: "brother goes to law against brother, and this before ἀπίστων"
> 7:12: "if any brother has an ἄπιστον wife"
> 7:13: "if any woman has an ἄπιστον husband"
> 7:14: "the ἄπιστος husband is sanctified by the wife, and the ἄπιστος wife is sanctified by the husband"
> 7:15: "if the ἄπιστος separates, let him separate"
> 10:27: "if one of the ἀπίστων invites you to dinner"
> 14:22: "tongues are a sign not for believers but for ἀπίστοις, and prophesy not for ἀπίστοις but for believers"
> 14:23: "if outsiders or ἄπιστοι come in"

The first of these references relates to the courts in Corinth while the references in ch. 7 relate to mixed marriages. In 10:27 the reference is to hospitality from an unbeliever and in ch. 14 the references are to unbelievers who come into the Christian assembly. It is fairly clear that, in all of these cases, the term is applied to the unbelieving Corinthian people who find themselves in some kind of association with the Christians, either as magistrates, spouses, hosts, or visitors to the Christian assembly. There is, of course, in 1 Cor. 6 no suggestion

---

[8] The patristic use of this section is quite varied. Cyprian (*Treatises* III.62) uses 2 Cor. 6:14 in regard to marriage, along with Tob. 4:12, 1 Cor. 7:39-40, 6:15-17, and 1 Kings 11:4 ("And foreign wives turned away his heart after their gods") to support his thesis that marriage is not to be contracted with Gentiles. Tertullian (*Adv. Marc.* 5.7) takes the view that Christians must not marry heathens, on the basis of 1 Cor. 7:39, without any reference to 2 Cor. 6:14. The evidence for prohibition by ecclesiastical authority of marriage to an unbeliever is widely found later (cf. The Councils of Elvira, Agda, and Laodicea), though it was often widely disregarded, (cf. Jerome's complaint [*Adv. Jovin.* 1] that the greater part of Christian women marry heathens). A more open view is represented by Augustine (*Fide et Operibus* 19) who reports that in his time marriage to an unbeliever had ceased to be regarded as a sin. Tertullian (*Pudititia* 13-16) discussed at some length the problems of contact with evil in the Corinthian letters. In his essay on Idolaters (13) he uses 2 Cor. 6:14 against involvement in the pagan festivals cf. also *Spect.* 26, where the verse is used in regard to the Spectacles. Ignatius (*Eph.* 16) uses 2 Cor. 6:14-16 as support for exhortations not to follow "an unskillful shepherd, and receive a false opinion for the truth." Similar use in regard to truth and error in relation to Marcion is to be found in Tertullian, *Adv. Marc.* 3.8.

that the believers in Corinth would not gain fair justice at the hands of the unbelieving judges. Rather, the point is that it is a shame to the Christian fellowship that they should air their Christian-to-Christian disputes in public before unbelievers. In the case of the material relating to marriage, there is no suggestion at all that continued matrimonial contact with unbelievers is, in itself, wrong. On the contrary, Paul's attitude is that the Christian believer ought to stay with the unbelieving spouse and ought not to be the one who departs. In the case of hospitality, the same applies. The Christian ought to accept pagan hospitality and deal with the problems of conscience if and when they arise. In the case of visitors to the Christian assembly, it is clear that they are not to be excluded, although they may be startled when they come into the assembly.

There is a single reference in 2 Corinthians, at 4:4, where Paul states that the God of this world has blinded the minds of the unbelievers to keep them from seeing the light of the Gospel of the glory of Christ who is the likeness of God. In all probability this is again a reference to those who do not receive and accept the Gospel preached by Paul and his associates in Corinth.

It seems unlikely to be a specific reference to those who are preaching an alternative gospel, that is to say, Paul's opponents in Corinth, as Collange has suggested.[9] Nonetheless, it is certainly the case that this reference to unbelievers comes in a context where Paul's preaching of the Gospel, as to its substance and as to the manner in which he preaches it, is set in the sharpest contrast to the activities and the Gospel of his opponents in Corinth. It is also particularly noticeable that, in 2 Cor. 4:4 and 4:6, Paul uses the imagery of light and darkness in order to highlight the character of his Gospel as light. Furthermore, there is a reference here to the god of this world who has blinded the minds of the unbelievers to keep them from seeing this light. This light and darkness contrast and the reference to the god of this world is echoed in the rhetorical contrasts of 2 Cor. 6:14ff.

We are faced then with a very interesting situation in regard to this exhortation in 2 Cor. 6:14. On the one hand, we have the use of the term "unequally yoked" which, from such evidence as we can see, refers to an allegiance which someone undertakes or commits himself or herself to and, in the New

---

[9] J. R. Collange, *Enigmes de la Deuxième Épître de Paul aux Corinthiens* (Cambridge, England: Cambridge University Press, 1972), pp. 126ff. See also H. D. Wendland, *Neue Testament Deutsch* (Göttingen: Vandenhoeck & Ruprecht, 1968), p. 104; H. Lietzmann, *An die Korinther I, II* (Tübingen: Mohr, 1910), p. 181.

Testament material in particular, an allegiance which has a religious connotation. One might say, not unreasonably, that the term suggests a relationship to a religious leader such as for example in Matt. 11, Jesus himself.

On the other hand, the allegiances here are said not to be unequal in relation to unbelievers. The term "unbelievers" in Paul's letters to the Corinthians seems clearly to be used to describe those people in Corinth who did not believe the Christian Gospel as preached by Paul. Furthermore, there is ample evidence to show that Paul does not seek any kind of exclusiveness for the Christians' relationships with these Corinthian unbelievers.

There is some suggestion in the 2 Cor. 4 passages that, when Paul is talking about unbelievers, he has in mind the preaching of his opponents which he describes in the starkest and darkest possible terms. The combination of these two terms, then, simply does not make sense in terms of the accustomed usage. It is this point which has prompted commentators to suggest that this is not a Pauline idea and that, therefore, this passage cannot be regarded as having been written by Paul. The crux of the suggestion in this essay is that the second term in this exhortation, ἀπίστοις, refers, in this case, to Paul's opponents, in which case, of course, the exhortation would make very good sense in terms of the characteristic usage of the yoke imagery.

A2. The Rhetorical Pairs

It can be seen from the text, as set out above, that the rhetorical questions which follow the opening exhortation have a certain symmetrical character to them. The first two rhetorical questions stand together stylistically and the third and fourth, similarly, stand together while the last leads on to the concluding statement in the section that we, ourselves, are the temple of the living God. It is not uncommon for Paul to use a series of rhetorical questions as he does here in order to emphasize a point.[10] One might compare, for example, Rom. 8:31-36 where a series of rhetorical questions emphasizes the certainty of the Christians' assurance.

The terms of the contrast are drawn in various ways and each, perhaps, contributes something to the picture and thereby adds to the reinforcement that the

---

[10] See generally R. Bultmann, *Der Stil der paulinischen Predigt* (Göttingen: Vandenhoeck & Ruprecht, 1910); N. Schneider, *Die rhetorische Eigenart der paulinische Antithese* (Tübingen: Mohr, 1920); B. N. Kaye, *The Thought Structure of Romans* (Austin, Texas: Scholia Press, 1973), pp. 14ff.

whole set gives to the initial exhortation. Righteousness, as a term, is widely used by Paul, particularly in Romans and Galatians, but in 2 Cor. 3:9 it is used directly to refer to Paul's ministry.

That ministry refers to a dispensation of righteousness, in contrast to the ministry of Moses. In 2 Cor. 6:7 Paul argues that he promotes his ministry by means of the weapons of righteousness. It is important to notice that, in this passage, the catalog of contrasts moves from physical sufferings to those of accusation and opposition to his ministry. In other words, in both 2 Cor. 3 and 6, righteousness is used as a term to characterize Paul's preaching ministry and to characterize it in a situation where it is contrasted with other ministries. The term ἀνομία is not used elsewhere in the Corinthian letters although it is interestingly used in Romans 6:19 in contrast to righteousness and in combination with the term ἀκαθαρσία.[11]

The light and darkness imagery is used in 2 Cor. 4, 6 and 6:14 where Paul's ministry is contrasted to that of others. One might note as well that, in 2 Cor. 11:14, Paul claims that Satan disguises himself as an angel of light.

The third contrast involves the terms "Christ" and "Beliar." The term "Christ," of course, is widely used in Paul, but "Beliar" is used by Paul only here. One might, not unfairly, compare the usage of Satan at 1 Cor. 5:5 and 7:5 and again at 2 Cor. 2:11. Here Satan is to be the accuser of the individual Christian and of the Christian community. In 2 Cor. the question at stake is the restoring of an offender. Barrett refers the term at 2 Cor. 2:11 to would-be leaders in Corinth, that is to say, Paul's opponents who, according to Titus, had been voted down.[12] It is clear from 2 Cor. 2:9 that the test is allegiance or obedience to Paul and his ministry. One might refer, as well, to 2 Cor. 11:13ff. where the false apostles are described as deceitful workmen disguising themselves as apostles of Christ. By way of explanation Paul adds that this is no wonder since even Satan disguises himself as an angel of light.

The contrast, fairly clearly, is between the Christ whom Paul preaches and who is represented by Paul's ministry and "Beliar" and his agents. Paul's opponents disguise themselves as if they were ministers of the same Gospel but are, in fact, false apostles and deceitful workmen.

---

[11] See 2 Cor. 7:1.

[12] C. K. Barrett, *A Commentary on the Second Epistle to the Corinthians* (New York: Harper & Row, 1973), p. 23, and "Ο ΑΔΙΚΗΣΑΣ (II Cor. 7:12)," in *Verborum Veritas,* ed. O. Bocher and K. Haaker (Wuppertal: Brockhaus, 1970), p. 155.

The fourth contrast between faith and unfaith or belief and unbelief is much more general, and its antecedents in the Corinthian letters are more difficult to determine. On the other hand, the image of the Christian community at Corinth as being the temple of God has been used by Paul at 1 Cor. 3:16ff. and, in a more individual way, the Corinthians' bodies are said to be a temple of the Holy Spirit at 1 Cor. 6:19. Idols, of course, have been subject to some discussion in 1 Corinthians and they are clearly representatives of that foreign opposing power of darkness which stands against the Christian and the Christian community. In Paul's mind, idols do not have any substance or reality but, nonetheless, one cannot imagine that there can be a correspondence between idols and Christ, between the cup of the Lord and the cup of demons. It is clear, not only from the structure of the rhetorical pairs in this verse, but also from the terms which are used, that the last contrast, between the temple of God and idols, is a preparation for the concluding statement in vs. 17. This, in turn, is an introduction and connection with the scripture material which follows. One might note here, as well, that the ἀπιστοῦ at 2 Cor. 6:15 at the end of the fourth rhetorical question may well be intended to correspond to the ἀπίστοις in 2 Cor. 6:14. The last contrast serves to introduce the next argument in support of the exhortation at 6:14.

A3. The Scripture Material

There are, essentially, three quotations in this section at 2 Cor. 6:16, 17 and 18. It is possible that, in 2 Cor. 6:16, an allusion is being made to Lev. 6:12. However, Ez. 37:27 is textually closer and, in terms of sense, more immediately relevant. Ez. 37:15-28 is an oracle on the reunification of the divided nation under King David. It begins in vss. 15-20 with the image of two sticks which the Prophet is to lay out. In vss. 21-28, the meaning of this image is explained. God will bring the nation back to the land which he had promised them (37:21). Then God himself will make them into *one* nation, not two, under *one* King (37:22). The people will then not defile themselves, but God himself will cleanse them: "They shall be My people and I shall be their God" (37:23). Thus, David will be their king and shepherd and they will keep the ordinances and dwell in the land. God will make a covenant of peace and will set his sanctuary in their midst, "I will be their God and they shall be my people."

There are a number of terms in this passage in LXX Ezekiel, apart from the quotation, which have associations in 2 Cor. 6:14-7:1:

Ez. 37	2 Cor. 6:14-7:1
vs. 23: ἀνομιῶν	6:14: ἀνομία
vs. 23: καθαριῶ	7:1: καθαρίσωμεν
vs. 26: τὰ ἅγιά μου	7:1: ἁγιωσύνην
vs. 27: ἡ κατασκήνωσίς μου	6:16: ναὸς θεοῦ
vs. 28: ὁ ἁγιάζων	7:1: ἁγιωσύνην

The quotation from Ez. 37:27 is the second occurrence of the theme as it is stated in the oracle in Ezekiel. The point of the oracle in Ezekiel is the uniting of Israel into one nation under one ruler or shepherd, namely, King David. The passage refers to God's "holy place" being amongst his people rather than them being the temple as in 2 Cor. 16:16.

The quotation in 2 Cor. 6:17 seems most probably to be from Isa. 52:11 which, like Ez. 37, refers to the return of Israel, after the exile, to the Promised Land. The prophetic oracle comes just before a Servant Song and begins in 52:7 with a reference to the preacher and the watchman. The quotation comes from the end of the section and has numerous Exodus overtones.

It is less easy to discern the allusion being made in 2 Cor. 6:18. It is most likely to 2 Sam. 7:14, although this reference is addressed to the King in Israel.

It is striking that the two most clearly identifiable Scripture references are cast in the context of the restoration and the uniting of the nation of Israel and, in the Ezekiel passage, it is quite significant that that uniting of the nation will take place under one single leader. What the Scripture passages, therefore, contribute to the 2 Corinthian passage is not just simply some sense of the peculiarity and distinctiveness of Israel's vocation but the central necessity of the nation being united under the one leader or shepherd. The question at stake is as much the unity of the nation under one leader as its restoration. The appeal, therefore, is not simply to a restoration in quite general terms, but to a restoration under a single leader. In the context of 2 Corinthians and Paul's occupation throughout the letter with the false apostles and his opponents in Corinth who are dividing the Corinthian community, that contextual background has powerful connotations.[13]

---

[13] By way of contrast, the corruption of Israel is often attributed by the prophets to the

A4. The Concluding Exhortation

The terms of this last exhortation are fairly clearly drawn from Scripture material. The call to cleansing and the term used here is not at all common in Paul's letters. Indeed, the verb occurs only in Eph. 5:26 and in Tit. 2:14. However, it does occur quite significantly in Ez. 37:23. In regard to the term καθαρίζειν, one perhaps, compare the passage in Jer. 23:15 where the term is used in the Septuagint and refers to the pollution of the land because of the false prophets in Jerusalem. The exhortation is fairly clearly connected with, and draws its strength from, the immediately preceding Scripture material. The term ἐπιτελοῦντες connotes bringing something to a conclusion which has already been started and, here, might well suggest the completing of the restoration of Paul's standing in the Corinthian community which has already begun, as described in 2 Cor. 2.

This examination of the terms and structure of the passage 2 Cor. 6:14-7:1, and the Scriptural material which is such a central part of the argument in support of the exhortations contained in the passage, suggests a clear area of thought which fits well with the conflict of authority which underlies the whole of 2 Corinthians. That conflict of authority is between Paul and his opponents and the acceptance by the Corinthians of Paul's apostolic authority rather than the false and benighted authority of his opponents. The imagery of the Scripture material and the terms and connotations of the rhetorical questions point in this same direction. Unbelief, therefore, is the mark of those who stand over against Paul and his Gospel.

The use of ἀπίστοις in 6:14 in this context, therefore, can be reasonably regarded as an extension of the meaning of the term elsewhere in 2 Corinthians and, thus, to refer to Paul's opponents.

B. The Immediate Context

The most directly adjacent material to this passage are the exhortations contained in 2 Cor. 6:11-13 and 7:2-5. These adjacent exhortations are worth noting for our purposes and, as well, we will need to look at the developing argument.

---

national leaders. For example, Jereboam in 2 Chr. 13:8ff., Amaziah in 2 Chr. 25:14ff., Jezebel and the prophets of Baal in 1 Kings 18, Korah in Nu. 16. There are general references to leaders in Isa. 3:12. See also Jer. 5:31; 14:14; 23:21-22.; 27:9; Ez. 13:4; Micah 3:5-8; Zech. 13:2ff., and compare Wis. 2:24.

B1. The Adjacent Exhortations

The exhortations in 2 Cor. 6:11-13 have a clear connection with the preceding material in so far as vs. 11 is a statement of Paul's attitude towards the Corinthians which he has just spoken of in the preceding part of ch. 6 with deep feeling and emotion. When he says, in 6:12, "you are not restricted by us," he refers to the fact that he has placed no obstacle in anyone's way (compare 6:3). The point of 2 Cor. 6:12 is in the second half of the verse, namely, that the Corinthians do not reciprocate this openhearted approach that Paul has towards them. "They are," he says, "restricted in their own affections," that is to say, in their affections towards him. Therefore, the appeal in 6:13 is that they should widen their hearts also towards Paul.

It has often been pointed out that this exhortation in 2 Cor. 6:12-13 leads naturally on to the exhortation in 2 Cor. 7:2. "Open your hearts to us," as it is often translated (although literally, "make room for us"), clearly contrasts with the statement in 2 Cor. 6:12 where he says that he is not restricted towards them. Three reasons are offered in support of this exhortation: We have wronged no one; we have corrupted no one; we have taken advantage of no one. In other words, just as in 2 Cor. 6 he stated that he set no obstacle in the way of the Corinthians' affections towards him, and that he, himself, was not restricted in his feelings towards them, so, now, again in a different form, he says that there is no ground for them being restricted in their affections towards him. There is no obstacle that he has placed in their way of having wronged, corrupted or taken advantage of anyone. 2 Cor. 7:3 quickly makes the point that Paul does not wish to condemn the Corinthians but rather he wants to establish the proper, fully open reciprocation for which he has appealed in 2 Cor. 6:13. he writes not to condemn but because "we live and die together."[14]

Both of these exhortations in 1 Cor. 6:13 and 7:2 clearly refer to Paul's relations with the Corinthians. On the one hand, Paul is open towards the Corinthians and full-hearted in his affections towards them. He has placed no obstacle in the way of their being able to reciprocate that, although, as a matter of fact, they appear not to do so. Therefore, he appeals to them to open their hearts to him, not to be restricted in their feelings, but to make a place for him in their affections.

---

[14] 2 Cor. 7:3.

Now it is quite possible, of course, to argue that the similarity of these exhortations means that the intervening material can be regarded as some kind of interpolation. However, it is just as reasonable, and, in the context of our earlier discussion, makes eminently good sense, to regard the intervening material as a more detailed and supported appeal to the Corinthians to withdraw themselves from those opponents of Paul in Corinth who have been attracting the Corinthians' affections away from Paul.

B2. The Developing Argument

C. K. Barrett analyzes the structure of 2 Corinthians as follows: introduction (1:1-11); Paul's plans for Corinth and their working out in the past (1:12-2:13); the purpose expressed in mission and ministry (2:14-7:4); Paul's plans for Corinth and their working out in the future (7:5-9:15); the future threatened (10:1-13:10); conclusion (13:11-13). In terms of this analysis, the passage 6:14-7:4 is entitled "Response to God is Exclusive." As the commentary makes clear, the appeal is that Paul's Corinthian readers should respond to God exclusively in the context of a discussion about the mission and ministry of Paul to them. Barrett thinks that, in 2 Cor. 7:5, the narrative is resumed from 2:13. These divisions, of course, are not by any means absolute and it is clear that narrative and biography are both integrally related in the expression of Paul's theological understanding, both of his own mission and of the position of the Corinthians and his opponents in Corinth.

We may, at this point, draw attention to some elements in the way in which the picture in chs. 5 and 6 develops in terms of the theme of Paul's mission, the Corinthians' relations with Paul and the position of Paul's opponents. The first ten verses of ch. 5 give Paul's personal orientation on life, and how he views his situation, Then, in vs. 11, he says it is because of this that he persuades men. In other words, his mission arises from that personal orientation which he has expounded in the first ten verses of ch. 5. That orientation is founded on Christ's representative death, a point to which he returns in vs. 16 and which leads him, again, to the conclusion that it is because of this that we are ambassadors. Indeed, he goes so far as to say that God actually makes his appeal through vs. [15]. In the first ten verses of ch. 6, Paul extends this point and says that he, in his mission, works "together with God." Thus, he raises no obstacle so that no fault may be

---

[15] 2 Cor. 5:20.

found in his work and, as servants of God, "we commend ourselves in every way." All this is by way of exposition of Paul's understanding of how he views them.

There are, of course, underlying hints of an indirect kind to difficulties in his mission, perhaps even difficulties at Corinth. But it is clear that Paul regards himself, in a very direct and immediate way, as God's representative as an Apostle in Corinth to the Corinthians.[16] Because of this, the Gospel which he preaches, and which they receive, is intimately and directly related to the way in which they view him as an Apostle. Then, in 2 Cor. 6:12b, Paul explicitly refers to difficulty in the matter of the Corinthians' response to himself. This is the first time we have had such an explicit and direct reference since 2:5 and the implied difficulties in 2 Cor. 1.

If we now move to the context as it develops after 7:4, Paul discusses the news which he has received from Corinth. The problem had been the Corinthians' attitude towards Paul. He tells them that he has received news, through Titus, of their zeal for Paul himself. Paul here refers to the letter which he had written to them and his anxiety about it, and them. Now, however, he is comforted by Titus' news, and not only by the news which Titus brings but also by the report which Titus himself gives of his own reception at Corinth. Titus himself had been received with fear and trembling.[17] It is interesting to notice that the person of Titus, as a representative of Paul, reflects the attitude which Paul is looking for in the Corinthians towards himself. Zeal, affection and allegiance from the Corinthians toward Paul as their Apostle and ambassador of God is what he is looking for. Ch. 8 then goes on to talk about the collection and the role of the Macedonian churches in that regard.

In this context, from ch. 5 to the end of ch. 7, the dominant theme is the question of Paul's attitude towards the Corinthians, his understanding of his mission to them as an Apostle and as an authoritative representative of God to them, and the difficulty that the Corinthians appear not to have received him as just such an Apostle. This cannot have been a universal rejection of Paul and, as ch. 7 shows, it was not a permanent one since the news and the experience of Titus reassure Paul about the Corinthians. The argument is a mixture of general points and particular personal issues and there is a continuing background of Paul's opponents

---

[16] Cf. 1 Cor. 4:14-21 where, having conceded a complementary role for himself and Apollos, he nonetheless claims a special and unique relationship to them as father, because by his preaching they were "begotten."

[17] 2 Cor. 7:15.

in Corinth. His mission is thought of in divine terms and hence rejection of it is a rejection of the Gospel which Paul preaches. The direct appeal to the Corinthians at 6:11 is the first sustained direct appeal of its kind and it comes as the climax to what Paul has been saying about himself and his mission. It stands as the most obvious and natural thing that he should then go on to say how the Corinthians ought to regard the opponents who appear to have been causing such difficulty in Corinth: They are not to be "unequally yoked with them."

"To Predestine" (Προορίζω): The Use of a Pauline Term in Extrabiblical Tradition

Robert Sloan

Professor of Religion, Baylor University
Waco, Texas

In the spring of 1976, in what the University of Basel, Switzerland calls the "summer semester," I attended Professor Bo Reicke's lectures on the book of Romans. My sporadic notes in no way reflect Professor Reicke's orderly progression through the epistle, but they remind me nonetheless of what were for me the most thought-provoking comments of the semester. The occasion was May 12, according to my notes, and Professor Reicke was dealing with ch. 8. It was at vss. 29-30 that my notes reflect—by an infusion of detail—a certain upsurge of interest on my part. A lecture that was already interesting became engaging. What kept us talking for some time after the lecture was Professor Reicke's contention that the sorites, or "heaping up" of terms, of 8:29-30—the references to God's foreknowing (προέγνω), predestining (προώρισεν), calling (ἐκάλεσεν), justifying (ἐδικαίωσεν), and glorifying (ἐδόξασεν)—was not an *ordo salutis* after the fashion of the orthodox theologians of the seventeenth century. Rather, our professor maintained, no temporal progression or successive chronological linkage was presupposed at all; instead, the theologically loaded words of the passage referred to different dimensions of the salvation of God. The justly famous passage related

128 *Good News in History*

not chronologically different moments, but logically distinguishable aspects of salvation that lay, as it were, "within" one another. I have since both heard and read somewhat similar viewpoints, but for me none was more engagingly stated than Professor Reicke's observations of that May 12. His remarks continue to serve as a touchstone and point of departure for my present thinking regarding the Pauline soteriology as it relates to that passage.

The fact is, however, that viewpoints which see 8:29-30 as some kind of *ordo salutis* involving a temporal progression which begins in "prehistory" are very common. The remarks of C. E. B. Cranfield are typical. Regarding προέγνω:

> The thought expressed by the προ- is not just that God's gracious choice of those referred to preceded their knowledge of Him, but that it took place before the world was created (1:431).

προώρισεν:

> This divine predestination or decision which appoints for the elect their goal is, like their election, to be thought of as taking place πρὸ καταβολῆς κόσμου (1:432).

and ἐκάλεσεν:

> With this third link of the chain we are in the realm of historical time.[1]

Such assertions, however, seem more dependent upon certain theological assumptions than hard evidence gained from texts reflecting the historical use (sacred and secular) of προορίζω.

A forthcoming article[2] will examine the *Pauline* uses of the word "to predestine" (προορίζω). Indeed, that work (though not quite the finished product) actually preceded and generated this one. My study of the use of προορίζω in 1 Cor. 2:7, Rom. 8:29-30, and Eph. 1:5, 11 has convinced me that, in Paul's writings at least, the term προορίζω has *no* contextual or theological association that automatically, or necessarily, predisposes its meaning to refer, without further qualification, to the eternal purposes of God executed and/or decided "before the foundation of the world." My study of Paul, in other words, convinces me (1) that Professor Reicke was correct in his assessment of the sorites of Rom. 8:29-30, that

[1] C. E. B. Cranfield, *The Epistle to the Romans* (Edinburgh: Clark, 1975-79), I, pp. 431-432.
[2] R. B. Sloan, "Predestination in Pauline Tradition: A Christocentric Hope" (forthcoming).

is, that there is no temporal progression implied in the sequence of given terms, and (2) that the term "to predestine" can be applied to any two points on a time-line, with no necessity for the predestining act to have occurred in a "before the foundation of the world" moment, only to be finally realized, as a predestined event, in history as we know it. Rather, to elaborate (2) above, I would maintain that the term προορίζω need only apply to two points on a time-line, the first, which I call the *"predestining* moment" or "act," and the second, a chronologically later point, which I call the *"predestined* moment" or "event." The predestining act or decision establishes or fixes "ahead of time" some predestined act or event now (at the predestining moment) "pre-determined" to come about. However, there is no necessity—at least within the term προορίζω itself, as used in the Pauline literary corpus—for the predestining act or decision to occur "before the foundation of the world" or "before the ages."

My study of Pauline occurrences of the term προορίζω soon led me to inquire as to its use in other Biblical/canonical literature and, especially, in nonbiblical Greek. As for Biblical literature, my search was brief. The only occurrences in the New Testament outside the five occurrences in the Pauline corpus is at Acts 4:28 where προορίζω seems to refer to the accomplishment of the divine will in the form of the fulfillment of Scripture: what the Scriptures predicted has come to pass.[3] As for the Septuagint, the word does not occur; but the notion of God's having pre-determined certain events is certainly not alien to Old Testament literature (see 2 Kings 19:25; Isa. 22:11), especially the prophets for whom God is the Lord of history and the one in whose hands Israel's future lies. Such predeterminations are inextricably linked no doubt to notions of promise, fulfillment, and covenant faithfulness, but *when* such predeterminations occur and *when* they come to fulfillment relates in the literature more to the historical situation of the given prophet and is not apparent from the terminology itself. Certainly the answer to such questions *vis-à-vis* the Old Testament is more likely to be in terms of prophecy and/or "history" than a putative "pre-history," or "before the foundation of the world." The study of extrabiblical uses of προορίζω, however, though difficult, did not prove in vain. Though the *theological subject* of "predestination" is difficult, if not maddening, the use of the term προορίζω in extrabiblical literature is less daunting. It is a matter of examining a relatively few texts and contexts.

---

[3] A brief look at Acts 4:28 is included in my forthcoming article (see n. 2) on the Pauline uses.

This study, therefore, seeks to bring clarity to a difficult subject at only one very limited, though important, point: the uses of the word "to predestine" (προορίζω) in extrabiblical literature dating from 100 B.C.E. to 200 C.E.

A compound of ὁρίζω ("to fix," "determine," or "appoint") and the preposition πρό ("before," "previously," or "in front of"), προορίζω means "to fix previously" or "ahead of time"—"to pre-determine." A computer-assisted search of the Greek textual databank of *TLG* (*Thesaurus Lingua Graece*, University of California at Irvine) using the Pandora software from the Harvard Perseus Project produced only two "hits" (terminology used in the software) using the parameters of 100 B.C.E. to ca. 120 C.E.[4] The first is in Ignatius of Antioch (*Ephesians, inscr.*), where the soon-to-be martyred Syrian bishop, in a conscious reminiscence of the earlier Pauline, Ephesian counterpart, refers to the Ephesian church as "predestined before the ages" (προωρισμένη πρὸ αἰώνων).[5] Two observations seem relevant. First, the Ignatian use of προορίζω here is almost certainly an imitation of Pauline language—in this case, however, since it uses πρὸ αἰώνων instead of πρὸ καταβολῆς κόσμου, it may be more 1 Cor. 2:7 that is being reflected than Ephesians 1:4-5. Second, the qualifying prepositional phrase referring the act of predestination to pre-history is deemed necessary; that is, it is apparently *not* redundant. Put another way, the term προορίζω does not *by itself* carry or imply pre-temporal, eternal notions.

The other extant use of προορίζω between 100 B.C.E. and 120 C.E. is in a nontheological text: Plutarch, *Quomodo adulator ab amico internoscatur*, in *Moralia* 70, "B," 3, where the discussion relates to the circumstances in which a true friend, as opposed to a flatterer, should be frank or even severe in the face of the moral failures of a friend. Plutarch writes: ὁ μὲν οὖν κοινὸς οὕτω προωρίσθω καιρός ("Let therefore the general occasion [for frankness and severity] be thus *set out*"). It is clear that this instance of προορίζω refers to the essayist's generalizing effort at defining "ahead of time" (for the moral benefit of his readers) the kinds of situations in which a true friend is compelled to frankness. There is of course no connection here to eternity or pre-history.

When the parameters of our search for προορίζω were extended to 200 C.E., the number of occurrences, particularly in Christian literature, began to increase.

---

[4] Unless otherwise indicated, the referencing system given is according to the *TLG* format.

[5] J. B. Lightfoot, *The Apostolic Fathers: Part II, S. Ignatius, S. Polycarp*, second ed. (Grand Rapids, Mich.: Baker, reprint 1981), p. 23.

We may note, first of all, however, three important, nontheological references in Galen and Pseudo-Galen. In Galen, *In Hippocratis librum de fracturis commentarii* III, 18, B, 540, 5, the author speaks of an issue in medical case study (related to swelling in singular or multiple bone fractures) not "previously set out," that is, which did not come under discussion in a prior, related passage (εἰρηκὼς γὰρ ὀγκηρότερα γίνεσθαι τὰ ὄστεα τῶν θεραπευομένων διὰ τῆς πρώτης παραγωγῆς, οὐ προωρίσατο πότερον ἁπάντων ἢ τινων, ἀλλ᾽ ἕν τε τῇ νῦν ῥήσει. . . .). An analogous use in Pseudo-Galen, *De Remediis Parabilibus* 14, 555, 5, employs προωρισθέντων to refer to the separation or setting apart of certain "previously set apart" substances. The force of the προ- is, as in the Galen passage cited above, something like "previously" or "formerly." Another occurrence of προορίζω, lying within a severely corrupted text, appears to function in a way similar to the other Galenic readings (Pseudo-Galen, *Historia Philosophica* 7,15).

As many as three theological uses of προορίζω were found (depending on the authenticity of the variants) in the Greek fragments of Irenaeus' *Adversus Haereses*. The first is from the Antiochene theologian Theodoret of Cyrus (c. 393-c. 458):

τοῦ πνεύματος οὖν κατελθόντος
διὰ τὴν προωρισμένην οἰκονομίαν. . . .[6]

It is in fact a variant reading and not the preferred reading in *Sources Chrétiennes*,[7] in which προειρημένην ("previously mentioned") is substituted for προωρισμένην. Whatever the correct textual reading, the meaning of προωρισμένην does not, in this context, refer to a divine determination "before the ages." Rather, if refers to certain scriptural anticipations (Isaiah 11:2, 61:1; Joel 2:28-32; Psalm 51:12, etc.) which came to pass with the descent of the Spirit.

The next two hits in Irenaeus were found in Greek fragments retained by John of Damascus (675-749). The text is II.33.5 in *Sources Chrétiennes* and contains two occurrences—προώρισε and προωρισμένης, though the latter instance could be προορίσεως. The fragment reads:

᾽Αλλ᾽ ὡς εἷς ἕκαστος ἡμῶν ἴδιον σῶμα λαμβάνει, οὕτως καὶ ἰδίαν ἔχει ψυχήν.
Οὐ γὰρ οὕτω πτωχὸς οὐδὲ ἄπορος ὁ Θεός, ὥστε μὴ ἕνι ἑκάστῳ σώματι ἰδίαν

---

[6] The reference in *TLG* is (liber 3), 1, 1, 1, 24, 2.

[7] Irénée de Lyon, *Contre les Hérésies*, in *Sources Chrétiennes*, ed. A. Rousseau and L. Doutreleau (Paris: Cerf, 1974), III, pp. 17, 4.

κεχαρίσθαι ψυχήν, καθάπερ καὶ ἴδιον χαρακτῆρα. Καὶ διὰ τοῦτο, πληρωθέντος τοῦ ἀριθμοῦ ὃν αὐτὸς παρ' αὐτῷ προώρισε, πάντες οἱ γραφέντες εἰς ζωὴν ἀναστήσονται ἴδια ἔχοντες σώματα καὶ ἰδίας ψυχὰς καὶ ἴδια Πνεύματα ἐν οἷς εὐηρέστησαν τῷ θεῷ, οἱ δὲ τῆς κολάσεως ἄξιοι ἀπελεύσονται εἰς αὐτὴν καὶ αὐτοι ἰδίας ἔχοντες ψυχὰς καὶ ἴδια σώματα ἐν οἷς ἀπέστησαν ἀπὸ τῆς τοῦ θεοῦ χρηστότητος. Καὶ παύσονται ἑκάτεροι τοῦ γεννᾶν ἔτι καὶ γεννᾶσθαι καὶ γαμεῖν καὶ γαμεῖσθαι, ἵνα τὸ σύμμετρον φῦλον τῆς προωρισμένης ἀπὸ Θεοῦ ἀνθρωπότητος ἀποτελεσθὲν τὴν ἁρμονίαν τηρήσῃ τοῦ Πατρός.[8]

These references occur in a passage which argues against the existence of souls in other bodies or in a prior state of being. Instead, Irenaeus argues (and the meaning is the same in each instance here of προορίζω), God gives each body its own soul, and thus the full number of bodies and souls and spirits corresponds to the "predetermined," "fixed," or "foreordained," will of God. The text does not indicate when this decision of God takes place as to the full or completed number of humanity. It certainly could be "before the ages," but our text does not say. It only demands that a meaning like "previously decided upon" be used. In any case, the Irenaean citations are fragments embedded within fifth- and eighth-century texts and may simply reflect Greek (re-)translations of the Latin *ante definiti* and *ante praefiniti*, respectively.

Other hits were recorded. The spurious "Clement of Rome" literature is suggestive, but its mixed origins and notorious difficulty with regard to date make it problematic for the researcher to project or deduce historical patterns or development for προορίζω based upon the five discovered occurrences. Nonetheless, it may be noted that one instance of the participle (*Homilies* 6, 1, 1, 1) refers to a "previously agreed upon" or "appointed" place of meeting (τρίτῃ δὲ ἡμέρᾳ εἰς τὸ προωρισμένον τῆς Τύρου χωρίον). A second instance refers to a "foreordained law" which those who were ignorant (of the given law) disobeyed and thus fell into the clutches of the king of this present age (Satan) and his demons (*Homilies* 8, 22, 2, 2). The "foreordained law" (τὸν προορισθέντα νόμον) in question, in the context of Homily 8, was a law, delivered by an angel of God to the half-breed (angel/human; cf. Genesis 6:1-6) survivors of the flood, to the effect that these demonic giants could have control over no human unless the human should voluntarily turn away from God's law to impurity by the practice of idolatry, adultery, murder, etc. Thus, the given allusion to a "foreordained law" refers to a previous *historical* (that

---

[8] The references in *TLG* are (libri 1-2), 1, 2, 54, 1, 5; (libri 1-2), 1, 2, 54, 1, 12.

is, not "before the ages") giving of a divine law as an act of revelation.

The Clementine evidence is, however, mixed. *Recognitions* 3, 26, 4, 4 does seem to refer, without a qualifying prepositional phrase, to a pre-historical divine determination (a number of "good souls predestined by God to fill the world"). On the other hand, two other uses (in virtually identical phrases) of προορίζω (*Homilies* 7, 6, 3, 1 and *Epitome Altera* 56, 6) combine traditional language with the use of προορίζω so that those things ("conditions") which are "predestined" are likewise, in an explanatory way, also said to be "fixed by God before the foundation of the world" (καὶ αὐτὸς παρὰ τοῦ θεοῦ ὁρισμούς). Thus, on the one hand, it is clear that the word προορίζω is at the time of these occurrences attracting to itself implicit pre-historical notions of things predestined "before the foundation of the world." On the other hand, it should not go unnoticed that explanatory expressions *are* still being provided: The force of the prefix προ- is being defined (but the definition is being given, not presumed) in terms of "πρὸ καταβολῆς κόσμου." Thus, some (especially theological) definition for προορίζω is still considered necessary. The meaning of "before the foundation of the world," though clearly possible in the second century, was not, as other examples have also shown, self-understood in the word προορίζω itself.

To sum up, the use of προορίζω in Plutarch, Galen, and Pseudo-Galen clearly indicates the fact that προορίζω, as a term, has no necessary connection to pre-historical events or realities "before the ages" or "before the foundation of the world." It could, perhaps, be argued that such is not surprising given the non-theological nature of these texts. However, the Clementine literature likewise indicates (1) a familiarity with and capacity to use προορίζω to mean "pre-determined" or "appointed" *without* thereby implying some notion of "before the ages" (*Homilies* 6, 1, 1, 1). Furthermore, (2) in a clearly theological context, the Clementine literature (*Homilies* 8, 22, 2, 2) also uses προορίζω to refer to a predestining act of God which is originally ordained *in history* and likewise comes to its predestined fulfillment *in history*. The same kind of evidence as summarized here for the Clementine literature is reflected in the Irenaean fragments, but the fact that two of the three Irenaean occurrences are textual variants, and all three are in literature considerably later (the fifth and eighth centuries) than our given parameters, makes us reluctant to make much use of these fragments.

Eventually, of course, the attachment of some such notion of "before the ages" to προορίζω did take place in Christian literature so that the use of such a qualifying phrase became theologically redundant and could be dropped. Clement of Alexandria and especially Origen illustrate this phenomenon. But such a phenomenon seems generally to be a Christian/theological development of the term. What we have seen of the extrabiblical uses of προορίζω, especially in non-theological contexts—but also evidenced in theological literature—shows the term used within what we are calling fully "historical" parameters. That is, *both* the predestining act and the predestined event occur within the range of this history, as opposed to a "before the foundation of the earth" setting for the predestining act or decision.

It is difficult, given the nature of the extrabiblical texts that we have examined, to establish any clear-cut patterns of development for the use of προορίζω between 100 B.C.E. and 200 C.E., though we suspect that the "eternalizing" of προορίζω—as a term that needs no qualification to be understood as a divine act "before the ages"—is a generally later, and developing, phenomenon. Certainly by the time of the literary career of Origen (c. 185-c. 254) προορίζω may be understood as a reference to the "pre-historical," "before the foundation of the world" decisions of God without any qualifying references.[9]

One conclusion at least is clear to this author based on the limited findings given above: A study of the uses of προορίζω in Pauline tradition which seeks to reflect and/or show some continuity with the extrabiblical usage of that term may not be approached with the kind of assumption reflected in Cranfield's remarks given above.[10] "Before the ages" is *not* without further ado packed into the word

---

[9] As the *TLG* evidence of occurrences in Origen clearly indicates.

[10] This kind of uncritical assimilation of προορίζω to notions related to the pre-temporal purposes of God is repeatedly evidenced in word books, commentaries on Rom. 8:29-30 and Eph. 1:5, 11, and other literature ancient and modern which in any way touches upon the Pauline idea of "predestination." In addition to Cranfield, as noted above, we could add the writings of John Calvin, *Institutes of the Christian Religion*, III, 21-22, and *passim*; K. L. Schmidt, "προορίζω," *TDNT*, V, p. 456; P. Jacobs and H. Krienke, "Foreknowledge, Providence, Predestination," *DNTT*, I, pp. 695-696; D. E. H. Whiteley, *The Theology of St. Paul*, second ed. (Oxford, England: Blackwell, 1974), pp. 89-98; E. P. Sanders, *Paul and Palestinian Judaism* (Philadelphia: Fortress Press, 1977), pp. 446-447; J. D. G. Dunn, *Romans 1-8*, (Dallas: Word, 1988), p. 482; J. Ziesler, *Paul's Letter to the Romans* (Philadelphia: Trinity Press International, 1989), pp. 225-227; P. Achtemeier, *Romans* (Atlanta: John Knox Press, 1985), pp. 144-148; M. Barth, *Ephesians: Introduction, Translation, and Commentary on Chapters 1-3*, (Garden City, New York: Doubleday, 1974), pp. 79-80, 105-109; F. F. Bruce, *The Epistles to the Colossians, to Philemon, and to the Ephesians* (Grand Rapids, Mich.: Eerdmans, 1984), pp. 254-264; Leon Morris, *The Epistle to the Romans* (Grand Rapids, Mich.: Eerdmans, 1988), pp. 330-334. Some commentators have rightly emphasized the eschatological *goal* of the predestining act: e.g., Achtemeier, *Romans*, pp. 143-148; Bruce, *Epistles to the Colossians, to Philemon, and to the Ephesians*, p. 264; Dunn, *Romans 1-8*, pp. 482-486, 495; but all that I have surveyed still relegate the initial predestining act to the realm of "pre-history" and/or the "willed" purposes of God.

προορίζω itself and certainly not the prefix προ-. Given this fact, the uses of προορίζω in Pauline tradition need another look.

The Concept of the Church in
Ignatius of Antioch

William C. Weinrich

Professor of Early Church History, Concordia Theological Seminary
Fort Wayne, Indiana

For nothing greater is Professor Bo Reicke to be remembered than for his strong commitment to the Church. He was not only an eminent scholar; he was a churchman. The leadership he provided for many years to the Lutheran community in Basel, as well as to other Lutheran congregations in Switzerland and Liechtenstein, witnesses to the ecclesial dimensions of his theological activity. It is appropriate, therefore, to honor Professor Reicke by proffering a few comments on an early Church figure who also was much interested in the concrete life of the *ecclesia Dei*, Ignatius of Antioch.

The letters of Ignatius of Antioch continue to elicit considerable interest among scholars, and nowhere is this more the case than in Ignatius' views concerning the Church.[1] In a recent book, P. Meinhold has published a collection

---

[1] We give here only a short selection of the literature: J. W. von Walter, "Ignatius von Antiochien und die Entstehung des Frühkatholizismus," in *Reinhold Seeberg Festschrift*, II: *Zur Praxis des Christentums*, ed. W. Koepp (Leipzig: Deichert, 1929), pp. 105-118; H. Schlier, *Religionsgeschichtliche Untersuchungen zu den Ignatiusbriefen* (Giessen: Töpelmann, 1929), esp. pp. 82-124; C. C. Richardson, "The Church in Ignatius of Antioch," *JR*, 17 (1937), pp. 428-443; V. Corwin, *St. Ignatius and Christianity in Antioch* (New Haven, Conn.: Yale University Press, 1960), esp. pp. 189-217; J. S. Romanides, "The Ecclesiology of St. Ignatius of Antioch", *GOTR*, 7 (1961-62), pp. 53-77; P. Stockmeier, "Bischofamt und Kircheneinheit bei den Apostolischen

of his contributions to Ignatian studies, and within this collection is his article, "Die Anschauung des Ignatius von Antiochien von der Kirche."[2] The reappearance of this article, along with the fact that Meinhold has evidently seen no reason to alter his opinions, gives us opportunity to present a view of Ignatius' idea of the Church which, in our opinion, is truer to Ignatius' vision and interest.

Following H. Schlier, Meinhold maintains that Ignatius derived his view of the Church from the background of the myth of the "Urmensch" or the "Redeemer." Through his suffering in the world the "Redeemer" gathers his scattered members in order to unite them with himself and to lead them back into the heavenly world. According to Meinhold, this myth forms the conceptual background of Ignatius' idea of the Church as the "body" of Christ.[3] For Ignatius, the Church is a metaphysical entity in which and through which the union of the "Redeemer" and his scattered members takes place: "So ist bei Ignatius die Kirche eine metaphysische Größe, und ihre Aufgabe besteht darin, die Einung des Getrennten herbeizuführen."[4] Organically connected with this view of the Church as the instrument of union is the view that God is essentially one, by nature passionless, at rest; God is the ultimate metaphysical principle of unity. Since the essence of God is harmony and unity, so also is the essence of the Church, in which union with the divine takes place, harmony and unity.

It is this view of the Church which, says Meinhold, Ignatius attempted to apply to the concrete circumstances of heresy and schism which he found in the churches of Asia Minor. Since the divisions in these churches had resulted in the rejection of the bishop and the cultus led by him, the principal intent of Ignatius in his statements concerning the Church is to justify the monarchical episcopacy.[5] This Ignatius accomplishes primarily through various correspondences between the

Vätern," *TTZ*, 73 (1964), pp. 321-335; A. van Haarlem, "De kerk in de brieven van Ignatius van Antiochië," *NTT*, 19 (1964-65), pp. 112-134; V. Remoundos, "The Ecclesiology of St. Ignatius of Antioch," *Diakonia*, 10 (1975), pp. 173-183.

[2] P. Meinhold, *Studien zu Ignatius von Antiochien* (Wiesbaden: Steiner Verlag, 1979). The article concerning Ignatius' view of the Church appears on pp. 57-66. The article earlier was published in *Wegzeichen,* ed. E. Chr. Suttner and C. Patock (Würzburg: Augustinus, 1971), pp. 1-13.

[3] Meinhold, *Studien zu Ignatius*, pp. 57-58. Cf. Schlier, *Religionsgeschichtliche Untersuchungen*, 102-110.

[4] Meinhold, *Studien zu Ignatius*, p. 58.

[5] Meinhold, *Studien zu Ignatius*, p. 59: "Das eigentliche Ziel, um das es Ignatius bei seinen Ausführungen über die Kirche geht, ist das praktische und durch die konkrete Lage hervorgerufene einer Rechtfertigung des monarchischen Episkopates und der beiden anderen kirchlichen Ämter der Presbyter und der Diakone."

heavenly and the earthly realities: As the heavenly Church exists in harmonious unity with God, so must the earthly Church reflect this heavenly unity through union with the bishop. "Der Bischof als das sichtbare Haupt der Kirche stellt so abbildlich Gott als das unsichtbare Haupt der Kirche dar."[6]

An interpretation such as that of Meinhold presents us with an Ignatius whose view of the Church is strongly dualistic, abstract (founded on an abstract conception of God), and primarily institutional (its order must reflect the heavenly order). This view of Ignatius, however, is dependent on the thesis that the Gnostic myth of the "Redeemer" (or at least a strong Platonic influence) is the proper background for comprehending Ignatius' thought. While Gnosticism was certainly an element of the general spiritual environment in which Ignatius lived, no cogent reason exists for adducing distinctly Gnostic concepts and texts for the interpretation of Ignatius. The considerable reserve concerning Gnostic thinking which William Schoedel reflects in his recent commentary is sound and helpful.[7] In those issues and themes which largely determine and motivate his thinking—incarnation, sending, unity, and passion—Ignatius is strongly Johannine, and to comprehend most of Ignatius it is not necessary to stray very far from the Johannine literature.[8] This is true also of Ignatius' statements concerning the Church.

The theology of Ignatius is essentially ecclesial. More than any other early Christian writer he speaks of the Church in laudatory terms. The Church is "blessed" (*Eph.* inscr.; *Mag.* inscr.), "established before the world for enduring glory" (*Eph.* inscr.), "elect" (*Eph.* inscr.; *Trall.* inscr.),[9] "beloved" (*Trall.* inscr.;

---

[6] Meinhold, *Studien zu Ignatius*, p. 60. Much of Meinhold's article consists of discussion concerning the various correspondences Ignatius uses in this "Urbild-Abbild-Spekulation." According to Meinhold, Ignatius uses also, albeit only as subordinate arguments, an idealized view of apostolic history and the motifs of sending and of initiation in his justification of the Church's offices.

[7] W. R. Schoedel, *Ignatius of Antioch: A Commentary on the Letters of Ignatius of Antioch* (Philadelphia: Fortress Press, 1985), p. 16: "There is scant evidence that the bishop was familiar with Gnosticism in a developed form. It is probably best, then, to consider the Gnostic religion a distinctive articulation of a widely diffused otherworldliness that variously affected forms of mystical and semi-mystical movements of the period. It is presumably such a spiritual climate that has left its mark on Ignatius."

[8] Some scholarship suggests that the Johannine literature is itself dependent upon Gnostic, mythic conceptions. Here it must suffice to indicate my agreement with that scholarship which emphasizes a Jewish background to John rather than the myths of Gnosis. For a balanced and persuasive account of the background of Ignatian thought, see R. M. Grant, "Scripture and Tradition in St. Ignatius of Antioch," *CBQ*, 25 (1963), pp. 322-335. Grant emphasizes Ignatius' use of Paul's letters, especially of 1 Corinthians, in addition to his use of John. Whether Ignatius knew John's Gospel, however, must remain an open question.

[9] With one exception, Ignatius speaks only of the Church as "elect," or "chosen." That

Rom. inscr.), "holy" (*Trall.* inscr.), "worthy of God" (*Trall.* inscr.; *Rom.* inscr.), "enlightened" (*Rom.* inscr.), the object of mercy (*Rom.* inscr.; *Phld.* inscr.; *Smyrn.* inscr.), "filled with faith and love" (*Smyrn.* inscr.), the "bearer of holy things" (*Smyrn.* inscr.), "most fit for God" (*Smyrn.* inscr.).

One does not, however, best approach Ignatius' idea of the Church through an analysis of these epithets. Rather, one must first consider the all-encompassing concern Ignatius has for unity, which in turn leads to a consideration of Christ and his work of salvation. The use of the terms themselves reflects the central importance unity has in the epistles of Ignatius. Within the Apostolic Fathers, the terms ἑνόω ("to unite"), ἕνωσις ("union"), and ἑνότης ("unity") occur only in Ignatius.[10] In the New Testament, ἑνότης appears only two times (Eph. 4:3,13). These terms, therefore, are characteristic of Ignatius. In addition to this unity word group, the idea of unity can be expressed by other terms, such as ὁμόνοια (*Eph.* 4:1,2; 13:1; *Mag.* 6:1; 15:1; *Trall.* 12:2; *Phld.* inscr.; 11:2), σύμφωνος (*Eph.* 4:1,2; 5:1), ὑποτάσσω (*Eph.* 2:2; 5:3; *Mag.* 2:1; 13:2; *Trall.* 2:1,2; 13:2; *Pol.* 6:1), ἐπὶ τὸ αὐτό (*Eph.* 5:3; 13:1; *Mag.* 7:1; *Phld.* 6:2; 10:1). Of course, the pivotal significance of unity for Ignatius' understanding of the Church is common knowledge. When Ignatius speaks of himself as a man made for unity (*Phld.* 8:1), it is within a context replete with major themes by which he expounds his notion of Church: the need for unity, the evil of division, the necessity of the bishop, the relationship of Christ and the Father (*Phld.* 7:2). When one notes how often the actual terms for unity are conjoined with statements concerning the bishop (*Eph.* 4:1-2; 5:1-3; *Mag.* 6:2; 7:1; 13:2; *Phld.* 3:2; 4; 7:2; 8:l; cf. *Pol.* 8:3), the crucial importance of unity for Ignatius' view of the Church—and, to be sure, the centrality of the bishop in that view—becomes all the more apparent.

Why, however, does unity become such an important ecclesiological concept for Ignatius,[11] and why is the bishop necessary for unity in the Church? To answer these questions it must be recognized that Ignatius' thinking concerning the

---

exception is *Phld.* 11:1 where Rheus Agathopus is "elect," presumably because he has been chosen out by God for martyrdom. The attempt by Schlier (*Religionsgeschichtliche Untersuchungen*, pp. 84-85) to perceive Gnostic myth (*Exc. ex Theod.* 41) behind Ignatius' designation of the Church as "elect" is unconvincing.

[10] Ἑνόω (*Eph.* inscr.; *Mag.* 6:2; 7:1; 14; *Rom.* inscr.; *Smyrn.* 3:3); ἕνωσις (*Mag.* 1:2; 13:2; *Trall.* 11:2; *Phld.* 4:1; 7:2; 8:1; *Pol.* 1:2; 5:2); ἑνότης (*Eph.* 4:2; 5:1; 14:1; *Phld.* 2:2; 3:2; 5:2; 8:1; 9:1; *Smyrn.* 12:2; *Pol.* 8:3).

[11] Richardson ("The Church in Ignatius of Antioch," p. 428) notes that ἑνότης can be virtually synonymous with "Church" (*Phld.* 3:2; cf. 8:1).

Church and the bishop has its roots in his understanding of Christ's work of redemption.[12] For Ignatius, the predicament of the world and of mankind is not so much sin as it is separation from God.[13] This separation from God has been occasioned by the "Ruler of this age"[14] whose rule is characterized by division, corruption, and death. Throughout his letters Ignatius explicitly or implicitly associates Satan with these woes.[15]

By contrast, salvation consists in the gifts of unity, incorruptibility, and life. How mutually related these are can be seen in a passage like *Eph.* 6:2 where Ignatius writes that the Ephesian bishop, Onesimus, praised his flock because they all lived according to the truth and there was no division among them (ὅτι πάντες κατὰ ἀλήθειαν ζῆτε καὶ ὅτι ἐν ὑμῖν οὐδεμία αἵρεσις κατοικεῖ). Here living "according to truth" and the absence of division are virtually synonymous.

Eph. 19:1-3 most vividly proclaims salvation as the destruction of Satan's kingdom and therewith the granting of eternal life:

> The virginity of Mary and her child-bearing, as well as the death of the Lord escaped the notice of the Ruler of this age. Three thunderous mysteries which were accomplished in the silence of God. How then was he made known to the ages? A star brighter than all the stars shone in the heavens. . . . And there was (fearful) perplexity whence this unique novelty had come. As a result all magic and every bond of evil perished. Ignorance was done away with. The ancient kingdom was utterly destroyed since God was revealing himself as man for the newness of eternal life. That which had been prepared by God had taken its beginning. Henceforth, all things were in confusion, since the destruction of death

---

[12] Although he sees perhaps too much of Eastern Orthodoxy in Ignatius, Romanides ("Ecclesiology of St. Ignatius") is very good at this point. It is surprising that a scholar like Meinhold, although tipping his hat to a Gnostic myth of redemption which he sees behind Ignatius, can discuss Ignatius' view of the Church without any special reference to Ignatius' understanding of Christ's work. It is a measure of how sterile much discussion of Ignatius' view can be.

[13] So correctly H.-W Bartsch, *Gnostisches Gut und Gemeindetradition bei Ignatius von Antiochien* (Gütersloh: Bertelmann, 1940), p. 82; Corwin, *St. Ignatius and Christianity*, pp. 162, 247.

[14] Ὁ ἄρχων τοῦ αἰῶνος τούτου is the usual designation of Ignatius for the enemy (*Eph.* 17:1; 19:1; *Mag.* 1:2; *Trall.* 4:2; *Rom.* 7:1; *Phld.* 6:2). διάβολος occurs four times (*Eph.* 10:3; *Trall.* 8:1; *Rom.* 5:3; *Smyrn.* 9:1). σατανᾶς occurs but once (*Eph.* 13:1).

[15] Division (*Eph.* 13:1; *Mag.* 6:2; *Trall.* 6:1; 11:2; *Rom.* 7:3; *Phld.* 2:1;, 3:1-3; 7:2; 8:1; *Smyrn.* 7:2); corruption (*Eph.* 16:1; 17:1; 19:3; *Mag.* 10:2; *Trall.* 11:2; *Rom.* 7:1; *Pol.* 2:3); death (*Eph.* 7:1-2; 17:1; 19:3; 20:2; *Mag.* 5:1; *Trall.* 2:1; 6:2; 11:1; *Smyrn.* 3:2; 5:1, 2; 7:1; *Pol.* 2:3). Also, deceit (*Trall.* 6:2; 8:1; *Phld.* 6:2; 7:1; *Smyrn.* 6:1); filth (*Eph.* 17:1; *Trall.* 7:2); strife (*Eph.* 8:1); wars, both cosmic and internal (*Eph.* 13:2; *Trall.* 4:2); ignorance (*Eph.* 17:2; 19:3; *Smyrn.* 1:1).

was being carried out.[16]

Ignatius expresses the organic association between Christ and "life" also in those passages which virtually identify the two: "Jesus Christ, our steadfast life" (*Eph.* 3:2); "Jesus Christ, our perpetual life" (*Mag.* 1:2); "Jesus Christ, our true life" (*Smyrn.* 4:1). According to *Eph.* 17:1, Christ was anointed in order that he might breathe incorruptibility on the Church. A passage such as *Phld.* 8:1 ("where there is division and wrath God does not dwell") and the many exhortations to unity are sufficient to show that unity is a characteristic of God's rule and kingdom (see *Phld.* 3:3).

The hymn of *Eph.* 19:1-3 primarily credits the incarnation for the defeat of Satan and the establishment of life. However, even here the death of Christ is mentioned, and elsewhere in the letters of Ignatius it is the passion of Christ which most closely is associated with the gifts of salvation (*Mag.* 9:1; *Trall.* 11:2; *Rom.* 7:3; *Smyrn.* 5:3). This is especially the case with unity. In some of Ignatius' most suggestive passages the passion of Christ is directly related to the unity of the Church. In *Trall.* 11:1-2 Ignatius warns against certain "evil offshoots" who bear "death-carrying fruit." These persons are not a plant of the Father, for if they were, they would be "branches of the cross . . . through which, in [his] passion he calls us who are his members to himself. A head is not able to be born without members, God promising unity which he is." This text is not easy to interpret in its details, but its general thrust is clear enough: The cross is the means by which Christ calls and gathers his members into unity with him. The head-members metaphor makes it clear that the unity of the Church is in view, and it expresses the organic relationship between Christ in passion and the unity of the Church. Where the passion of Christ is, there the Church is gathered together into unity. That Christ in his passion "calls us to himself" is the Ignatian equivalent of the Johannine thought that the dying grain bears much fruit (John 12:24) or that in being "lifted up from the earth" Jesus will draw all men unto himself (John 12:32; 11:51-52).[17]

---

[16] Although this "hymn" has been ascribed to Gnostic sources, the view of A. Cabaniss ("Wisdom, 18:14f.: An Early Christmas Text," *VC*, 10 [1956], pp. 97-102) that the Wisdom of Solomon lies behind it is more convincing.

[17] Schlier (*Religionsgeschichtliche Untersuchungen*, pp. 88ff.) thinks *Trall.* 11:2 especially clear evidence of the underlying Gnostic myth of the Redeemer who cannot return to the Pleroma without the redeemed. Meinhold (*Studien*, p. 57) appears to agree with this view. However, one need not go so far afield to account for Ignatius' thought here. The parallel with John 12:32 is

A second passage which connects the cross and the Church's unity is *Smyrn.* 1:2. Here Ignatius writes that Christ was "nailed in the flesh for us . . . in order that through the resurrection he might raise an ensign for the ages, for his saints and believers, whether among the Jews or among the Gentiles, in the one body of his Church." The words "raise an ensign" refer to the prophecies of Isaiah (5:26; 11:10, 12; 49:22; 62:10) that God will raise an ensign for his scattered people to which they shall gather. This would be the great eschatological act of God which would reverse the diaspora and unite his scattered people into the land of promise. For Ignatius this act of God occurred in the resurrection of Christ through which the cross was raised as an ensign. It is "in the body of his Church" that the ensign is raised, that is, the Church is gathered, made one, through the cross which is raised in its midst.

In a third passage, *Eph.* 9:1, Ignatius writes that the Christians are stones prepared for the temple of God and are "being carried into the heights by the machine of Jesus Christ, which is the cross, being hoisted by a rope, namely, the Holy Spirit."[18] Here again it is the cross which is the instrument of the Church's unity. Through it Christians are made into the temple of the Father.

In addition to the above three passages, other passages testify, albeit less vividly, to the foundational significance of the passion of Christ for the unity of the Church. Ignatius writes to the Ephesians that the Church has been united and elected in true passion (*Eph.* inscr.), and to the Philadelphians he writes that the Church has been "granted mercy and established in the harmony of God and made glad in the passion of our Lord" (*Phld.* inscr.). Here I would add also that much-debated verse, *Phld.* 4:1: "one cup for unity of his blood." Whether the genitive τοῦ αἵματος αὐτοῦ is best translated "by his blood" or "with his blood" is

---

quite sufficient to explain the meaning of the text. In both *Trall.* 11:2 and John 12:32f. the cross is the instrument of glorification and life which consists in unity with Jesus (προσκαλεῖτε, *Trall.* 11:2; πρὸς ἐμαυτόν, John 12:32). The κἀγώ of John 12:32 links the passage to 12:31 which speaks of the Ruler of this age being thrown down, defeated. In Jesus' death, his being lifted up, both the devil is defeated and unity and life with Christ is established. That *Trall.* 11:2 envisions also the defeat of Satan in Jesus' "calling" through the cross is clear from 11:1 which mentions the "evil offshoots who bear death-carrying fruit."

[18] It seems quite unnecessary to see a Gnostic background in the image of the machine (Schlier, *Religionseschichtliche Untersuchung*, pp. 110-124). Most simply it may be seen as a mere building metaphor. The essential background remains John, and, I would suggest, passages like 12:32 and 3:14. The salvific significance of Jesus "being lifted up" (ὑψωθῆσαι) is clear in both verses of John. Ignatius merely extends the language to the Christians: Since Jesus is "lifted up" (ὑψωθῆσαι) on the cross, so the Christians by the cross are lifted "into the heights" (εἰς τὰ ὕψη).

difficult to resolve (perhaps both are in view). In any case, the association between Christ's death and unity is clear.

The unity of the Church, therefore, is the result of Christ's passion by which the power of Satan is destroyed and division overcome. However, where in the concrete life of the Church is the passion of Christ to be found? That is, where is the uniting center by which the Church *now* is united? In view of the actual divisions within the churches of Asia Minor, this question was of existential importance to Ignatius, and there can be little doubt what the answer of Ignatius was. The primary form the passion of Christ takes in the Church is the eucharist. In the eucharist the passion remains as the instrument by which God gathers his people into unity with him; in the eucharist Satan continues to be defeated and separations overcome. For Ignatius the passion of Christ is not a dead act of the past which can only be remembered and recalled. For through the resurrection the cross has been erected in the Church like an ensign around which God now gathers his people (*Smyrn.* 1:2).[19] Through the resurrection the passion of Christ continues, in the eucharist namely, to be the means by which God gathers his people into one. In fact, on occasion Ignatius appears actually to use the term πάθος to designate the eucharist (*Eph.* inscr.; *Mag.* 5:2; *Trall.* inscr. 11:2; *Phld.* inscr. 3:3; *Smyrn.* 5:3). In one passage Ignatius identifies the eucharist as "the flesh of our Savior, Jesus Christ, which suffered for our sins and which the Father raised by His goodness" (*Smyrn.* 7:1). Since through the resurrection the passion continues in the Church, the passion is life-giving and produces the benefits of the resurrection.[20] It is not accidental, therefore, that Ignatius attributes to the eucharist the effects and benefits of Christ's passion and resurrection. Since the passion of Christ defeats Satan and overcomes division, the Church gathered in eucharistic fellowship experiences the defeat of Satan: "Be zealous, therefore, more often to come together into the eucharist of God and into glory. For when you are often together (ἐπὶ τὸ αὐτό), the powers of Satan are destroyed and his ruin is dissolved in your harmony of faith" (*Eph.* 13:1). But with the defeat of Satan comes the gifts of God's rule. Ignatius, therefore, frequently asserts that the Church in eucharist already possesses and enjoys the gifts of salvation: The Church is in union with God (*Eph.* 4:2; 5:1; *Mag.* 5:2; 6:1; *Trall.* 11:2; *Phld.* 3:2); the Church partakes of

---

[19] See W. C. Weinrich, *Spirit and Martyrdom* (Washington D.C.: University Press of America, 1981), pp. 124-127.

[20] Cf. *Smyrn.* 5:3: μέχρις οὐ μετανοήσωσιν εἰς τὸ πάθος, ὅ ἐστιν ἡμῶν ἀνάστασις.

immortality (*Eph.* 20:2; *Trall.* 2:1; *Smyrn.* 3:2), incorruptibility (*Mag.* 6:2; *Trall.* 11:2), life (*Eph.* 20:2; *Mag.* 5:2), peace (*Eph.* 13:2; *Trall.* inscr.; cf. *Phld.* 6:2), joy (*Phld.* inscr.).

We have answered our first question, why unity is for Ignatius a major ecclesiological concept. The Church is the place of unity with God, for in the Church the passion of Christ, the eucharist, continues to defeat the ancient kingdom of Satan with its separations and divisions and thereby continues to establish unity with God. For Ignatius, the Church is essentially the place of the eucharist.

But what of the second question, that concerning the necessity of the bishop in the Church? It is clear, first of all, that when Ignatius thinks of the Church in eucharistic fellowship he thinks of the Church gathered around the bishop: "Let nothing be among you which will be able to divide you; but be united with the bishop" (*Mag.* 6:2); "all who are of God and of Jesus Christ, these are with the bishop" (*Phld.* 3:2); "he who is within the sanctuary is pure, but he who is outside the sanctuary is not pure, that is, he who does anything without the bishop and the presbytery and the deacons, he is not pure in conscience" (*Trall.* 7:2); "let no one do anything which belongs to the Church without the bishop; let that eucharist be regarded as valid which is by the bishop or by him whom he may authorize" (*Smyrn.* 8:1). The opinion often voiced that this necessity of the bishop is grounded in a Platonic worldview whereby the heavenly order must be reflected in the earthly order[21] does not do justice to those passages in which the Father or Christ is said to be "bishop" of earthly communities (*Eph.* 1:3; *Mag.* 3:1,2; *Rom.* 9:1; *Pol.* inscr.). Nor are the analogies which Ignatius uses consistent enough to express the idea of a true reflection of a heavenly type in an earthly antitype. Rather, the necessity of the bishop must be understood within the context of what Ignatius says about the eucharist, for as we have noted, in Ignatius unity with the bishop and unity in the eucharist are correlative terms.

We will attempt to elucidate Ignatius' insistence on the bishop in two points. (1) As was clear already in *Eph.* 19:1-3, the incarnation of Christ as well as the passion is essential to the defeat of Satan. It is interesting to note how the anti-docetic creedal passages of Ignatius center upon the reality of the incarnation and

---

[21] E.g., Meinhold, *Studien zu Ignatius*, pp. 59-63. Corwin (*St. Ignatius and Christianity*, p. 197) correctly denies that Ignatius echoes Platonic thought but still thinks that Ignatius maintained a distinction between a "heavenly" (invisible, pre-eminent) Church and an "earthly" (visible) Church, the unity between which was maintained by a continuity of hierarchical structure.

death of Christ (*Eph.* 7:2; *Trall.* 9:1-2; *Smyrn.* 1:1-2). The point is essential for Ignatius precisely because the rule of Satan is in flesh, that is, is executed within history.

Death, corruption, and mortality are not understood by Ignatius as natural characteristics of the material order; they are caused by Satan, and, therefore, the conflict which God wages with Satan must be in the flesh, in the arena of the creation and, to be sure, in the reality of the passion. It is for this reason that Ignatius insists that the resurrection of Christ was also in the flesh. In a strongly antidocetic passage, Ignatius writes: "For I know and believe that even after the resurrection he is in flesh. . . . After the resurrection he ate and drank with them (the disciples) as one in flesh, although Spiritually, he was united with the Father" (*Smyrn.* 3:1,3). In *Smyrn.* 5:2 Ignatius calls the resurrected Lord "flesh-bearer" (σαρκοφόρος). The point is that after the resurrection Christ continues to work in a "sarkic," incarnational manner, namely in the real passion of Christ which now continues in the eucharist to be the unifying act of God. Ignatius is intensely concerned that the reality of the resurrection—incorruptibility, immortality, life, unity, harmony—which the Church receives in the passion of Christ be an experienced reality, that is, a reality which exists in the flesh, in time and in space, in the reality of the one Church. Since there are real divisions within the churches, since death and corruption continue to grip mankind, the work of Christ must continue to be in flesh. Satan is either defeated where he is, where he works his ways, that is, in the world of flesh, or he is not defeated at all. As we have seen, Satan continues to be defeated in the eucharist which is the form of Christ's passion in the Church. For this reason, Ignatius speaks of the eucharist as the "flesh of our Savior, Jesus Christ" (*Smyrn.* 7:1).

This soteriological concern of Ignatius helps us to appreciate his insistence on the eucharistic communion under the one bishop. Just as the defeat of Satan was not in the realm of the abstract and myth but occurred in a certain place and at a certain time, namely, in the passion of Christ under Pontius Pilate, so must the Church, which is the place of Christ's passion now, exist in a certain place and at a certain time. This spatial and temporal character of the Church takes its concrete form in the eucharistic fellowship under the one bishop. It is striking how often Ignatius uses spatial language in connection with the bishop: "*Wherever* the bishop should appear, *there* let the assembly be" (*Smyrn.* 8:2); "all who are of God and of Jesus Christ, these are *with* the bishop" (*Phld.* 3:2); those *within* the sanctuary do all things *with* the bishop (*Trall.* 7:2). We may note as well the use of the phrase ἐπὶ τὸ αὐτό to denote the eucharistic gathering as at one place (*Eph.* 5:3; 13:1; *Mag.* 7:1; *Phld.* 6:2).

First of all, then, the bishop as it were "localizes" the passion of Christ. The passion of Christ is bound to the bishop (*Smyrn.* 8:1; *Phld.* 3-4; *Trall.* 7:2). The local bishop is the "bishop in flesh" (*Eph.* 1:3) and as such is the center of the Church's life, which must be "sarkic."

(2) It may seem harshly "institutional" to say that the passion is bound to the bishop, and indeed Ignatius has often been interpreted as one primarily concerned with church order and discipline. Such a view must keep in mind the essentially eucharistic context of Ignatius' statements concerning the bishop. This much, however, must be said. For Ignatius, Church structure is not an indifferent matter,[22] for the place of the bishop is inherent within the economy of God's salvation.

As Grant has noted, the model for the relation between Christians and their bishop is the relation between Christ and the Father.[23] This relationship is described in terms which have close parallels in John's Gospel. As John speaks of Jesus as united with the Father (John 17:23), as sent by the Father (4:34; 5:23, 30, 37; 6:38, 44; etc.), and as doing nothing without the Father who sent him (5:30; 6:38; 7:16, 18; cf. 14:24), so also according to Ignatius Christ is united with the Father (*Eph.* 5:1; *Mag.* 7: 1; *Rom.* 3:3; *Smyrn.* 3:3), is sent by the Father (*Mag.* 7:2; 8:2; cf. *Eph.* 6:1), and is the very expression of the Father's will (*Eph.* 3:2; *Mag.* 7:1; *Rom.* 8:2; *Phld.* 7:2). Both in John and in Ignatius Christ is the very revelation of the Father's will, and Christ is this precisely in what he says and does. In other words, the sending of Christ consists *in* his words and works; or, Christ "comes" *in* his words and deeds. Ignatius expresses the revelatory character of Jesus' words and deeds in *Eph.* 15:1 ("who spoke and it happened, and whatsoever he did, being silent, was worthy of the Father") and in *Mag.* 8:2 ("there is one God who revealed himself through Jesus Christ, his Son, who is his word going forth from silence, who in all things was pleasing to him who sent him").

As we have seen, however, Ignatius considers Christ's revelation of the Father to consist in his incarnation and death, that is, in his passion in flesh

---

[22] See especially *Trall.* 3:1: "Without these [bishop, presbyters, deacons] the Church is not named." The fact that Ignatius often places presbyters and deacons alongside the bishop indicates the importance they had for him. However, it is clear that the bishop is of pre-eminent importance, and we shall restrict our remarks to him.

[23] Grant, "Scripture and Tradition," p. 329.

whereby Satan's division is overcome and unity restored. And as we have further observed, the passion of Christ in flesh continues within the Church in the eucharist. That is, the sending of Christ, by which the Father is revealed, continues in a concrete, incarnational, and sarkic way in the eucharist of the Church. As in the earthly Jesus the Father was revealed in visible form so that, to use the language of John, he who sees Christ sees the Father (John 12:45; 14:9), so now in the Church it is in the bishop administrating the eucharist that the sending of Christ, by which the Father is revealed, continues to take visible form. Thus, the bishop is a "type" (τόπος) of the Father (*Trall.* 3:1) and "in the place of God" (εἰς τόπον θεοῦ) (*Mag.* 6:1).[24]

The economy of the Father (sending of Christ in incarnation and death) is not located in the dead past but meets the Christian now in the person of the bishop whose ministry consists primarily in administering the eucharist. This is the significance of *Eph.* 6:1: "Everyone whom the householder sends to take care of his affairs (εἰς ἰδίαν οἰκονομίαν) it is necessary to receive as the sender himself. Therefore, it is clear that it is necessary to look upon the bishop as the Lord himself." The sending of Christ takes form in the Church in the ministry of the bishop. But this ministry of the bishop is no other than that of Christ in his incarnation and passion. In the bishop *as the one sent by the Father*, that is, in the bishop *as the administrator of the eucharist* Christ's passion becomes present revelation of the Father who is revealed precisely in His work of redemption through Christ Jesus, his Son.[25]

For Ignatius to assert the necessity of the bishop is simply for him to assert the necessity of Christ. Just as there is no work of Christ without the person of Christ, so also now in the Church there is no work of Christ (eucharist as the passion) without the person of Christ (the bishop as the one sent by the Father).[26]

---

[24] On occasion Ignatius likens the bishop to Christ (*Trall.* 2:1; *Smyrn.* 8:2). This is not just an inconsistency. It makes perfect sense within the "sending" scheme to liken the bishop sometimes to the Father and sometimes to Christ. Since Christ is the revealer of the Father so that in Christ the Father is perceived, to identify the bishop with the Father or with Christ is to express very similar ideas.

[25] The ideas of "sending" and "revelation" are closely related both for Christ (*Mag.* 8:2) and for the bishop (*Eph.* 6:1; *Phld.* 1:1). See H. Chadwick, "The Silence of the Bishops in Ignatius," *HTR*, 43 (1950), pp. 169-172.

[26] We emphasize again two points: (1) the concern of Ignatius is not institutional but soteriological. The bishop is not to be conceived apart from his ministry just as Christ is not to be abstracted from his work. The bishop, therefore, is not juridically conceived. He is not primarily a lawgiver, so obedience is not the essential relationship Christians have with him.

The following might serve to illustrate the point:

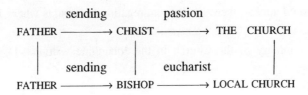

On the basis of this illustration, we may make several summary remarks:

(1) The economy of the Father in Christ has its present realization in the ministry of the bishop. In his ministry the work of Christ is "for us."

(2) Any correspondences between the top and the bottom is not due to any Platonic type-antitype schema. It is because the sending of Christ is itself present in the sending of the bishop that correspondence exists. Ignatius knows no distinction between a "heavenly" and an "earthly" Church. God is the true bishop of the Church (*Eph.* 1:3; *Mag.* 3:1,2; *Rom.* 9:1; *Pol.* inscr.). The bishop of the local church is bishop only because he is sent by the "invisible bishop" and therefore in His place.[27]

(3) The economy of the Father through the bishop is the means whereby the economy of the Father in Christ retains its incarnational character.

(4) A certain overlapping is involved in the persons of Christ and the bishop, categories, indicating two things: (a) Christ and the bishop are part of what might be called the sacramental direction of Ignatian thinking. In Christ and in the bishop the direction is from God to the world. (b) Yet, Christ and the bishop are never seen apart from the Christians, for Christ and the bishop are never seen apart from

---

Christians must order themselves under him (ὑποτάσσεσθαι) because to him has been entrusted the ministry of Christ in their midst. (2) Ignatius' ideas about the Church and the bishop take structural form because the economy of God in the Church is historical and fleshly, as was the economy of God in the earthly Jesus. But for the economy to be fleshly means for it to have a real subject of action. This subject of action is "the Father in Christ in the bishop."

[27] While one can make too much of Ignatius' analogies and correspondences between God and the bishop, one can also make too little of them. This seems to me to be a shortcoming in William Schoedel's fine commentary. Schoedel regards the language of correspondence as mere rhetorical formalities for the purpose of exhortation. Christians are to respect their leaders and to retain the integrity of their relations with the leaders (*Ignatius of Antioch*, p. 109, also 56, 57, 113, 116, 242-243). However, when Ignatius speaks of the Father as the invisible Bishop (*Mag.* 3:2), more than exhortation is intended. It is required to interpret Ignatius' view of the bishop within the context of his eucharistic theology, for as we have noted, in Ignatius' view unity with the bishop and unity in the eucharist are correlative.

passion/eucharist in which the Christians as the beneficiaries are already in view: "A head cannot come into existence without members" (*Trall.* 11:2); "Wherever the bishop should appear, there let the congregation be; just as where Jesus Christ is, there is the catholic Church" (*Smyrn.* 8:2).

In his summary of the Church in the Johannine writings, D. M. Stanley writes:

> It is however particularly in the Fourth Gospel that the Church emerges as the Church of the Incarnation. . . . In Jesus Christ, the incarnate Word of God, the divine presence has entered human history in a completely unprecedented way to redeem man and to reveal the God "no man has ever seen." Through the Christian sacraments, prefigured in the signs of the public life of Christ, the glorified Jesus remains and acts in the Church.[28]

It would be difficult to summarize the view of Ignatius of Antioch any better.

---

[28] D. M. Stanley, "Reflections on the Church in the New Testament," *CBQ*, 25 (1963), p. 399.

Luther's Understanding of
"The Obedience of Faith" (Rom. 1:5 and 16:26)

Daniel P. Fuller

Professor of Hermeneutics, Fuller Theological Seminary
Pasadena, California

"The faith that works itself out in love [avails everything]." This one proposition from Gal. 5:6, rendered literally from the Greek with its ellipsis (omitted words) filled in, was a *crux interpretum* for the Reformation and is an important proposition to construe correctly for the understanding of sanctification, that is, living the Christian life. Luther's objection to the way medieval theology interpreted this proposition can be seen from the following from his Galatians commentary:[1]

> We must needs say, that we be pronounced righteous by grace alone, or by faith in Christ, without the law and works. This the blind sophisters do not understand, and therefore they dream of a faith that justifies not, except it do the works of love. [In *CG*, p. 115 he said, "The wicked gloss of the schoolmen says that faith then justifies when love and good works are joined withal."] By this means faith which believes in Christ becomes unprofitable and of none effect; for the virtue of justifying is taken from it, except it be furnished with love. (*CG*, pp. 121-122)

---

[1] Quotations from Luther are from J. Dillenberger (ed.), *Martin Luther: Selections from His Writings* (Garden City, N.Y.: Doubleday, 1961). Abbreviations: *PR* = "Preface to Romans"; *FC* = *The Freedom of a Christian*; *TKR* = "Two Kinds of Righteousness"; *PNT* = "Preface to the New Testament"; and *CG* = *Commentary on Galatians*. Some archaisms in the Dillenberger anthology have been altered into more contemporary English.

In other words, medieval theology concerning Gal. 5:6 held that an earnest doing of the works of love would adorn one's faith because such works were the measure of its fervency. The problem with this construction, however, was that people could never be sure that their faith was sufficiently profitable for them to be forgiven. Luther's construction of Gal. 5:6 was totally opposite:

> ... when I have ... apprehended Christ by faith, and through him am dead to the law, justified from sin, delivered from death, the devil, and hell, then I do good works, I love God, I give thanks to him, I exercise love toward my neighbor. But this love or works following, do neither form nor adorn my faith, but [rather] *my faith forms and adorns love.* (*CG*, p. 122, italics added)

The battle lines of the Reformation can be stated in these two contrary propositions: "Faith adorns the works of love" (Luther), and "the works of love adorn faith" (Roman Catholicism). One objective in this essay is to clarify what Luther meant in saying that "faith adorns the works of love." My understanding of Luther on this subject is organized around three propositions.

I. Three Propositions in Luther's Teaching

Proposition 1: Faith in the trustworthiness of God's promises is the foundation for all proper (actual) righteousness.

Luther reasoned as follows:

> ... [faith] honors him whom it trusts with the most reverent and highest regard since it considers him truthful and trustworthy. There is no other honor equal to the estimate of truthfulness and righteousness with which we honor him whom we trust. Could we ascribe to a person anything greater than truthfulness and righteousness and perfect goodness? On the other hand, there is no way in which we can show greater contempt for a person than to regard someone as false and wicked and to be suspicious of him or her, as we do when we do not trust a person. So when the soul firmly trusts God's promises, it regards him as truthful and righteous. Nothing more excellent than this can be ascribed to God. The very highest worship of God is this, that we ascribe to him truthfulness, righteousness, and whatever else should be ascribed to one who is trusted. When this is done, the soul consents to his will. Then it hallows his name and allows itself to be treated according to God's good pleasure for, clinging to God's promises, it does not doubt that he who is true, just, and wise will do, dispose, and provide all things well.
>
> Is not such a soul most obedient [righteous!] to God in all things by this

faith? What commandment is there that such obedience has not completely fulfilled? (*FC*, p. 59)

That faith in God's integrity to keep his promises is the essence of proper (actual) righteousness becomes clear when we understand what a terrible thing it is to regard God as untrustworthy. So Luther went on to say,

> On the other hand, what greater wickedness, what greater contempt of God is there than not believing his promise? For what is this but to make God a liar or to doubt that he is truthful?—that is, to ascribe truthfulness to one's self but lying and vanity to God?[2] . . . Therefore God has rightly included all [sinful] things, not under anger or lust, but under unbelief. . . . (*FC*, p. 59)

In his statement quoted above, "Is not such a soul most obedient [righteous!] to God in all things by this faith? What commandment is there that such obedience has not completely fulfilled?" Luther was subsuming all righteous attitudes and activities under the rubric of faith.[3] According to Luther, the most all-embracing of God's promises to be believed is Rom. 8:28, "God works all things together for good to them that love him, to them that are called according to his purpose."[4]

After thus paraphrasing Rom. 8:28 Luther concluded:

> . . . [consequently] the cross and death itself are compelled to serve me and to work together with me for my salvation. This is a splendid privilege, and hard to attain, a truly omnipotent power, a spiritual dominion in which there is nothing

---

[2] It has helped me understand the ultimacy of this wickedness (and conversely what essential righteousness is) to realize that in human relationships, whenever I have indicated to someone that I no longer trusted that person, it has been virtually impossible thereafter to be friends again. Not to trust another is the greatest insult we can render, and by the same token, not to entrust ourselves to God's promises is the greatest wickedness in that in so doing we render to God the worst possible insult. Since we have all done this innumerable times, we are indeed totally depraved. Yet the surprisingly good news of the Gospel is that God will forgive the repentant for their sin of unbelief and goes so far as to make them his children, so they are joint-heirs with Jesus Christ, his only begotten Son! So nothing in human forgiveness bears an analogy to God's forgiveness of our sins.

[3] The importance of this concept that all sin is disbelief in God's promises and all righteousness is believing them can hardly be overemphasized. In *PR*, p. 22, Luther put the concept into one sentence: "Just as faith *alone* gives us the spirit and the desire for doing works that are plainly good, so unbelief is the *sole* cause of sin" (italics added).

[4] This promise is for everyone, for it is conditioned only on loving (delighting in) God. If we choose to believe God's promise that he wants to love us so much as to work all things together for our good (so present stumbling blocks eventually become stepping stones!), then we most certainly will love him in the sense of delighting in him, and thus we surely will fulfill the condition necessary to receive this promise.

so good and nothing so evil, but that it shall work together for good to me, *if only I believe. (FC*, p. 64, italics added)

The delight in God involved in believing such a promise brings joy to our souls, and this joy shines out from us to the surrounding world. According to Luther,

> Faith is a living and unshakable confidence, a belief in the grace of God *so assured* that a person would die a thousand deaths for its sake. This kind of confidence in God's grace, this sort of knowledge of it, makes us *joyful* and *high-spirited*, and *eager in our relations with God and with all humankind.* That is what the Holy Spirit effects through faith. Hence, the person of faith, without being driven, willingly and gladly seeks to do good to everyone, serve everyone, suffer all kinds of hardships, for the sake of the love and the glory of the God who has shown that person such grace. It is impossible, indeed, to separate works from faith, just as it is impossible to separate heat and light from fire. (*PR*, p. 24, italics added)

The second proposition shows why we need a very different kind of righteousness as the foundation for the actual righteousness of doing good works.

Proposition 2: Faith, which is the basis for proper righteousness, is imperfect, and so there is need of an alien righteousness to atone for our lack of proper righteousness.

Luther is emphatic that the Bible teaches that there are two completely different kinds of righteousness, as the following quotation from his *Commentary on Galatians* makes clear:

> . . . Christian righteousness consists in two things; that is to say, in faith of the heart [proper righteousness], and in God's imputation [alien righteousness]. Faith [of the heart] is indeed a formal[5] righteousness, for after faith there remain certain amounts of sin in our flesh. . . . Wherefore the other part of righteousness [alien righteousness] must be added also [to proper righteousness] . . . that is to say, God's imputation [of righteousness]. For faith [of the heart] does not give enough to God formally [to be fully righteous], because it is imperfect, yea rather our faith is but *a little spark of faith,* which only begins to render to God his true divinity [by trusting his promises]. Yea, the holiest that live have not yet a full

---

[5] Here I am interpreting Luther's "formal" to mean "that which is the essential constitution or structure of [in this case, of *proper righteousness*]," the first meaning given in *Webster's Seventh New Collegiate Dictionary,* 1972.

and continual joy in God, but have their sundry passions, sometimes sad, sometimes merry, as the Scriptures witness of the prophets and Apostles. But such faults are not laid to their charge because of their faith in Christ, for otherwise no one could be saved. (*CG*, p. 127, italics added)

It is helpful to sort out the elements contained in Luther's concept of "alien righteousness." Negatively, there is justification, or more simply, God's forgiveness for our lack of proper righteousness, for our sinfulness and sins, which consist of a reluctance to entrust our future to God and his promises. Luther said, ". . . alien righteousness, that is the righteousness of another, [is] instilled from without. This is the righteousness of Christ by which he justifies through faith. . . ." (*TKR*, p. 86). This forgiveness is instant and complete, for alien righteousness ". . . . swallows up all sins in a moment" (*TKR*, p. 88; cf. p. 66). Furthermore, this alien righteousness not only swallows up our sins but also our sinful nature. ". . . [the godly] know that the remnant of sin which is in their flesh, is not laid to their charge, but freely pardoned" (*CG*, p. 149). A necessary implication from this is that alien righteousness not only obviates all sins committed from the past to the present but also forgives all future sins, since they will all arise from the sinful nature that remains in us until "the last day" (*FC*, p. 67).

He felt that great emphasis needed to be given to these negative aspects of alien righteousness: ". . . whoso does not understand or apprehend this [passive, alien] righteousness in afflictions and terrors of conscience, must needs be overthrown. For there is no comfort of conscience so firm and so sure, as this passive righteousness is" (*CG*, p. 101). As a deduction from his insistence that alien righteousness must be the foundation for proper righteousness, Luther could make the following statement, from which the original Latin phrase, *simul iustus et peccator*, "both righteous and a sinner," has become a technical expression in theology for representing the concept of the believer's possessing both a proper and an alien righteousness:

Thus a Christian person is both righteous and a sinner,[6] holy and profane, an enemy of God and yet a child of God. These contraries no sophisters will admit, for they know not the true manner of justification. And this was the cause why they constrained people to work well so long, until they should feel in themselves

---

[6] The Christian is *righteous* by virtue of being accounted righteous by faith. But the Christian is also a *sinner* because of an inability always to be at rest and hopeful in adversity and to do truly beneficial things to others with joy.

no sin at all. Whereby they gave occasion to many (which, striving with all their endeavor to be perfectly righteous, could not attain thereto) to become stark mad; yea an infinite number of those which were the authors of this devilish opinion, at the hour of death were driven into desperation. Which things would have happened unto me also, if Christ had not mercifully looked upon me, and delivered me out of this error. (*CG*, p. 130)

But Luther also strongly emphasized the positive side of alien righteousness. In that God has forgiven all our sins, he no longer needs to deal with us on the basis of justice, but now with full joy deals with us in terms of mercy and love.[7] Consequently, in his love God does not withhold any good thing from those who believe in Jesus.

[Jesus] is entirely ours with all his benefits if we believe in him, as we read in Rom. 8:32: "He who did not spare his own Son but gave him up for us all, will he not also give us all things with him?" Therefore everything which Christ has is ours, graciously bestowed on us out of God's sheer mercy. . . . (*TKR*, p. 87)

This is because

whatever [Christ] did, he did it for us and desired it to be ours, saying, "I am among you as one who serves"[8] [Luke 22:27]. . . . Through faith in Christ, therefore, [his] righteousness becomes our righteousness and *all* that he has becomes ours; rather, he himself becomes ours. (*TKR*, p. 87, italics added)

So we see that alien righteousness brings the greatest positive benefits and is not

---

[7] Luther declared that there was no Gospel in the Old Testament but that it contained only "God's laws and commandments. . . . [and] the records of men who kept [them], and of others who did not," whereas "the New Testament is a volume containing God's promised evangel, as well as records of those who believed or disbelieved it" (*PNT*, p. 14). Therefore it is ironic that he wrote, in "A Preface to the Psalms" for his German translation of the Bible (Dillenberger, *Martin Luther*, pp. 37-41), "that Psalms clearly describes the nature and standing of *all Christian people*" (p. 38, italics added), and preached many sermons from the Psalms. Furthermore, when he felt the deepest need of being reassured of having the forgiveness of sins proclaimed in the Gospel, he turned for comfort to passages in Ezekiel (*CG*, p. 155) where God said, "As I live, I have no pleasure in the death of the wicked, but that the wicked turn back from his way and live; turn back, turn back from your evil ways; for why will you die, O house of Israel?" (Ez. 33:11; cf. 18:23, 32.). For these and other reasons I have been forced to conclude that Luther's characterization of the Old Testament as law in contrast to the New Testament as Gospel represents a needless inconsistency in his thinking.

[8] This is also part of the reason why the Christian is so gloriously free in Luther's thinking, for how could he or she be otherwise if Christ, God's only begotten Son, is among us to *serve* us?

merely the concept of justification or the forgiveness of sins.

We have chosen to discuss Luther's concept of alien righteousness as coming after proper righteousness, because it is easier to see our need of God's forgiveness after we see how far short our actual, proper righteousness falls from perfection. But in reality we should think of alien righteousness as coming first in that it is the indispensable foundation without which it would be impossible to believe God's promises and thus make progress in overcoming our sins. For Luther, "This [alien] righteousness is primary; it is the basis, the cause, the source of all our own actual righteousness" (*TKR*, p. 88). We now seek to understand how this can be true.

Proposition 3: Alien righteousness is the requisite for proper, actual righteousness.

The first way alien righteousness serves as a basis for actual righteousness is that it removes from our souls any sense of God's anger and impending judgment for our terrible sins of unbelief. The Bible's promises of God's forgiveness lay an indispensable foundation for confidently claiming God's "very great and precious promises" (2 Pet. 1:4) for oneself. So Luther says,

> . . . it behooves us . . . to mark well the distinction between the righteousness of the law [proper righteousness], and the righteousness of Christ [alien righteousness]. And this distinction is easy to be uttered in words, but in use and experience it is very hard . . . for in the hour of death, or in other agonies of the conscience, these two sorts of righteousness do encounter more near together than you would wish or desire.[9]
>
> Wherefore I do admonish you . . . that you exercise yourselves continually by study, by reading, by meditation of the Word and by prayer, that in the time of temptation [an agony of conscience] you may be able to instruct and comfort both your own consciences and others', and to bring them from law to grace, from active and working righteousness to passive and received righteousness, and . . . from Moses to Christ.[10] For the devil is wont in affliction and in the conflict of

---

[9] I interpret Luther's saying that passive righteousness and proper righteousness get too close together in times when we experience agonies of conscience to mean that we are more inclined then to think about our own behavior and thus see its many imperfections than we are to dwell on how God, through Christ, has given us full pardon for our sins because Jesus made an atonement for them in his incarnation and death on the cross. So at such times we must fight back by focusing on Biblical passages that declare that God has indeed forgiven all the believer's sins (Ex. 34:6-7; Mark 3:28; 1 John 1:9; and many others).

[10] According to my interpretation, Luther is not pitting Moses against Christ here; rather, he is using their names as ways of distinguishing active righteousness (Moses) from passive righteousness (Christ in his atoning death, not in his Moses-like teaching). This necessarily implies that the prophets and apostles also taught proper righteousness (the law!) in their

conscience, by the law to make us afraid and to lay against us the guilt of sin, our wicked life past, the wrath and judgment of God, hell and eternal death, that by this means he may drive us to desperation . . . and pluck us from Christ. Furthermore, he is wont to set against us those places of the Gospel[s], wherein Christ himself requires works of us, and with plain words threatens damnation to those who do not do them. Now, if here we be not able to judge between *these two kinds of righteousness*, if we take not by faith hold of Christ . . . who makes intercession unto the Father for us wretched sinners [Heb. 7:25], then we are *under the law [of proper righteousness]* and not under grace [alien righteousness], and Christ is no more a savior, but a lawgiver.[11] Then there can remain no more salvation, but a certain desperation and everlasting death must follow. (*CG*, pp. 107-108, italics added)

This passage clearly shows, I believe, how the negative aspects of alien righteousness make it possible for us sinners to be freed from a sense of condemnation, so that we are free to "work with that first and alien righteousness" to "make progress" in improving our proper righteousness (*TKR*, p. 88). But then Luther says, ". . . alien righteousness is not instilled all at once, but it begins, makes progress, and is finally perfected at-the-end through death" (*TKR*, p. 88). How can Luther say this about alien righteousness that "swallows up sin in a moment" (*TKR*, p. 88; cf. p. 66)? Did not Luther really mean to speak here about "the proper righteousness" in which progress is made during our lifetimes in casting out the sinful nature? (cf. *TKR*, p. 88).

It is possible, of course, that Luther uttered a malapropism here. But the interpreter should be chary in drawing such a conclusion about an author. The interests of truth are more apt to be served by trying to see if a strange statement of an author could make sense in some way that would not create additional contradictions with the other statements. My guess is that Luther meant that none of us, in this life, possesses and appropriates all the positive blessings of alien righteousness, which is the foundation for producing proper righteousness. Consequently, in the claim that "alien righteousness is not instilled all at once," I regard "alien righteousness" to be a metonymy for the proper righteousness made possible by alien righteousness. Evidence in support of this hypothesis comes from near the top of p. 88, where Luther talks about how alien righteousness is the cause

---

instructions as to how people are to obey. In support of this construction, see what Luther goes on to say, and note the next words in italics.

[11] In other words, when we let regrets for our past behavior and our foolish inclinations gain the ascendancy in our thinking, we can easily lose sight of the forgiveness of sins given us in Christ's passive righteousness.

and source of actual righteousness; it also comes from near the bottom of page 88 where the believer is to "work with that first and alien righteousness" (*TKR*, p. 88) to gain more of proper righteousness. Just how one works with alien righteousness to produce proper righteousness is made understandable by the following, beginning with God's promise:

> "If you wish to fulfill the law and not covet, as the law demands, come and believe in Christ in whom grace, righteousness, peace, liberty, and all things are promised you [the positive aspects of alien righteousness]. If you believe, you shall have all things; if you do not believe, you shall lack all things." That which is impossible for you to accomplish by trying to fulfill all the works of the law—many and useless as they all are [without faith]—you will accomplish quickly and easily through faith. . . . Thus the promises of God give what the commandments of God demand and fulfill what the law prescribes, so that all things may be God's alone, both the commandments and the fulfilling of the commandments. . . . Therefore the promises of God belong to the New Testament. Indeed they are the New Testament.[12] (*FC*, pp. 57-58)

This quotation from Luther is very helpful in understanding that the "obedience of faith" (Rom. 1:5; 16:26) is not merely justification, as Calvin affirms in his Romans commentary (*ad loc.*), but also affirms that faith in God's promises is essential for progress in sanctification. There are other places where Luther puts the law into a positive light, and these should now be cited before we consider what to make of Luther's negative statements regarding the law. In commenting on Rom. 3:28-31 in the Preface to his translation of Romans he said,

> We reach the conclusion that faith alone justifies us [alien righteousness] and fulfills the law [proper righteousness]; and this [proper righteousness comes] because faith brings the spirit gained by the merits of Christ [the positive aspects of alien righteousness]. The spirit, in turn gives us the happiness and freedom at which the law aims; and this shows that good works really proceed from faith. That is Paul's meaning in Romans 3:31 when, after having condemned the works of the law [3:28], he sounds as if he had meant to abrogate the law by faith; but he says on the contrary, we confirm the law through faith, i.e., we fulfill it by faith. (*PR*, p. 22)

Luther regards Paul's crucial term, "works of law" to mean the attempt to please God as though one were performing needful services for God out of an

---

[12] But we have seen how much Luther preached from the Psalms, and in his darkest moments found comfort in God's promise of mercy in Ezekiel. See above, note 10.

ability that one already possesses. He did not believe that the law itself enjoined such "works," for he stated clearly that the law itself taught that it was to be obeyed in a spirit of joy that comes from believing God's promises. In commenting on our innate hostility to the law of God set forth in Rom. 7:22-23. he declared,

> St. Paul therefore asserts at this point that if the law is rightly understood, and if it is construed in the best way, it only reminds us of our sins [of unbelief], uses [this knowledge of our sinfulness] to kill us, and makes us liable to everlasting wrath. All this our own conscience learns perfectly by experience when it meets the law face to face. Hence, if we are to be upright and attain salvation, we shall require something different from, and better than the law [understood as commands to be obeyed apart from faith]. Those people who fail to understand the law aright, are blind; in their presumptuous way, they think they can fulfill it with works. They are unaware how much the law demands; in particular, a heart that is free and eager and joyful [e.g., Deut. 28:47]. Hence they do not read Moses aright; the veil still covers and conceals his face [2 Cor. 3:14]. (*PR*, p. 31)

Unlike Calvin, who said that we should use the law as a whip to a balky ass to get ourselves to produce proper righteousness,[13] Luther affirmed that sanctification, as well as justification, is attained by faith alone: ". . . in the same faith whereby [true saints] are justified . . . [they] do abstain from the desires of the flesh [sanctification]" (*CG*, p. 164, italics added). Furthermore,

> When we have thus taught faith in Christ [to receive alien righteousness], then do we teach also good works. Because you [my reader] have laid hold upon Christ by faith, through whom you are made righteous, begin now to work well. Love God and your neighbor, call upon God, give thanks to him, praise him, confess him. Do good to your neighbor and serve him fulfill your office [of serving others in the vocation to which God has called you]. These are good works indeed, which flow out of this faith and this cheerfulness conceived in the heart, for that we have the remission of sins freely by Christ. (*CG*, pp. 111-112)

Now it should be clear how in Luther's thinking "faith forms and adorns [the works of] love" (*CG*, p. 122). Faith *forms* good works because it releases us from fear of God's punishment for our sins and promises us that, along with Christ, God will give us all things (Rom. 8:32) so that everything works together eventually for our good (Rom. 8:28). And the joy of believing the faithful God who makes such

---

[13] Cf. John Calvin, *Institutes of the Christian Religion*, II, 7, 12. I have been unable to find where Calvin ever said that sanctification, or progress in gaining more proper righteousness, was produced by faith in God's promises.

promises *adorns* our good works and makes them beautiful. So, for example, Paul commands that those who do acts of mercy do them with cheerfulness (Rom. 12:8).

II. An Insufficient Emphasis in Luther's Teaching

It troubles me, in the quotation cited above from the Galatians commentary (*CG*, pp. 111-112), that Luther exhorts those who have assurance of alien righteousness simply to go ahead and produce genuine righteousness. He tells his reader to "begin now to work well," and goes on to list off some basic things belonging to proper righteousness. But the only thing he mentions that *forms* and *adorns* good works is the joy one derives from the negative aspect of alien righteousness, namely the forgiveness of sins, whereas we have cited passages where a positive aspect of alien righteousness, namely the promises of God, plays a large role in making good works adorned or "beautiful." Luther's teaching would have been much less apt to produce mere nominal Christians if he had continued to emphasize how the promises of God, the positive aspect of alien righteousness, produce good works understood as the obedience of faith. If, instead of telling his readers just to go out and "do well," he had continually reiterated how various promises in Scripture would overcome hearts expressing unbelief in such attitudes as covetousness, bitterness, anxiety, jealousy, impatience, regret, and so on, and if he had stressed the absolute necessity of fighting the fight of faith in order to gain the joyous heart necessary for the doing of good works, the history of Protestantism might have been very different.

It is significant that Luther himself, in describing how he regained the "joyful, high-spirited" (*PR*, p. 24) heart that is able to fulfill the law's commands, merely talked of having "laid hold of any place of Scripture, and stayed myself upon it as upon my chief anchor-hold, . . . [and] straightways my temptations did vanish away" (*CG*, p. 155). To be sure, all scripture is profitable. But we have seen Luther's statements about the ultimate importance of faith in the *promises* of God as the foundation on which to build a proper righteousness. So he should have emphasized the portions of the Bible containing God's promises as most valuable for regaining the happy heart that is essential for truly complying with the law. He should have emphasized that "faith [in the promises] battles with sin" (*PR*, p. 29) as much as he stressed the forgiveness of sins through Christ's atonement. Calvin was an avid student of Luther (through his writings), and if Luther had made this equal emphasis, perhaps Calvin would have taught faith in the promises as the

Good News in History

mainspring for making progress in sanctification instead of the lash of the "bare" law regarded as something opposite from faith.[14]

So if the subsequent Calvinism had taught an obedience of faith that embraced sanctification as well as justification, church history since the Reformation might not have had so many dreary chapters about Christian nominalism in it. The emphasis I received in the Protestant tradition in which I was raised was that all one needed to do to be saved was to believe in Christ's atoning work for the forgiveness of sins. The following quotations from Luther aptly sum up the emphasis that I received in my upbringing: " . . . like as neither the law nor any work thereof is offered us but Christ alone: so nothing is required of us but faith alone, whereby we apprehend Christ, and believe that our sins and our death are condemned and abolished in the death of Christ" (*CG*, p. 121). Also, "Wherefore we also do acknowledge a quality and a formal righteousness in the heart [proper righteousness] . . . and yet so notwithstanding, that the heart must behold *nothing* but Christ the Savior" (*CG*, p. 110, italics added).

So it is no wonder that Luther complained that "if we teach faith, then carnal people neglect and reject works: if works be required, then is faith and the consolation of conscience lost" (*CG*, p. 150). But would he have had that trouble if he had made an equal emphasis on both the negative and positive side of alien righteousness? I think not. John's Gospel emphasizes in many places that Jesus provides for forgiveness of sins (e.g., 1:29 and 3:16). But it also emphasizes that true faith in Jesus results in a slacking of heart thirst and hunger (4:11-12; 6:35), which produces good works (5:28-29). Only those who continue in Jesus' word are truly his disciples (8:29). It seems that John would have agreed that a person only worships what he or she hopes in, and serves what he or she worships. So if Luther had always taught a faith in the negative as well as the positive aspects of alien righteousness, he would not have had to complain about any dichotomy between faith and works. Furthermore, had Luther stressed both aspects equally, he would have had more credibility when he said, " . . . we are the children of God as long as we obey and strive to put sin to death" (*PR*, p. 31).

Luther could have avoided several other objectionable emphases in his teaching if he had only stayed with faith both in the negative (forgiveness) and positive (righteousness-producing) aspects of alien righteousness. We could show

---

[14] See Calvin, *Institutes*, III, 2, 29, and all of III, 19, for Calvin's unambiguous teaching about the contrast between law and faith.

why he would not then have felt compelled to call James "an epistle full of straw" (*PNT*, p. 19). We could also show that Jesus was preaching an essential of the Gospel when he told the rich young ruler and the lawyer that they must keep the law in order to have eternal life, so that Luther would not have had to dichotomize Christ both into a Savior and into another Moses (*PNT*, p. 17). Neither would he have needed to subordinate the Old Testament to the New Testament (*PNT*, p. 14), nor the Synoptic Gospels to the Gospel of John, the epistles of Paul and I Peter (*PNT*, p. 19).

The historic problem Luther was facing probably best explains his failure to emphasize the positive, as well as the negative, aspects of alien righteousness. But I am grateful to him for the times when he did speak about faith in the positive aspects of alien righteousness as the key for being a loving person. It is my conviction that conservative evangelical theology should have done with all carry-over from Calvinism and covenant theology that dichotomizes faith and good works, and insist rather (with Calvin himself) upon keeping these together in Christ though never conjoined.[15] Nominalism would have a difficult time surviving in the presence of a Christianity that, like Luther, declared that only if you persevered (though admittedly with some lapses) in believing that in Christ God works all things together for one's good, would you enjoy eternal life, but if you did not persevere in believing this you would know only eternal misery. It is my conviction that Protestantism needs to start teaching that the law is a law of faith (Rom. 9:32) complied with by an obedience of faith (Rom. 1:5; 16:26), which produces the works of faith (1 Thess. 1:11; 2 Thess. 1:3; cf. Heb. 6:10).

[15] Cf. Calvin: "Repentance [Calvin's term for what we today call "sanctification" today] and faith, although they are held together by a permanent bond [in union with Christ], require to be joined rather than confused" (*Institutes of the Christian Religion*, III, 3, 5, ed. J. T. McNeill, tr. F. L. Battles, in *LCC*, XX and XXI [Philadelphia: Westminster Press, 1960]).

One God—Two Covenants

Wendell W. Frerichs

Professor of Old Testament, Luther Northwestern Theological Seminary
St. Paul, Minnesota

Graduate studies after seminary are obviously intended to accomplish more than develop research skills. Some of us can attest that they are also challenging to cherished theological positions and presuppositions. As a result, one could write not only a dissertation but also an autobiographical piece entitled, "How my mind has changed." For some these mind-changing experiences are more painful than for others. For those of us working with Professor Bo Reicke the pain was minimal due to his gentleness and kindness. Yet, even so, there was considerable stretching, even tearing, involved in giving birth to new ideas. The two most difficult but enduring of these changes which graduate studies worked in my life were the acceptance of the historical-critical method of Biblical interpretation and of Judaism as a living faith. The latter of these two will be addressed here.

The world Jewish community is small. Had they not been decimated time and again, most recently in the Holocaust, someone has estimated that the Jewish people might today number two hundred million. Because they were so often killed or forcibly converted to Christianity they now number less than a tenth of that total. Thus one may grow up in America or Europe not knowing any Jewish person. Even where there were a few of them in the community, as in my particular case, one could effectively ignore them and in church pretend that they did not exist. That is what we did. In our church the Jews were talked about a great deal, but not the Jews who lived among us. We learned about Pharisees and Scribes, about hypocrites and legalists, about Jesus' opponents and Paul's antagonists, about Judaizers and synagogues of Satan in New Testament times. We learned about stiff-necked enemies of the prophets and God's unfaithful people who worshipped Baal in Old Testament times. No one bothered to ask whether the Jews of our town continued to worship God. It was enough to know that they were the dispersed descendants of those who rejected Jesus and who had clamored for his death. There was no possibility of any of them being saved unless they converted to Christianity. Yet, even with such views, who knows whether anyone cared enough about them to invite them to church.

Professor Reicke's courses, "Das Judentum" and "Neutestamentliche Zeitgeschichte," and Professor Oscar Cullmann's "Geschichte des Judentums im Mittelalter" changed all that. The years since have been a kind of pilgrimage for discovering the faith and people of Judaism. For that I am grateful to these two fine professors. It is sad to contemplate that most of the members of our churches are probably as isolated from the synagogue and as parochial as their parents were a generation ago. That is why some of us use every opportunity we get to tell congregational and seminary classes about Judaism as a living faith. One hopes that there are many more opportunities for them to learn than we had, including sermons which sensitively and appreciatively portray these neighbors rather than caricature them. One might also hope that personal contacts such as living room dialogues and synagogue visits will take people farther than merely removing stereotypes.

We also need to learn and repent of the church's long, cruel history of mistreating the Jewish people. Are the current college and seminary church history textbooks more adequate in portraying the history of the Jews than the books we studied? Do students read books like E. Flannery's, *The Anguish of the Jews*?[1] Are they made aware of past and present effects of anti-semitism or anti-Judaism? Already in New Testament times a conflict between church and synagogue was going on. The belligerent way in which "the Jews" are referred to in the Gospel of John or "the synagogue of Satan" in Revelation indicates how heated the battle had become. Choice denunciations and epithets used by the sainted Church Fathers[2] to allude to the Jews of their communities carried on the tradition and heightened

[1] E. H. Flannery, *The Anguish of the Jews* (London: Macmillan, 1965).
[2] See in D. D. Runes, *The War Against the Jews* (New York: Philosophical Library, 1968), pp. 1, 5, 10, 13, 42, 46, 48, 54, 67, 69, 85, 86, 91, 96, 105.

it. The difference was that, by Constantinian times, Christians not only called names, but also had enough political clout to use sticks and stones to break bones. The miserable fate of the Jews in the western Christian world needs to be told and confessed by the church. Not only some of the hideous deeds done against them (Professor Cullmann told us that the cultured people of Basel once locked the Jews of their city in a house which they then burned down), but the hatred and suspicions which led to such acts also need to be recognized. The problem has not gone away just because everyone now has gone to high school. Ignorance is not its only cause. Well educated, articulate church people continue to be prejudiced against Jews, just as their ignorant, unlettered ancestors were. Some tentative answers as to why this was true and continues to be so will follow.

Christians have singled out Jews for contempt because they need scapegoats to blame for their troubles. In the fourteenth century was it not convenient to have the Jews to blame for the Black Death? Now centuries later we can see that vermin in their own unkempt houses spread the plague among our ancestors. But it was opportune for these ignorant, threatened people to spread the unfounded rumor that Jews had poisoned the wells. Of course, killing the Jews did not stop the plague. Another basis of anti-semitism was that people usually do not love those who lend them money, especially when it comes time to pay it back. Due to their exclusion from various businesses, the trades, farming and owning land, Jews were forced into the unpopular business of money lending. It was a service which was needed since Christians were short of money for crusades and wars. But the temptation to legalize the defaulting of loans and to expel Jews from realms where prince and pauper were indebted to them proved too great in one country after another. A further reason for distrust and prejudice derived from the Jewish exclusivism and from cultural differences between the Jews and the rest of the population. Saturday rather than Sunday observance, eating kosher food and refusing to share in what was non-kosher cut them off from intimate relationships with Christians. They became the butt of jokes and rumors rather than respected as neighbors. Yet the most serious bases of Christian anti-semitism were, and still are, theological.

Jews as well as Christians claim to be elect and chosen by God, to be in covenant with God. We but not they claim Jesus to be their Messiah. We but not they proclaim, teach, and believe in an exclusive way of salvation which they have knowingly rejected. According to our theology they can pass muster on the great day of judgment only by having previously converted to the Christian faith. Because we have been hounding them about their lost state for nearly two millennia, mostly without success, we do not know what to do with them. Most Christians have believed that the only Jew acceptable to God is a converted Jew, and so we have been desperate to explain why most of them have not done so. They are therefore said to be stubborn as well as lost. Like Luther,[3] Christians have over the centuries considered an appropriate response the expropriation of Jewish property, the destruction of synagogues, and the expulsion of their persons from our lands. It is clear that we Christians will not leave the Jews in peace until the last of them is converted (an unlikely prospect) or until we have theologically rendered it legitimate to be Jewish. It is the latter alternative which will be supported here. Some of the reasons which have compelled me to adopt this position follow.

A major reason for Christians to accept Jews as they are is that Jews are already a community of faith, worshipping the same God as we do. They are the ones who introduced us to their God in the first place. Their God is the God of both their Scriptures and our Bible. Their Bible even now constitutes the bulk of our Sacred Scriptures. Our God and theirs is the Redeemer of Israel, creator of the universe. The promises which God has made in the Hebrew Bible only include us Gentiles in a derivative way. They were made initially only to Israel. Further, the direct descendants of the first recipients still live in hope of those things not yet fulfilled. It is their faith in God, their prayers and praise of God, their obedient response to God which convince us that they are already a community of faith accepted by God without the need of being converted to our faith. Together the two communities, Christians and Jews, look forward to the same blessed future era of peace and justice. Together we pray for it and struggle to make it a reality in God's good but fallen world.

One aspect of that future era on which we both agree and disagree profoundly is that it will be the time of the Messiah. We believe, teach and confess that Jesus, our crucified Savior and risen Lord, will return to usher in that perfect age. Jews are unconvinced that he will be the one, since his initial coming did not change the world in the way that the promised Messiah was expected to do it. Christians will, into the foreseeable future, disagree among themselves as to how important Jewish rejection of Jesus as their Messiah is. Some will be satisfied with

---

[3] Martin Luther, "On the Jews and Their Lies," in *Luther's Works*, XLVII, ed. H. Lehmann, tr. M. H. Bertram (Philadelphia: Fortress Press, 1971), pp. 121-306. For a reasoned contemporary understanding of Luther's tract, see G. Forde, "Luther and the Jews," in *Luther, Lutherans and the Jewish People*, (Minneapolis: The American Lutheran Church, 1977), pp. 6-20.

Jesus' mediation as *the* or *a* way to God for Gentiles, though not for Jews. Others, convinced by passages like John 14:6 and Acts 4:12, will insist on full conversion of Jews to Christianity as the only way for them to experience eternal salvation. Hopefully both liberal and conservative Christians can agree that it is not our generosity or our exclusivism but rather God's grace which will ultimately decide the issue.

Since it is our Messianism (Christology) which most decisively separates Jews from Christians, theologians on both sides have recently been giving attention to this subject.[4] Jewish contributions range all the way from utter rejection of anything Messianic about Jesus to willingness to entertain the possibility of Jesus' resurrection. Christian appraisals run the gamut from the traditional "Jesus is the fulfillment of Biblical Messianic prophecy" to "Jesus was a Jewish man." The dialogue does not seem to be leading anywhere. The conservatives and the traditionalists on each side hold out for positions which perpetuate the millennia-long impasse between the two faiths. The unorthodox and the liberals tend to go so far beyond the majority of the members of their own faith as to render themselves out of touch, so that they really speak only for themselves. Where it is suspected that they have compromised too much for the sake of more successful dialogue, there they become alienated from their own kind.

It may be that the Jewishness of Jesus, his humanity and his solidarity with his people, is a fruitful avenue to explore together. It may also prove useful to study together just what Messianic expectations the Hebrew Bible projects, and to ask which of these the New Testament claims to have been fulfilled in Jesus' life, death and resurrection. Some Christians already suggest that we entertain another term than "Messiah" for the one who came and did fulfill those aspects of Biblical promise which Christians consider crucial. Another matter is what we can do in dialogue with those promises as yet unfulfilled and which we are content to await in the second coming. To expect Jewish participants to share our enthusiasm for Jesus' *parousia* would seem unrealistic. The Christological impasse will not likely

---

[4] See E. B. Borowitz, *Contemporary Christologies: A Jewish Response* (New York: Paulist Press, 1980). This volume by a Jewish theologian surveys modern Christian Christological positions in terms of their consistency, their acceptability to the Jewish community, and their relationship to the Christian faith. Also R. H. Levine, *Two Paths to One God: Judaism and Christianity* (New York: Collier, 1962). Through a question and answer format, Rabbi Levine shows great respect for his neighbor's faith as a valid way to God and also clarifies what is distinctive about Judaism. He does not suggest two covenants as the way to mutual recognition for the two faiths.

It is, therefore, with cautious hope that a separate but equal, two-covenant approach is proposed. This route does not force Jews to do more than the majority of them have long ago been prepared to do: to acknowledge that Christianity is an acceptable path to God for Gentiles. What is asked of Christians is to acknowledge that God's promises to Abraham and his covenant with Israel are still valid and in place. Do the two faiths need to agree in their Christologies to say that much? Let us hope not.

Numerous models have been developed by Christians and Jews which seek to accommodate the awkward fact that both groups claim to be covenanted with the same God. The earliest rapprochement came from the Jewish side, acknowledging that the *goyim* need not become Jewish and observe the 613 commandments of the Torah in order to be accepted by God.[5] Instead, the covenant of God with Noah, in conjunction with the observance of but seven commands was deemed sufficient. Unfortunately, and even though this gesture was generous, the Noahide covenant does not correspond with the self-understanding of any Christian. It thus provides a two-covenant model with which only the people on the Jewish side will find affinity.

A more hopeful approach is one made a generation ago, again from the Jewish side. F. Rosenzweig and his Christian friend, E. Rosenstock-Huessy, found it necessary to reflect upon the religious side of their friendship.[6] Out of this came Rosenzweig's proposal of two valid covenants existing side by side. On the one side is God's covenant with Israel. On the other is the covenant which God offers through Jesus of Nazareth and which is necessary for Gentiles. Rosenzweig thus offers an alternative to the traditional Jewish willingness to accept non-Jews on the basis of the Noahide Covenant. He simply accepted the covenant mediated by Jesus as valid, even as necessary, for the nations. Not many Jewish writers seem to have followed his lead.

One Jewish theologian who does follow Rosenzweig is W. Herberg.[7] He

---

[5] A. Cohen, *Every Man's Talmud* (New York: Dutton, 1949), p. 65.

[6] E. Rosenstock-Huessy (ed.), *Judaism Despite Christianity: The Letters on Christianity and Judaism Between E. Rosenstock-Huessy and Franz Rosenzweig* (University, Ala.: University of Alabama Press, 1969). A fine, clarifying summary interpretation of this position is: M. G. Bowler, "Rosenzweig on Judaism and Christianity—Covenant Theory," *Judaism*, 22 (1973), pp. 475-481.

[7] W. Herberg, "Judaism and Christianity: Their Unity and Difference," *JBR*, 20 (1953), pp. 67-78. Herberg is followed by H. Matt, "How Shall a Believing Jew View Christianity?" *Judaism*, 24 (1975), pp. 391-405. Herberg proposes that, through Christianity, God's covenant with Israel is opened to all people. His is then a one covenant theology with Christians becoming,

proposes that Christians abandon their one-covenant theology, the position that God's covenant with Israel has been superseded by the New Testament covenant. Not many Christians initially responded to this proposal though their numbers are growing.[8] I wish to join them for reasons already stated—in brief, that the synagogue is clearly a living community of faith. Further, aside from a few places

---

in effect, Israelites. In spite of differences the two faiths have so much in common as to be equal before God. Both are covenant faiths. Two covenant communities now exist, each with a different vocation. The new covenant community does not replace or displace the Sinai covenant community. Matt is more resistant to Jews responding to the Christian claim that Christ makes God available to humans. Jews sense no need of Christ to mediate a covenant for them. Following Rosenzweig and Herberg, he seems to allow Christ to fill this role for the Gentiles, yet he uses considerable space and energy portraying the supposed differences between the two faiths. He is especially interested in dispelling Christian misportrayals and caricatures of Judaism such as that it is a legalism or is this-worldly and materialistic. What finally matters is that God's presence and power are evident in the lives of both Christians and Jews, so that each should then willingly acknowledge the validity of the covenant in which the other lives.

[8] Cf. P. Borchsenius, *Two Ways to God* (London: Vallentine, 1968). This Danish Lutheran pastor affirms God's covenant with the Jews and also the one with Christians, the new covenant (Ch. 16, "The Two Ways"). Both Judaism and Christianity are "ways" built by God. Borchsenius is also keenly sensitive to the church's guilt for its many past evil acts against the Jews and for a lingering anti-semitism. Also, H. H. Ditmanson, "Judaism and Christianity: A Theology of Co-existence," *Dialog*, 15 (1977), pp. 17-24. Ditmanson approves of mutual recognition of each other's covenants by the two communities. Also, D. McCarthy, S.J., "Covenant in the Old Testament: The Present State of the Inquiry," *CBQ*, 27 (1965), pp. 217-240. McCarthy traces the study of covenant from Wellhausen to the present day and in the process gives us a brief overview of covenant in the Ancient Near East as well as its development in Israel. This includes both the history of the various covenants and the history of the theological motif. The complexity of the subject, the several covenants, in the Hebrew Bible and in Israel in Biblical times, which McCarthy describes, should enliven the current discussion between Christians and Jews. If God established covenants with Abraham, with David, and with all Israel at Sinai, there is already precedent for more than one covenant operating between the one God and different people and even simultaneously. Also, J. T. Pawlikowski, O.S.M., *Christ in the Light of the Christian-Jewish Dialogue* (New York: Paulist Press, 1982). This author affirms Judaism as a living faith, and renounces deliberate attempts at converting Jews to Christianity, though each faith should enrich the other *via* respectful dialogue. Pawlikowski describes and evaluates one and two covenant theories, emphasizing the creative distinctiveness of rabbinic, pharisaic Judaism as important for the emergence of Jesus and Christianity. Rather than dialogue about Christ as the fulfillment of Jewish Messianic hopes, he finds Christian incarnational Christology a better place to begin discussion. Also, J. C. Rylaarsdam, "Jewish-Christian Relationship: The Two Covenants and the Dilemmas of Christology," *JES*, 9 (1970), pp. 249-270. The author in this article presses the distinction between the covenants of Sinai and David, both of which exercise an influence in Judaism and in Christianity. The tension between these two covenants is never resolved in either faith, but lessened in both by the predominance of one covenant in each faith, Sinai in Judaism and David in Christianity. Thus, Rylaarsdam does not propose a usual two-covenant theology which would press Jews and Christians to affirm each other's faith. Instead he contrasts the two faiths at this one point. Yet his outlook as a Christian is strongly positive and open as over against Judaism.

such as in Hosea 1:9, the Hebrew Bible nowhere calls God's covenant with Israel into question. The canonical form of even Hosea (1:10 and 2:1), together with the whole of the Pentateuch, the Prophets and the Writings, affirms the covenanted status of Israel. This is true in spite of the unfaithfulness and disobedience which were punished in 722 and 587 B.C.E. God, if not always his people, is faithful to the covenant(s) he has made.

It will not do to cite extra-canonical sources (whether New Testament, Apocrypha, Qumran, or the Book of Mormon) to document our own disinheriting of Israel. Any convincing evidence must come from Israel's own sacred Scriptures or from the Talmud, where it is not to be found. Nor is it in the New Testament, say scholars such as K. Stendahl.[9] Even if such evidence were in the New Testament it would scarcely be convincing to Jews for whom this literature is not Scripture. It seems both unnecessary and precarious for Christians to insist upon their own covenanted relationship to God while denying the validity of God's earlier covenants with Israel. It would seem that God's faithfulness is required for either one or both covenants to be still in effect. By affirming God's covenant with the Jews, we are affirming the faithfulness of God which that community also attests. We are also affirming something which we have experienced ourselves, namely the witness of Jews that they are in covenant with the God of Abraham and Moses.

---

[9] K. Stendahl, *Paul Among Jews and Gentiles* (Philadelphia: Fortress Press, 1976). Stendahl contends that Paul's theological focus was on justification rather than on forgiveness and that Paul's Damascus Road experience was a call to service rather than a conversion. These two views alone should set the stage for a rather different stance of Christians toward Jews. His views on St. Paul (specifically Rom. 9-11) and the Jews likewise change the whole ground of the centuries-old debate between church and synagogue. Stendahl believes that Paul taught the coexistence of the two faiths, further that God never intended to Christianize the whole world. See also J. C. Beker, *Paul's Apocalyptic Gospel* (Philadelphia: Fortress Press, 1982), pp. 30-35. Beker lays great stress on God's faithfulness to Israel, though he does not use two-covenant language to describe the relationship between Christians and Jews.

Unity and Diversity
in New Testament Theology

Bo Reicke

Late Professor of New Testament, University of Basel
Basel, Switzerland

Translated by Ed. L. Miller*

As a rule, presentations of New Testament Theology proceed from the whole of the New Testament as contained in the Canon, and the reason for this is that the church has admitted this collection of writings into its Holy of Holies.

I

Sometimes, however, the question arises about the *unity* of the collection of New Testament writings. The fact is, the church—even if according to God's will—singled out the twenty-seven writings of our New Testament over a period of three centuries and combined them into a Canon which was first definitively established at the time of Athanasius. Doubtless, *historical* factors contributed to this development. But were not the Holy Scriptures bound to one another by virtue of a certain unity of *content*? Do they constitute the present Canon only *thēsei*, that is, from outside by edict or decree? Were they not chosen also *physei*, by virtue of

---

*From "Einheit und Vielfalt in der neutestamentlichen Theologie," *Lutherische Kirche in der Welt*, 35 (1988), pp. 15-34.

their inner *nature*, as the authoritative foundation of the Christian proclamation? And even if the aforementioned *thēsis*, the historical formation of the Canon, is understood not as the product of human but rather divine decree, Biblical theology demands nonetheless a verdict concerning the *physis* or content, the essential unity of the New Testament message.

But if one seeks for the inner unity of the New Testament, a complication immediately arises as a result of critical considerations. Specifically, the New Testament representations of faith turn out to be quite varied when the Synoptics, John, Paul, the Catholic Epistles, and Revelation are compared with one another. This has led several Biblical theologians to reject any unified representation of New Testament theology. Thus the leading German books, for example that of R. Bultmann, M. Meinertz, R. Schnackenburg, H. Conzelmann, W. G. Kümmel, J. Jeremias, and L. Goppelt, treat the main groups of New Testament writings separately. By contrast, the New Testament is treated as a theological unity, for example, in an earlier book by E. Stauffer and more recently by K. H. Schelkle, as well as in the British works of M. Burrows and A. Richardson (see notes 1 and 2 below). There are grounds for both sorts of approach, but what are these grounds and which is the right approach? Should one divide everything according to various categories traditionally employed in teaching [*Lehrbegriffe*], as it was called in the nineteenth century, or present the material as a whole? Here we examine first the arguments for unity and then for diversity.

1. In general, the advocates of the *unity* of the New Testament try to establish this perspective on the basis of a common teaching or idea in the New Testament: One points to the concept of God, the doctrine of justification, the teaching about reconciliation, the love commandment, or eschatology; another emphasizes such ideals as the brotherhood of man or the worth of the soul.

But it is impossible in this way to achieve a solution acceptable to all. This impossibility does not derive from the fact that the Synoptics, John, Paul, etc. have expressed the message in different ways—differing forms do not exclude a common substance. Rather, the New Testament in general has no interest in any systematic doctrine or *Weltanschauung*. It propagates no particular ideal, dogma, principle, or the like. Much rather is it the concern of the New Testament to announce *facts* connected with Jesus Christ. It is not a question of doctrine, but of Gospel, *kerygma*, proclamation of pressing facts. From these facts men and women should draw practical conclusions: the necessity of conversion, of faith, etc.

There is no question that all of the New Testament writings concern themselves with *the same Jesus Christ*, with the same events connected with him and their consequences. There is an identity between the proclaimer Jesus and the proclaimed Christ which from the start was expressed in the name, title, and confession: "Jesus Christ." According to the uniform witness of the texts, apostles and others recognized, in spite of a temporary uncertainty, the proclaiming Jesus in the resurrected Christ (Matt. 28:9, Luke 24:3, John 20:14, 1 Cor. 15:5-8), and this Jesus Christ became immediately the subject of their proclamation (Acts 2:22, etc.). The experienced facts were understood by the believers and represented in the documents as an organic and vital salvation-history along with its consequences for men and women, a history [*Geschehen*] connected with the election of Israel, with the Old Testament, and above all with Jesus. For the post-apostolic time too this salvation-historical context determined the proclamation, instruction, and fixing of the Canon as the legendary and Gnostic productions were relegated to the periphery as apocryphal.

Here is found the answer to the question concerning the unity of the New Testament message: The unity of the content of the New Testament lies in the central idea, the *Christ-event*. Because the writings of the New Testament concern themselves without deviation with Jesus Christ, directly and immediately with the events connected with him, with the proclamation by him and about him, the unity of the content of the New Testament is a given. Thus the New Testament is a unity not merely *thēsei*, but also *physei*.

2. There are, nevertheless, also reasons for an arrangement of the material according to different *categories*. Notwithstanding the unity of the person of Jesus Christ, it is a fact that the Synoptics, John, Paul, and other authors of the New Testament present the same Christ-event in somewhat different perspectives.

This coheres with the fact that no two people ever experience the same facts in exactly the same way. Moreover, the New Testament writers lived and worked in different environments. They each possessed a distinct individuality, enjoyed a different training, and wrote for different readers. Because of such diversities among the Synoptics, John, Paul, etc., noted theologians of our time have been inclined to organize the presentation of New Testament theology in terms of several groups of writings.[1]

---

[1] Representation according to various groups of writings may be found in the following textbooks, which have also appeared repeatedly in new editions: R. Bultmann, *Theologie des Neuen Testaments* (Tübingen: Mohr, 1948-53); M. Meinertz, *Theologie des Neuen Testaments*, (Bonn: Hanstein, 1950); H. Conzelmann, *Grundriß der Theologie des Neuen Testaments* (Munich:

176 *Good News in History*

To be sure, it is misguided if this parceling out is done only for the sake of cultural and historical factors, because fundamentally the concern is not merely with forms and mediums of expression. One has no sufficient basis for a division of the material among the aforementioned primary authors when it is undertaken merely out of regard to its variety of expression, personalities, and cultural circumstances. They are simply the means of the presentation.

An illustration from the physical world may clarify the matter. As the natural sunlight is broken and tinted by a prism, so does the divine heavenly light radiate through human witnesses in the world and become thereby variously colored. It is the same light. Though it assumes varying colors depending on the situation the various reflections can be traced back to the same beam. Likewise in the New Testament, many concepts which are generally characteristic for the most important groups of writings, such as the Kingdom of God in the Synoptics and the reign of Christ in Revelation, or truth in John and Righteousness in Paul, fit together in a common framework. Purely formal differences, such as occur at times with respect to varying images and language, do not alter the fundamental message of Jesus Christ. The human prisms through which the heavenly light is variously broken provide in and of themselves no basis for a theology split up and arranged according to fixed headings. Moreover, a splitting up on such a basis would mean a *metabasis eis allo genos*, namely a crossing over from Biblical theology to the religious and ecclesiastical history of early Christianity. The concern should be with revelation, with the heavenly light, not with the prisms by which the light is broken, not with the external medium of the manifestation.[2]

Nevertheless, there is within the New Testament a significant, substantial, and above all theological basis for the arrangement of the Biblical-theological

---

Chr. Kaiser-Verlag, 1967); W. G. Kümmel, *Die Theologie des Neuen Testaments nach seinen Hauptzeuge Jesus, Paulus, Johannes* (Göttingen: Vandenhoeck & Ruprecht, 1968); Joachim Jeremias, *Neutestamentliche Theologie: Die Verkündigung Jesu* (Gütersloh: Mohn, 1971); G. E. Ladd, *A Theology of the New Testament* (Grand Rapids, Mich: Eerdmans, 1974); E. Lohse, *Grundriß der neutestamentlichen Theologie* (Stuttgart: Kohlhammer, 1974); L. Goppelt, *Theologie des Neuen Testaments: 1, Jesu Wirken in seiner theologischen Bedeutung; 2, Vielfalt und Einheit des apostolischen Christuszeugnisses*, ed. J. Roloff, (Göttingen: Vandenhoeck & Ruprecht, 1975-76).

[2] Representatives of the common thematic: E. Stauffer, *Die Theologie des Neuen Testaments* (Gütersloh: Bertelsmann, 1941); M. Burrows, *An Outline of Biblical Theology* (Philadelphia: Westminster Press, 1946); A. Richardson, *An Introduction to the Theology of the New Testament* (New York: Harper & Row, 1958); K. H. Schelkle, *Theologie des Neuen Testaments*, (Dusseldorf: Patmos, 1968-76).

material according to definite types: and that in the following: In the Synoptics, John, Paul, and also in other authors of New Testament books, Jesus is presented under differing Christological perspectives, and this difference of perspective is a sufficient basis for treating the main groups of the New Testament authors separately.

To be sure, the diversity was sometimes presented in a one-sided manner. If one portrays the Redeemer predominately in accordance with the Synoptics, as was the custom of the liberal theologians of the nineteenth century, one does John and Paul a great injustice. If one throws him into relief primarily in terms of John or Paul, as was the case for a long time with the Orthodox or Anglican preoccupations with John or the Protestant alignment with Paul, one likewise does the other New Testament witnesses an injustice. Who is qualified to judge whether the Synoptics, John, Paul, or others should be the standard? People cannot arbitrarily decide that, nor is it the business of the church traditions to judge. It is the mark of a one-sidedness to shove aside other parts of the Bible as less instructive, and the result is that some of its available wealth is inevitably lost. Also, the funneling of the material to the Synoptics, to John, and to Paul (to be taken up below) means a theological constriction, though it seems to be unavoidable for the sake of the overall view. It is, thus, not a concern for history of religion or history of culture but rather a concern for Christology that best allows the abundance of the heavenly light (shining in the New Testament through various prisms) to appear in its true form. For this reason one must make sure that the parceling out of the material to the Synoptics, John, and Paul is theologically rooted.

Questions about religious history and literary criticism should not cloud the overall theological picture as has unfortunately happened so often in research. In the case of the Synoptics, for example, one pushes into the foreground supposed original elements of the life of Jesus, or, in the case of John and Paul, apparent Hellenistic features of their theology, and emphasizes how the theological ideas developed from originating circumstances and in various stages. And in regard to the Synoptic tradition there is a widespread practice of ranking the material in a mechanical-historical way. Thus Mark taken as a source is played against Matthew and Luke, though, first, the Markan priority is by no means a certain hypothesis and, second, the application of this hypothesis results in an unnatural mixture of historical and theological treatments whereby Matthew and Luke are accorded only secondary value. When such questions are permitted to dominate in theological contexts they lead to theories of development as employed by religious studies and literary criticism.

Consequently, New Testament theology must occupy itself, without commitment to naturalistic hypotheses, with the content of the proclamation of the New Testament, a proclamation respected as revelation. The historical and theological approaches should be kept distinct, though they are directed to the same object and each has its own significance. They can supplement one another and enrich knowledge, but they can only do so when they run parallel, not when the message is accommodated to a reconstructed pre-history. This does not imply an anti-historical Fundamentalism, but rather a respect for the principle of the *analogia fidei* (Rom. 12:6).

In a New Testament theology, therefore, the primary authors of the New Testament should be presented with a regard for their respect for and individual treatment of Christology, and certainly, therefore, in every case theologically.[3]

II

How this principle can be applied to the Synoptics, John, and Paul is suggested in the following.

1. In the case of the *Synoptics* the focus is on the appearance of Jesus the proclaimer in predominately earthly and human terms. Here is depicted his birth and humanity, his travels in Galilee, his interaction with the disciples and the people, his proclamation of the Kingdom of God, and his suffering in Jerusalem.

If this fundamental perspective is understood Biblically and theologically, an understanding which defines the Synoptics' Christological contribution to the whole New Testament, their concept of the *Incarnation* must be emphasized.[4] This comes to expression in the oft-cited designation from the Synoptics, "Son of Man," because here the human character of Jesus the proclaimer is emphasized (as in Matt. 11:19). The Synoptics produce even among themselves various representations, so that Jesus already at the beginning steps forward in Matthew as

---

[3] Examples of other discussions of methodology: R. Schnackenburg, *Neutestamentliche Theologie: Der Stand der Forschung* (Munich: Kösel, 1963); B. S. Childs, *Biblical Theology in Crisis* (Philadelphia: Westminster Press, 1970); J. Barr, "Trends and Prospects in Biblical Theology," *JTS*, 25 (1974), pp. 265-282; J. Giblet, "Unité et diversité dans les écrits du Nouveau Testament," *Istina*, 20 (1975), pp. 23-34; J. D. G. Dunn, *Unity and Diversity in the New Testament: An Enquiry into the Character of Earliest Christianity* (London: SCM Press, 1977).

[4] Rightfully emphasized by J. W. Bowman, *The Intention of Jesus* (London: SCM Press 1945), pp. 44-45 and 75-105.

Matthew as King of the Jews (Matt. 2:2), in Mark as Son of God (Mark 1:1), and in Luke as Savior (Luke 2:11); nonetheless, the earthly character of the Son of Man is among them a generally predominate perspective. Jesus appears in the Synoptics as the Son of Man proclaimed by Daniel and Enoch, who on earth laid aside his divine glory and stepped forth in humility and meekness as a human (e.g., Matt. 8:20).

This way of thinking can be compared to the concept of the so-called *kenosis* of Phil. 2:6-11. What is significant here is that the heavenly Christ "emptied" himself, that is, laid aside his other-worldly glory with God and took on a this-worldly existence as a human. To be sure, the Synoptics have expressly developed no such *kenosis* doctrine, but their depiction of the Son of Man is a counterpart to it. If one wants to make good the Christological distinctiveness of the Synoptics in the framework of the whole theology of the New Testament, then the concept of the *kenosis* fits as a characterization of their theological standpoint. The Synoptic Gospels reflect the equation of Jesus the Son of Man with Christ the Son of God especially in the context of the Easter experiences. The latter yielded the insight that Jesus of Nazareth was in actuality the Christ sent from God (Matt. 27:54 par.; 28:9,17; Mark 16:7; Luke 24:31, 45). As is indicated by the title and confession "Jesus Christ," the identity between "Jesus" and "Christ" was, since Easter, a fact for the Christian community. The Johannine report about Thomas who, after a preliminary doubt, came to the confession of the identity (John 20:28: "My Lord and my God") also attests to this general conviction. Only with a Docetic implication can it be denied that the Synoptics concern themselves with the earthly appearance of the same Jesus who is portrayed by the other writings of the New Testament as the heavenly Christ who is from eternity and lives in eternity.

At other points too the Synoptic Gospels betray a conviction as to the heavenly status and mission of the Son of Man, although they have not emphasized the pre-existence of Jesus as explicitly as other books in the Canon. Jesus of Nazareth appears in the Synoptics certainly first of all as a man, who grew up in a family known to contemporaries and in a town insignificant at the time. In spite of this human horizon, nevertheless, his divine nature meanwhile forces itself through, most notably in the baptism, transfiguration, and crucifixion (Matt. 3:17; 17:2; 27:54; all with par.), but also in the miracles (Matt. 8:1-4 par., etc.).

Temporarily, the Messiahship of Jesus should remain externally a secret, but it is for those to discover who have eyes to see and ears to hear (Matt. 13:16; Mark 8:18; Luke 10:23). In the Synoptic drama the Messianic secret betrays itself more and more through Jesus' powerful deeds and compelling words. It is the negative powers in the spiritual world which first suspect the Messianic secret. Because they belong to the spiritual world, although enemies of the Messiah, they can react before people can to the appearance of the Messiah. Despite a repeated command to silence, the secret of Jesus is then spread more and more among people. In Caesarea Philippi, beyond Galilee, Peter ventures on behalf of the Apostles to confess his insight that Jesus is the Messiah or Christ (Matt. 16:16 par.). Jesus acknowledges this, but, to the horror of Peter, immediately directs attention to his Messianic suffering (16:1 par.). Only when Jesus enters Jerusalem by way of the Mount of Olives is the Messianic secret revealed, because it is in the context of suffering and death that the divine majesty of Jesus should come to expression (Matt. 26:28 and 64; 27:37, 54 pars). Consequently this Messianic claim, revealed in the capital city, brings about his death, while unrecognized by his countrymen as the suffering servant of God prophesied by Isaiah (Isa. 53:3). He dies here publicly as the Messiah but, according to the Synoptics, has fulfilled this role earlier though secretly and in an anticipatory way. That is a basic idea which characterizes all three Synoptic Gospels, and their development of the Messianic secret is, in fact, the counterpart of the Pauline *kenosis* doctrine.

But is not the so-called Messianic secret a redactional invention of the Synoptics, and above all of Mark, as is often emphasized? Did it not conceal the fact that the community had actually experienced Jesus, the Master from Nazareth, not so much in the Messianic and Christological categories as was imagined by those writing after the crucifixion of the Lord and the development of the church? Not a few theologians of our time defend such a view. It is a question of a hypothesis which goes back to a book of the year 1901 by W. Wrede.[5]

In itself this theory constitutes only an artificial construction for the benefit of liberal theology's picture of a decidedly immanent Jesus, and in spite of its wide dissemination it is not tenable for historical reasons: If the Synoptics had wanted to harmonize the reminiscences of the historical Jesus with a later, developed Christology, they could have produced a harmony of remembrance and pronouncements much more simply and more naturally through concrete legends and proclamations than through this complicated motif of the Messianic secret. Moreover the Messianic secret and the motifs connected with it, like the

---

[5] William Wrede, *Das Messiasgeheimnis in den Evangelien* (Göttingen: Vandenhoeck & Ruprecht, 1901), pp. 227-228.

stubbornness and misunderstanding on the part of the disciples, are found generally in the Synoptics where they are essential from a dramatic standpoint. One cannot exclude them from tradition without destroying the whole context. A historically satisfying solution to the problem presents itself only on the assumption of sporadic but factual reminiscences of the Son of Man's discretion concerning Messianic claims, both in his life and teaching, which shows that he consciously distinguished himself from contemporary pseudo-Christs. On the whole, the material shows that in humility Jesus stepped forth as the Messiah who is hidden to outsiders, and that reminiscences of that are reflected in the Synoptic traditions.

This historically oriented excursus concerning the Messianic secret has been included in order to demonstrate an essential feature of the Synoptic Christology as being pertinent and not merely speculative.

On the other hand, it must be granted that in the Gospels Jesus has been portrayed inevitably from the standpoint of the post-Easter company of disciples. After the surprising encounters with the resurrected Jesus (1 Cor. 15:5-8) one saw him in a different light than before (Matt. 28:18; Luke 24:45; John 20:28; Acts 2:24; Acts 2:24; e.g., 2 Cor. 5:16). During his life the disciples were not prepared to believe in him without reservation, for frequently they doubted and denied, and this the Evangelists repeated and clearly reported. It was only after the resurrection that the disciples could first grasp the true nature of the historical Jesus, and the Evangelists conceal nothing of their preliminary impediment and subsequent enlightenment (Matt. 16:22/Mark 8:22; Mark 9:6,32/Luke 9:45; Matt. 26:13/Mark 14:9; Matt. 26:34 par., 26:40 par.; 26:56/Mark 14:50; Matt. 28:7 par.; Luke 24:25-26, 44-48; John 1:50; 2:22; 3:14; 8:28; 12:16).

Consequently, two historically different pictures of Jesus are to be distinguished in the Gospel reports, and this holds essential significance for Biblical theology. These two pictures correspond to Jesus (1) as the apostles perceived him *before* his death, and (2) as they understood him *after* his death.[6]

But not even the first picture of Jesus (J^1) is as "historical" or "authentic" as a self-assured exegesis of yesterday and today would like to think. It concerns itself specifically with the apostles' pre-resurrection picture of Jesus, with a picture limited and incomplete in respect to the Apostles' later representations. Not the

---

[6] For discussion of the "historical" Jesus and the kerygmatic Christ, see Bo Reicke, "Der Fleischgewordene," in *Der historische Jesus und der kerygmatische Christus*, ed. H. Ristow and K. Matthiae (Berlin: Evangelische Verlaganstalt, 1960), pp. 208-218 = "Incarnation and Exaltation: The Historic Jesus and the Kerygmatic Christ," *Interpretation*, 16 (1962), pp. 156-168.

reality but a subjective picture is present there, and this picture can only be hypothesized, not historically reconstructed. The following fact stands out everywhere in the Gospel material: Jesus of Nazareth, as the apostles and their associates saw, heard, and understood him during his earthly life, was in reality more exalted than they at that time suspected. In this respect, the Synoptics' references to Peter's betrayal are significant (Matt. 16:23/Mark 8:33; Matt. 26:34 par.). The human incapacity to grasp the majesty of Jesus to the full measure reveals itself also in the following citation from the Gospel of John: "Jesus did, however, many other signs before his disciples, which have not been written down in this book" (John 20:30; cf. further, below).

Only after the Resurrection were the disciples able better to grasp the historical nature of Jesus, and then they completed the previous picture. The second picture of Jesus, which took shape in this way (J^2), was no product of the theologizing community, as is commonly asserted, but rather a result of the Christ-event and an amendment to the earlier limited and inadequate reminiscences and interpretations. For this reason the second picture of Jesus was, in the eyes of the disciples as well as of the traditions and of the Evangelists, even more historical and authentic than the first. The disciples, formerly slow to believe, had constructed for themselves the first inadequate picture of Jesus; according to the witness of the New Testament, it does not correspond to the historical Jesus but rather was the product of limited, human imagination—as is also sometimes the diminished picture of modern representations of the life or the mission of Jesus. According to the witness of the texts, only the post-Easter retrospective view of this Jesus, who had dealings with his own and with the people but who was not correctly understood by the disciples until after his death, corresponds to the historical [*historischen*] or to the historic [*geschichtlichen*] Jesus.

Here the concept "historic" ["*geschichtlich*"], in reference to Jesus, should be treated consistently with respect to the meaning of the texts. From this standpoint it is impossible, in the case of the Synoptics, to play off the "historic" [*das "Geschichtliche"*] against the "theological."[7] It is as impossible here to separate out a non-theological tradition as it is for one to find a core in paring an onion. That holds also for the Gospel of Mark which, with its great interest for human details, concerns itself throughout with a dramatic event. To be sure, a

---

[7] E. Hoskyns and N. Davey, *The Riddle of the New Testament* (New York: Harcourt, Brace & Co., 1931), pp. 23-24 and 142.

purely profane historicity [*Geschichtlichkeit*] is a feature which the Synoptics tacitly ascribed to the Master from Nazareth, inasmuch as Jesus was in no way portrayed as a mythical figure. The reason why the Synoptics have not taken the trouble to document this historicity [*Geschichtlichkeit*] is because it was something generally known in the community. Also in rabbinic polemic against Christianity, the historicity [*Historizität*] of Jesus was not doubted—it was his authority and legitimacy that was disputed. But the Synoptics were not really interested in history [*Geschichte*] and biography in the modern secular sense. If they had been, they would have cited more concrete details—perhaps noted the age of Jesus and described his appearance—but this they certainly did not do.

What the person of today understands by the "historicity" ["*Geschichtlichkeit*"] of Jesus—namely his life, as witnessed to by sources, in the milieu of a spatially and temporally identifiable past—was for the Synoptic tradition and Evangelists not as important as the *Great Commission*, the purpose of the advent and activity of the God-Man. Factuality is here joined with finality. Tradition and Evangelist did not look back to the life of Jesus as some merely bygone event, and they did not desire to reconstruct his career in space and time. For them only the end was decisive, the purpose for which God allowed his Son to live and work in the world. Accordingly, the Synoptics consciously cite out of the mouth of Jesus such sayings as, for example, "The Son of Man has come *in order to. . . .*" (Matt. 5:17; Mark 10:45; etc.). For them it was important not only *that* Jesus lived, but even more *why* he came. And, to be sure, for them the mission of the Son of Man had an active and passive side: active in that he was sent in order to bring the Kingdom of God to people, passive in that he was sent in order to suffer and die for them.

The interpreter of the Gospels can rightly understand this purpose-oriented historicity of Jesus only by attending to the peculiar character of the reality before us.

a) One can view Jesus in a purely human light without reference to God, eliminating the divine elements in the New Testament picture. In that case the interpreter obtains a picture of Jesus devoid of the faith factor, a picture such as Pilate or the scribes no doubt had. But this picture is found nowhere in the New Testament, and can be postulated only in the interest of the indifferent person or the skeptic in the community.

b) Further, the interpreter can attempt to retain a few faith factors and reject the rest as products of the theologizing community. Such a reduction is often and enthusiastically undertaken in modern research: One starts out from an accepted picture of Jesus and throws out everything that does not fit this basic conception. But this method involves, unmistakably, a *petitio principii*, because what serves as a point of departure is not the objective material but rather a subjective bias of the interpreter or the community. This unchecked arbitrariness has led to a diversity of individualistic pictures of the imagined historical Jesus. Generally overlooked is the conviction of the Apostles that their understanding, achieved after Easter, of Jesus' true majesty enabled them to present a genuinely historical picture of him, whereas previously their lack of preparation to perceive and to believe had, according to Jesus' own judgment, limited their understanding (thus especially, Matt. 16:9/Mark 8:17: "Do you not yet understand?"). In the critically reduced Jesus-picture of many a great and small Biblical scholar of modern times the same limitation reveals itself, and the post-Easter discovery of the disciples concerning the full reality of the historical Jesus is suppressed.

c) The difficulties identified under (a) and (b) can be escaped only through consideration of the understanding of the historical Jesus achieved by the Apostles after Easter. Owing to the references to stubbornness and misunderstanding, the Gospels contain certain indications of the Apostles' pre-Easter picture of Jesus (J^1), but according to the witness of the texts this changed in the light of the events of Easter and Pentecost, so that there arose a Christologically more exact picture of Jesus Christ (J^2). Only the second was considered by the disciples to be historical in view of the fact that they were convinced that they were able, on the basis of reminiscences and Easter experiences, to report reliably about the human and divine reality in the Son of Man. Behind the Jesus-picture of the Gospels stands the historical Jesus who at first was comprehended only imperfectly by his own but whose nature and reality they were able to render more fittingly in the post-Easter retrospect.

Therein lies the peculiarity of the Synoptic concept of "historical": With the emphasis on finality, there was seen and portrayed in connection with Jesus a simultaneously earthly and heavenly reality.

2. Such a union of earthly and heavenly reality is found still more clearly in *John's* witness to the life of Jesus.

Christologically, the Gospel of John stands in the middle between the Synoptics and Paul, although it employs a special terminology. While the Synoptics represent the Son of Man predominantly in his earthly appearance as the proclaimer, Jesus of Nazareth, and while Paul attends primarily to the crucified, resurrected, and exalted one, now proclaimed as Christ, the Fourth Gospel so portrays the incarnate Word of God that already the earthly proclaimer Jesus appears as bearer of the glory proclaimed in the Gospel. Because their attention is concentrated either on the earthly or the heavenly plane, the Synoptics, John, and Paul differ, as with the letters S, J, and P in this diagram:

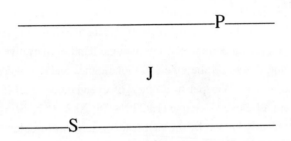

In reading the Gospel of John one is pointed again and again, by means of the earthly form of Jesus as it appears in its historical context, to the heavenly reality which here reveals itself. The whole action is played out on two levels at once, one earthly and one heavenly. In the Gospel of John, Jesus appears to be transparent, as with the painted figures of ancient Christian or Byzantine art which, certainly, possess human elements but spiritual substance.

One thereby beholds in this incarnate Logos not only the heavenly world, but the prophet from Nazareth also presents himself during his earthly life as Lord of a growing Kingdom which is not of this world, namely the Church. This emerges, for example, from the shepherd image of the Gospel (John 10:1-18) or from the allegory of the vine and the branches (15:1-17). Also in the First Epistle of John, which shares a common terminology with the Gospel of John, the Church plays a fundamental role. This and similar witnesses show that in the Fourth Gospel Jesus as the Logos of God (John 1:14) not only is called the Shepherd of the sheep (10:11), but actually serves as the Lord of the Church. For this Gospel the proclaimer and the proclaimed are one, since Jesus in word and deed reveals himself as the Christ. He is the Logos both as person and in content.

It must therefore be observed that, contrary to a popular opinion, the author or authors of the Fourth Gospel had no interest in presenting an ecclesiastical revision of the life of Jesus—it only appears so from an anachronistic viewpoint of literary criticism. Much rather, the Evangelist—whether an apostle or circle of disciples (John 19:35; 21:24)—wished on the basis of eyewitnesses' reminiscences to expand the picture of Jesus based on traditions already known (20:30-31: "Jesus also did many other signs before the disciples which are not recorded in this book. But these have been recorded that you may believe. . . ."; 21:25: "There are also many other things which Jesus did. . . ."). Certainly also in the Gospel of John, traditions were presented which are remarkably parallel to the Synoptic Gospels (above all, John 6:1-71, involving the events from the feeding of the 5000 to the confession of Peter, and particularly 18:1-20, 31, the Passion story). But Johannine characteristics appear predominately, one the one hand, in narrative pericopes and topographical notes, and, on the other, in monologues and dialogues.

References in this Gospel to a circle of eyewitnesses (1:14; 19:35; 21:24) and, among them a Beloved Disciple (13:23; 19:26; 20:2; 21:7, 20) who is nowhere named but was clearly known by the first readers, serve as forceful evidence of the reliability of its account. When this disciple appears at Christologically decisive moments, namely the Last Supper, the crucifixion, the empty tomb, and the encounter in Galilee, he demonstrates his intimate connection with Jesus. Because the Beloved Disciple had recognized the Logos and Messiah even better than had Peter and other disciples, the Fourth Gospel could supply other accessible traditions (suggested in 20:30 and 21:25), extended and intensified (20:31: "that you may believe").

Thus the achievement of the Fourth Evangelist is analogous to the process which led to the portrayal of Jesus in the Synoptic Gospels in which the disciples, with Peter at the head, remedied and supplemented the pre-Easter picture by means of a post-Easter picture. To a higher degree, John filled out and heightened earlier elements of the picture so that a third picture of Jesus can be spoken of. Whether the Synoptic Gospels were accessible to him as written documents is not at all certain, but in any case it is to be noted that in relation to the Synoptic traditions his Gospel involves an enrichment of the Jesus-picture with respect to the heavenly and ecclesial meaning of the Son of God.

Still, for the author of the Gospel of John, or the community originally responsible for it, it is a matter of historical reality and not of theological speculation. Already in the Prologue it is expressly declared (John 1:14): "And the Word became flesh, and we *saw* his glory." That involves a self-declaration by eyewitnesses who had experienced and recognized the glory of God's Son during his life. Likewise, the Johannine disciples provide attestation by appeal to the Beloved Disciple at the cross (19:35): "That one has *seen* and has testified, and he knows that what he says is true, so that you may believe."

No proper consideration of the Gospel of John is possible unless this intention of his, or of the original author or authors, is first taken into account. Independent of literary- and religious-historical questions concerning the identity of the Evangelist and possible analogies to his thought among the Essenes, in Hellenism, or in other movements, the claim of this Gospel to contain eyewitness reports must be heeded.

Biblically and theologically, what is significant in the end is that John wanted to expand and enrich the existing witnesses to Jesus in order to awaken and strengthen the faith of the reader (20:31, etc.). In this he may have had earlier oral traditions in view rather than written ones, and these could have been in some cases sources of our Synoptics. But that is a purely historical question, certainly not a theological one. If the theology of the entire New Testament Canon is taken into account, the Johannine picture of Jesus must be welcomed as an expansion and enrichment of the Synoptic picture. And, to be sure, the enrichment consists above all, as already emphasized, in the fact that in relation to the Synoptic picture of Jesus the Johannine picture expresses, first, somewhat more strongly the spiritual reality and, second, somewhat more clearly the ecclesial significance.

Let it be said again: For the Johannine circle the enrichment resulted from personal impressions and historical reminiscences. The Johannine witnesses certify that they had actually seen the glory of the only begotten Son (John 1:14), and they shared with further readers what was from the beginning and what they had personally heard and seen (1 John 1:1).

3. As the above outline shows, *Paul* has primarily interpreted the significance of the crucified and resurrected one for the present, while certainly touching on specific points in the Master's activity in the past without elaborating on them. This coheres with the Apostle's career, since, as far as is known, he did not see the earthly Jesus and thus he could not supplement the disciples' previous reminiscences of the Master. He surely knew that those travelling with him who were members of the original community, such as Barnabas, Mark, Silas, and other sources of tradition, could enlighten the congregations concerning Jesus of Nazareth better than he. On the other hand, according to the witness of Acts and the Pauline letters, since his conversion at Damascus (Acts 9:5; Gal. 1:15-17) Paul experienced especially intensely the nearness, guidance, and help of the crucified, risen, and living Christ (Acts 16:17, etc.; Rom. 1:5, etc.).

Thus Paul did not contribute to the picture of Jesus through his own experience, though, on the other hand, neither was he, in opposition to a widely held opinion, indifferent to (a) the teaching and (b) the life of the Master from Nazareth, which will be demonstrated below and documented by examples. Likewise, it is necessary to protest the superficial judgment that for Paul (c) the enduring contact with the exalted figure of the Lord signifies no practical experience but only theoretical speculations.

(a) Notwithstanding the concentration on the post-Easter reality, for Paul the historical activity of the Incarnate One was fundamental, primarily in view of the *teaching of Jesus*. From accessible traditions, Paul has quoted several "sayings of the Lord" as support for his admonitions or counsel. A few of these have analogies in the canonical Gospels, others do not. But since our Gospels certainly did not exist before the Pauline Epistles, the apostle quoted in both cases from an early widespread tradition of the *logia* of Jesus. Already in Damascus, Jerusalem, and Antioch, Paul may have become acquainted with this tradition, which has been preserved quite amply in the double tradition of Matthew and Luke, and then utilized relevant sayings of Jesus in oral instruction as well as written correspondence (cf. 1 Cor. 11:23: "what I also passed on to you").

In 1 Corinthians Paul repeatedly alludes to imperative sayings of Jesus. The first example, 1 Cor. 7:10, reads as follows: "To the married I command—not I, but the Lord—that a wife should not be divorced from her husband." According also to Matt. 5:32 and 19:9 (and pars.) Jesus had expressed this view. The subsequent instruction by Paul in 1 Cor. 7:12 was, on the contrary, identified as his own counsel and was not traced back to a saying of the Lord. Further, through allusions to Jesus' sayings Paul underscored his admonitions concerning interruptions of the preacher in 1 Cor. 9:8-14, concerning discipline in the Lord's Supper in 11:23, and concerning the silence of women in 14:34 and 37. Counterparts to the first two of these allusions are found in the Gospels (to 9:14 in Matt. 10:10 and Luke 10:7; to 11:23 in Matt. 26:26-28 par.). In 1 Tim. 5:18 the Moses-saying quoted in 1 Cor. 9:9 is connected with the Jesus-saying in 9:14, while both quotations appear as declarations of "the Scripture." That a *logion* of Jesus was likewise represented as a word of Scripture depends, possibly, on an early existence of written notes on the life and teaching of Jesus. In any case, the combination of declarations by Moses and Jesus in 1 Tim. 5:18 also illumines Paul's tendency to ascribe high authority to the traditional sayings of the Lord.

Moreover, already in 1 Thessalonians Paul had clarified eschatological problems of the congregation with the aid of Jesus-sayings, while in 1 Thess. 4:15-

17 he explained the position of deceased Christians in relation to the Parousia, and in 5:2 he likened the suddenness of the Last Judgment to the breaking in of a house. These are analogies to apocalyptic sayings of Jesus which have been recorded in Matt. 24:30-31 par. and 4:43/Luke 12:39.

Thus it is clear that Paul, in his instruction and in his correspondence, sometimes refers to elements known to him from the teaching of Jesus, and that means that in such cases he points to the historic activity of Jesus. Moreover, he held the Lord's sayings, imparted by apostles or other sources, to be absolutely reliable and binding.

b) Paul has cited no episodes from the *life of Jesus*, and yet he considered the earthly life of the Lord to be an absolute fact. Contrary to a Judaism and Docetism which did not wish to acknowledge any identity between the earthly Jesus and heavenly Messiah or Christ, and likewise against any dogmatism which led to factions and sects, Paul in various Epistles emphasized (i) the historical incarnation of God's Son, as well as (ii) Christ's humble condescension and obedient sacrifice.

(i) The historical incarnation and human existence of Jesus Christ constituted for Paul an argument against the outbreaking Judaism in Galatia (Gal. 4:4): "When the fullness of time came, God sent his Son, born of a woman, placed under the Law." Paul drew attention here to the human birth of the divine Son and his obedient life under the Holy Law in order to oppose the readers' return to the works of the Law.

Since a party of Docetic Christians in Corinth came out against Jesus as a historical person and even blasphemed him, the apostle solemnly announced that only a confession of Jesus as Lord confirms the possession of the Spirit (I Cor. 12:3). Because those Docetics also rejected the resurrection of Christ, the reference to the Lord's bodily death maintained a primary place in the *kerygma* or summary of the Gospel with which Paul recalls to the Corinthians his fundamental proclamation (1 Cor. 15:3-4a): "I delivered to you first of all what I also had learned: that Christ died for our sins according to the Scriptures, and that he was buried. . . ." With the special reference to Jesus' burial Paul wanted to demonstrate the Lord's death as a physical fact and thereby to give his readers to understand that Jesus had lived as a historical person.

(ii) The *kenosis* or self-emptying of the Son of God which he recalls to the Christians in Philippi (Phil. 2:6-11) was directed against the tendency, suggested by the context, of some members of the congregation to dogmatic factionalism, and explains the previous and subsequent specific admonitions to unanimity: ". . . think the same way, have the same love, be united, be of one mind without contentiousness and presumption" (2:2-3a); "Do all things without grousing and argument" (2:14). In laying aside his divine nature, in humility taking on the form of a human and servant, and out of love of people allowing himself to be crucified (2:6-8), the Son of God reclaimed the divine majesty and omnipotence (2:10-11). Here Paul applies the historical life and death of the Son of God in humility, love, and obedience on behalf of people, as an argument for a similar renunciation of the believers' self-affirmation relative to fellow Christians. Each should have respect and provide support to the others. It is not here a matter accommodation or compromise with respect to doctrine, because when Paul summoned Christians to unity of mind he meant the focusing of their entire interest in Christ and the coming salvation (3:13-14): "Only one thing [is important]. . . : I pursue the goal, in view of the prize involved with God's calling from above in Christ Jesus." Slight differences in the teaching and regulation of various groups should not, according to Paul, undermine the unity of all Christians in the pursuit of the triumph of Christ and the Kingdom of God. With his reference to the *kenosis* of the heavenly Christ and the sacrifice of the historical Jesus, the apostle wanted to secure this unanimity of all believers.

Over and over again, when necessary, Paul thus appealed to (a) the authentic teaching and (b) the historical life of Jesus. The latter he did sometimes to counteract a Docetic one-sidedness in Christology, and at other times as a summons to Christian unanimity with respect to standards of conduct. Contrary to widespread opinion, according to which Paul had no relation to the historical person of Jesus, his references to the Lord's teaching and life (occasioned from time to time by pertinent and pressing problems) must be emphasized.[8]

(c) It is, moreover, evident and well-known that Paul occupied himself

---

[8] Many incline even yet to the same judgment about Jesus and Paul as taught by W. Wrede in his widely read popular book on Paul (1906) where the distance between the two was stressed: One could "never demonstrate that he [Paul] . . . had understood the work of Jesus; moreover, Jesus, whose disciple and servant he wanted to be, was emphatically not the historical man Jesus but rather another" (*Paulus* [Tübingen: Mohr, 1906], p. 95). Any such claim involves a *petitio principii*, because through a Christological reduction the interpreter himself produces that altered picture of Jesus which he distances from the Pauline picture. This negative judgment concerning the relation between Jesus and Paul is often found also in more recent literature. G. Bornkamm provides an example in "Paulus," in *Die Religion in Geschichte und Gegenwart*, 5 (1961) col. 175. To be sure, earlier in the same reference work a positive opinion was expressed: G. Sevenster, "Christologie," *ibid.*, I (1957), col. 1747.

primarily with the crucified and risen *Christ* and in this connection called him *kyrios* or Lord. While the name "Jesus" occurs in Paul 213 times, "Christ" is found 379 times and *kyrios* 275 times.

It is to be noted that Paul invoked the designation "Christ" and *kyrios* not as objective honorary titles but as subjective confessions. The message of the Church was for him a Gospel "of Jesus Christ our Lord" (Rom. 1:4), and this signifies that it was the believers' experience of the personal efficacy of this Christ that lent to these titles their significance. Since his experience at Damascus Paul always proceeds from his own experience of the efficacy of the Lord Jesus Christ, and his claims about the Savior rest for him completely on overpowering *experience* and not religious doctrine.

This experiential orientation of the Pauline Christology may be illuminated by a couple of chronologically arranged examples.

The risen Jesus was proclaimed at first by Paul as a Son of God "who will save us from the coming wrath" (1 Thess. 1:10). During his early activity Paul therefore emphasized that everyone will stand before Christ as judge (cf. Acts 17:32). This majestic aspect of the Messiah was already decisive for Paul at the time of his commission and call to be a servant of Christ (Gal. 1:10, 12, 15). Later, Paul understood himself as crucified with Christ (2:19) and experienced Christ's life within himself (2:20). For him the resurrection of Christ was no intellectual concept but rather the active agent of God's power and wisdom (1 Cor. 1:24). In his temptation he understood the meaning of Christ's comforting words to him: "My grace is sufficient for you. For strength is perfected in weakness" (2 Cor. 12:9). The power experienced in association with Christ was also the motive for Paul's declaration concerning the Christian message: "I am not ashamed of the Gospel. For it is a power of God for salvation, for everyone who believes" (Rom. 1:16). For Paul faith meant nothing other than peoples' readiness to allow the activity of God in Christ, which reveals his righteousness, to work on the heart (3:22, 24). In baptism every confessor is bound in a physical manner to the crucified one, and in the future consummation shall be united with the resurrected one (6:5). Paul lived continually in this substantial union with the resurrected Lord and thus declared solemnly: "For me, to live means Christ and to die means a gain" (Phil. 1:21).

Owing to such sayings of Paul it is manifestly misleading to speak of a special theological doctrine of the Apostle to the Gentiles and perhaps to canonize his doctrine of justification. For the apostle himself it is a matter, fundamentally and consistently, of a personal experience of the activity of the crucified and resurrected one, and although he proceeded from his own experiences, he assumed at the same time this same lordship of the Son of God over all confessors and baptized: "All of you who have been baptized into Christ have put on Christ. Here there is neither Jew nor Greek, slave nor free, man nor woman, because you are all one in Christ" (Gal. 3:27-28).

In light of this experiential perspective, Paul's predilection for statements about the exalted Christ is to be understood, which earlier in our diagram was represented as a shift of interest in comparison with the testimonies of the Synoptics and John. In spite of this graduated difference, in all three cases unmistakably the same Jesus Christ was meant.

A musical image may clarify the difference and congruence encompassed within the Christological perspective of the Synoptics, of John, and of Paul. The Synoptics, the Gospel of John, and the Pauline Epistles can for practical purposes be treated as the primary witnesses to New Testament Christology. In spite of certain differences they depict the same Jesus Christ and harmonize together like a three-part contrapuntal composition. In regard to the tone of the instruments and pitch of the parts there are differences, but the parts are in the same key and express the same theme. Only if the ear opens itself to the contrapuntal three-parts can the richness of the New Testament message be grasped. If, in view of further nuances, but without dogmatic prejudice, one adds the remaining canonical writings, namely Acts, the General Epistles, and Revelation, then sounds this three-part composition even more impressively.

Professor Bo Reicke:
A Biographical Appreciation

Bruce N. Kaye

Master, New College, University of New South Wales
Kensington, NSW, Australia

Born in Stockholm and having received his education and theological training in Sweden, Bo Reicke spent the greater part of his teaching life in Switzerland. For 31 years he held the chair of New Testament at the University of Basel. More than forty doctoral students made the pilgrimage to Basel to work under the supervision of Bo Reicke, and his work during that period is probably the best known aspect of his career, particularly to his students. However, his years in Sweden were of fundamental importance in shaping the professor who gained such endearing respect from both students and colleagues.

Bo Ivar Reicke was born on the 31st of July 1914 at the beginning of the first World War. He grew up in Stockholm, the son of a merchant in that city and was educated at the Gymnasium, where he received basic training in German, English, French and Latin. Military service was compulsory for all young men in Sweden, and students from Stockholm were sent to the north of the country to serve as subaltern officers or even officers. Reicke was no exception and he was sent to the quiet garrison city of Boden not far from the arctic circle. He used his spare time to teach himself Greek from a Langenscheidt course. The decision to study theology was taken during this time, not as the result of some conversion, but as the fruit of a growing interest in this field of study.

Reicke first matriculated at the University of Stockholm, spending three semesters studying history of religions. In 1935 he transferred to the University of Uppsala. While remaining in the Faculty of Arts, he took Classical Greek and Philosophy. Graduation in these three fields allowed him to enter the Faculty of Theology in 1938 without prior language courses. He must have started to learn Hebrew by himself early in 1937, since in August 1938 he took his first examination in Old Testament. He spent the whole of the following winter studying the New Testament and his examination in this subject went so well that Anton Fridrichsen, the professor of New Testament, offered him a place in his *Doktorandenseminar*. Reicke declined this offer preferring to finish his degree, taking examinations in New Testament, church history, systematic theology and practical theology. It was not until 1942 that Reicke returned to the offer of his New Testament professor and joined the circle of doctoral students. Before that, however, he had undergone, after the graduation, a university-based training for the ministry of the church of Sweden and was ordained by the archbishop in December 1941. The bishop had given him leave to study for his doctorate and he was only to be called up for parish service in special cases.

Since the early twentieth-century theology and the life of the church in Sweden had been dominated by Nathan Söderblom (1866-1931), the former professor of *Religionsgeschichte* in Uppsala and Leipzig who, as the Archbishop of Uppsala, had arranged the first ecumenical meeting in Stockholm in 1925. The influence of Söderblom was felt strongly even after his death, and so it was quite natural that Reicke was first attracted to the study of the history of religions. The heritage of Söderblom was kept alive in Uppsala in the circle of academic teachers who formed the "Nathan Söderblom Society" of which Reicke was elected a member in 1947. Reicke shared Söderblom's conviction that all forms of religion were worthy of interest and respect. Christian belief in the person of Jesus Christ, however, was to be seen as of a different quality. All syncretism was to be dismissed—the "living God" (the title of Söderblom's Gifford Lectures) will solve any antinomy in the last days.

Most influential among the members and initiators of the Söderblom Societies were Anton Fridrichsen (1888-1953), Professor of New Testament, and Henrik Samuel Nyberg, (1889-1974), Professor of Semitic Languages. Nyberg is best known internationally for his work on Iran, but his work also covered the Old Testament and he was a powerful adversary of literary criticism. Nyberg had inoculated generations of Swedish theologians against belief in the results of this literary critical method. Anton Fridrichsen was born and raised in Norway, coming from a family of pastors, where the typically Norwegian pietistic tradition was represented as well as the more outwardly church tradition such as one finds in the Dane, Grundtvig. Fridrichsen studied in Germany with Ernst von Dobschütz and obtained his doctorate from Strasbourg University, where this sociable Norwegian, with his gourmet taste, was an almost legendary figure. In his "realistic" method of exegesis we find many of the elements which are typical of his later students. He underlined such concepts as the Messianic consciousness of Jesus, the church as the body of Christ, and the role of the apostle in the later church. Nyberg and Fridrichsen were personal friends and in 1943 they invited Reicke, who was then a doctoral student, to be the secretary for the editing of a Swedish Bible encyclopedia. Reicke took the job and remained active (with the help of his wife) until the first volume appeared in 1948. The editorial work for this encyclopedia was taken over by Ivan Engnell.

Since Reicke's name is associated with the so-called Uppsala school, of whom Ivan Engnell and his friend Geo Widengren, Professor of History of Religions, are the most well-known representatives, his name is also sometimes associated, somewhat inappropriately, with that of Engnell, and thus it is necessary to clarify the situation at that time. Widengren and Engnell were slightly older and already established in their academic careers. They were, in fact, never Reicke's teachers. He certainly received inspiration from the ideas dominant in the circle around those two professors, but he was never one of their close circle, and when giving attention to cultic factors he always put the accent differently.

On the other hand, Carl Martin Edsman did inspire Reicke and was also a friend. He also shared with him an interest in patristics. Edsman, a former doctoral student of Fridrichsen, was at that time a *docent* in the history of religions, and also, like Reicke, stood for a strong engagement with the church in theological work. Long before he was ordained Reicke was firmly convinced that theological research had to be seen as a service to, and in, the church.

In Sweden at this time, doctoral students were required to take an intermediate exam, the licentiate, which included a main field and also a second field. Reicke chose the New Testament as his main field and never hesitated that Old Testament would be his second. Professor Fridrichsen had a large group of doctoral students; some of the more well-known are represented in *The Root and the Vine*, edited by A. G. Hebert (1953). His methods as a teacher were unconventional. Some students with good training in Greek, such as Reicke and

Harald Riesenfeld, were invited to help him with the revision of the Greek-Swedish dictionary of the New Testament. A characteristic mode of working would be that on an evening at Fridrichsen's home, an entry of the dictionary was thoroughly discussed and then the evening and the study exercise ended in the kitchen with a opulent meal from the refrigerator.

Reicke wrote his New Testament paper for the licentiate on 1 Peter 3:19, and his professor simply gave him the credits without further examination. A year and a half of intense study followed, as his copy of the *Biblia Hebraica* bears witness with its many pencil marks and annotations. He also learned Syriac and published his first scholarly paper on "Joseph's Story in Genesis." The dissertation, *The Disobedient Spirits and Christian Baptism*, was written, translated into English with the help of a Scottish lady, and printed, during one winter. At the latest possible date, in May 1946, Reicke presented his dissertation. He had to defend his dissertation before the faculty, and the appointed opponent was Nils Dahl who was then professor in Oslo. The second opponent chosen by Reicke was C. M. Edsman. A position as *Docent*, with the obligation to lecture two hours per week and to pursue scholarly research, was open in the university and Reicke was appointed to the position. It was not a tenured position but was limited to a maximum of seven years.

A new period now began which was marked, above all, by many international contacts. Especially because of Fridrichsen's European horizon, Uppsala was a mecca for travelling theological professors in the late 1940's. Contacts were also made by Reicke during journeys abroad. Among scholars who visited the Reickes in their Uppsala home were Old Testament professors such as H. H. Rowley (with whom Reicke corresponded for three months), S. Mowinckel, W. F. Albright, and also Rudolf Bultmann. At one point Bultmann was, in fact, a paying guest in the Reickes' spare room for three years. Other visitors were F. Schlier, J. Munck, A. Wikgren, A. Wilder, O. Cullmann, and J. Danielou. One should note the ecumenical as well as the international character of this group of visitors.

In the spring of 1947 Reicke spent six weeks in London and four weeks in Paris working in the British museum library and in the Bibliotheque Nationale. From London he visited Cambridge and Oxford and in the latter city he was able to take part in the first post-war meeting of the *Studiorum Novi Testamenti Societas*, to which he was, at that time, elected a member. In the summer term of 1948 he was a guest professor of the Evangelical Faculty of Theology at the

University of Vienna. On the journey home he and his wife were able to visit Italy for the first time, spending two weeks in Rome.

Reicke was the first scholar in Sweden to react to the discovery of the Qumran documents. He immediately wrote an article on the finds and took up contacts with the finder, J. C. Trever, with W. H. Brownlee and M. Burrows. In 1952 his Swedish translation of the *Habakkuk Scroll* and the *Manual of Discipline* was published. His interest in the Holy Land was expressed also in his work for the Swedish Jerusalem Society. He edited its journal and wrote a number of articles for it himself. He was also the secretary of the society and as such handled arrangements for two or three missionaries. A Swedish theologian of high reputation, Bishop Gustav Aulén, was the president of the society, and remained in personal contact with Reicke even after the move to Basel.

On the retirement of Rudolf Bultmann the Faculty of the University of Marburg inquired of Reicke whether he would be interested in an appointment at Marburg. He thought it unwise to accept such a position because he was a foreigner who had not shared the pre-war and wartime experiences of Nazi Germany. In 1953 he first received an inquiry from the University of Leiden which was seeking a New Testament professor, but before the offer from Leiden had been officially communicated, Professor Cullmann visited Sweden and invited Reicke to join the University of Basel. In June he was interviewed by the Faculty in Basel and accepted the invitation. Much later the lost letter from Leiden turned up, which, thus, had not reached Reicke at the crucial time of the decision!

When in 1953 the Reickes moved to Basel they commenced a long and profound involvement with the city and the university. Within a year of their arrival they had managed to purchase the house in Spalentorweg 24, which is so well-known to generations of students in Basel. Within the University of Basel Reicke played a full role as Professor of New Testament. When he arrived in Basel, it was a time of giants among the faculty members, Karl Barth, Oscar Cullmann, Walter Baumgartner, Walther Eichrodt, and the church historian Ernst Staehelin. Reicke worked closely with Cullmann and he soon took over various responsibilities in the faculty. In 1955 he became editor of the *Theologische Zeitschrift*, a position he occupied for nearly twenty-five years. He was Dean of the theology faculty in 1956 and on three subsequent occasions, and he served also as a member of the governing council of the university in addition to various committees. He took a particular interest in the house in which Karl Jaspers and his wife had lived and enjoyed his role a president of the committee which administered the house.

Reicke's publication output was extensive, to say the least. Numerous articles, papers, and a considerable number of books came from his pen. From the Uppsala days his dissertation, *The Disobedient Spirits and Christian Baptism*, was published (1946), and as well the monumental survey of the early church, *Diakonie, Festfreude und Zelos* (1951). After his arrival in Basel, he completed a commentary on the epistles of Peter and Jude for a Swedish publisher which, in expanded form, was subsequently published in 1964 as part of the Anchor Bible series: *The Epistles of James, Peter, and Jude*. Throughout this period his writing on the early church and on New Testament topics is known through his survey, *Neutestamentliche Zeitgeschichte* (1964), and in its English translation, *The New Testament Era (1968)*. The diversity of his interests is indicated by his book on the Ten Commandments, *Die Zehn Worte in Geschichte und Gegenwart* (1973), and even more so by his co-editorship of the four-volume *Biblisch-historisches Handwörterbuch* (1962-66). His book, *The Roots of the Synoptic Gospels*, published in 1986, reflects a continuing interest over many years in the synoptic problem, an interest which surfaced many times in lectures and seminars. It also indicates the originality of his approach to this critical question of New Testament studies, as well as his special and continuing interest in the Gospels. Reicke wrote in English, German, and Swedish, a testimony to his remarkable linguistic skills.

Reicke did not remain narrowly within the university when he came to Basel. He and his family were members of the Lutheran Church in Basel, and Reicke himself was President of that church. He later represented the Lutheran Church in the *Arbeitsgemeinschaft christliche Kirchen in der Schweiz*, which had been founded in 1972. In 1971 the whole family took up Swiss (Basel) citizenship, giving up their Swedish passports.

The contributors to this *Festschrift*, however, remember particularly Reicke the man and the teacher. His lecturing style was not the sparkling rhetorical affair that one found in some others, but his range, his knowledge, and his sympathies were immense. He was at his best in smaller groups and in individual discussion, where the depth and quality of his knowledge became apparent. There was no doubt that he knew the material, that he had considered it in depth, and had arrived at his own independent judgments. He did not, however, force his judgments on his students. Rather, he made available to them the extraordinary resources of his scholarship and acumen so that they could reach their own conclusions in a properly scholarly fashion. It is because of these skills and qualities that he attracted research students and was so successful a supervisor of doctoral students.

Reicke never liked the expression *Doktorvater,* which is perhaps a sign of his willingness to let the doctoral student work along his or her own lines as long as the method was scholarly. Forty doctoral students at the University of Basel have reason to be grateful to him for his gentle guidance of their research.

Many aspects of Reicke's academic career and life and his contributions to the cause of theology and Christian culture could be noted at further length than has been done here. However, since this is a *Festschrift* presented by his doctoral students it is perhaps appropriate to conclude this biographical tribute on a more personal note. For the doctoral students represented in this *Festschrift,* and for this particular writer, three significant characteristics marked Reicke's work: his scholarship, his humanity, and his partnership with Mrs. Reicke.

From the earliest days Mrs. Reicke had been a fellow worker in the academic activities that occupied her husband. Their first publishing enterprise was a joint venture of editorial work. The editorship of *Theologische Zeitschrift* over many years was largely a joint enterprise. A linguist of the highest qualities, Mrs. Reicke contributed significantly to the publishing and academic activity of her husband. She has published translations of theological works in her own right as well. Spalentorweg 24 is a house with many associations for many doctoral students. Some have stayed there for periods of time; others have had the benefit of using some of the domestic equipment which was kept in the house for that purpose. Their chalet at Salvan, in the mountains of French-speaking Switzerland, has been for many of us a place to visit or a place for rest or for work. In all of their hospitality Mrs. Reicke ordered the household with a businesslike efficiency and a highly civilized courtesy.

Professor Reicke's scholarship was not of the aggressive kind but rather of a moderate and highly informed kind. He exposed his students to a depth of knowledge and an independence of thought which provided a model for their own work. He was content to promote discipline and scholarship with his students and aimed to cultivate scholarly method. Scholarly method was much more important to him than the opinion or the conclusions that the student might reach. This reflected a modest sense that neither he nor others knew everything, and certainly not the whole truth. His interest in the Synoptic problem is perhaps a good example. Recent discussions among a group of New Testament scholars designed to restore to some broader acceptance the theory of Griesbach attracted his sympathetic encouragement although he himself was never really convinced by the Griesbach theory. He had developed a more independent line on the question

reflecting to some extent his Swedish origins and his broad approach to questions
of New Testament interpretation. The fruits of that reflection and a detailed
explanation of his views has been made available to us in the *The Roots of the
Synoptic Gospels*, already mentioned.

Because, in a certain sense, he stood in a mediating position on some critical
matters pertaining to New Testament interpretation, Reicke did not attract vast
popularity nor was he protected from criticism from those who would wish to take
a more extreme point of view. One cannot but speculate as to whether his declining
to succeed Bultmann at Marburg did not have something to do with his different
outlook from that of Bultmann, combined with a certain respect for the integrity
and continuity of the New Testament chair in that university. His presidential
address to the annual SNTS meeting in 1982 was on an earlier Basel theologian,
and one speculates that it held a certain autobiographical significance: "W. M. L.
de Wette's Contribution to Biblical Theology." He had not been dismissed from
any chair as de Wette had been, but he certainly was not without his critics, and
his attempt to combine devotion and scholarship was, in many respects, very
similar to that of de Wette.

For the contributors to the *Festschrift*, these three characteristics have been
in varying degrees formative in their own scholarly development. The kind of
scholarship which Reicke inculcated, his interests in the broad experience of
humanity, and his capacity to work with people, as demonstrated in his partnership
with Mrs. Reicke, were all significant elements in the kind of professor and teacher
whom we seek in this *Festschrift* to honor. These characteristics were combined in
a gentle humanity which endeared him to all those who came to know him. He was
somewhat formal in manner but he revealed a generosity and a warmth to those
who came to know him and a continuing and gentle encouragement for the
development of his students after they graduated. When Reicke died unexpectedly
on May 15, 1987, many colleagues and friends were deeply saddened. His doctoral
students shared in that sadness, but at the same time they remember a teacher and
a friend. This *Festschrift* is a testimony to the personal and scholarly qualities or
our friend and teacher.